To: Regius Prof. Scanlon,

With appreciation!

The Palace of Established Happiness

Cordially,

Ronnie C. Chan

To: Prof. Eileen Scanlon   July 29, 2015
at Asia Society Hong Kong Center

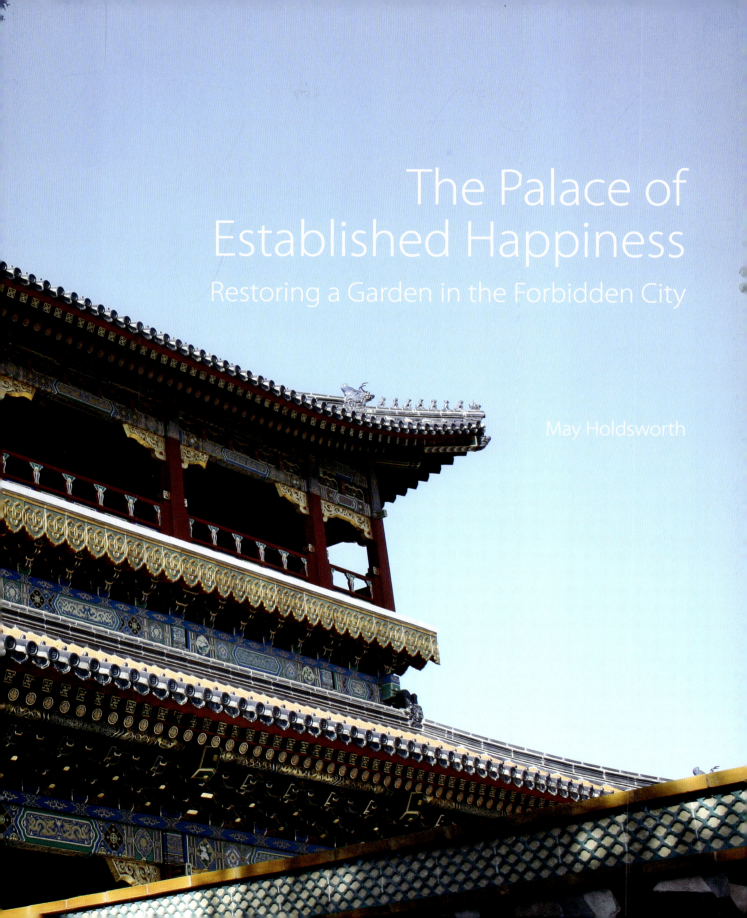

The Palace of Established Happiness
Restoring a Garden in the Forbidden City

May Holdsworth

The Garden of the Palace of Established Happiness
建福宫花园

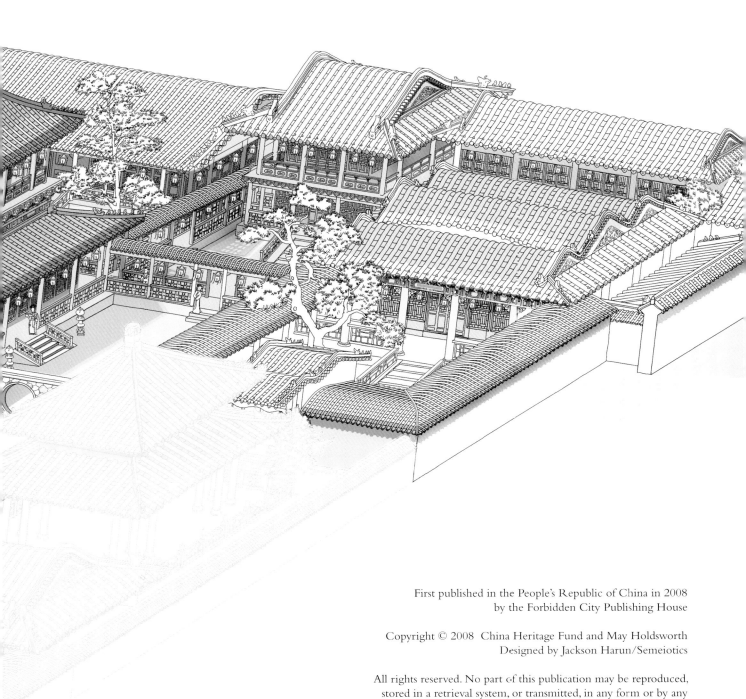

First published in the People's Republic of China in 2008
by the Forbidden City Publishing House

Copyright © 2008 China Heritage Fund and May Holdsworth
Designed by Jackson Harun/Semeiotics

All rights reserved. No part of this publication may be reproduced,
stored in a retrieval system, or transmitted, in any form or by any
means, without the prior permission in writing of the publisher, nor be
otherwise circulated in any form of binding or cover other than that
in which it is published and without a similar condition including this
condition being imposed on the subsequent purchaser.

ISBN 978-7-80047-331-9

Printed and bound in the People's Republic of China

Contents

(Pages 2-3) The Pavilion of Prolonged Spring.

(Pages 4-5) The Palace and Garden of Established Happiness. According to the artist, this is not so much a true isometric drawing as an aesthetic representation that emphasizes the style of traditional Chinese architecture. The Garden — the area of the restoration — is highlighted.

(Left) Interior of the Pavilion of Prolonged Spring.

Contents

Preface — 8
Ronnie Chan, *Founder and Chairman, China Heritage Fund*

Foreword — 10
Zheng Xinmiao, *Director, Palace Museum, Beijing*

Map — 12
The Forbidden City

1 | The Fire — 14
A Vase and a Dish

2 | Qianlong Builds a Garden — 24
The *Admonitions* Scroll

3 | The Garden in Twilight — 44
A Painting and a Photograph

4 | What Caused the Fire? — 62
with Zou Ailian, Tang Yinian *and* Yang Yongzhan, *First Historical Archives of China*
How Much Was Lost?
with Tang Yinian, *First Historical Archives of China* and Yuan Hongqi, *Palace Museum*

5 | China Heritage Fund — 80
Conserving the Architecture of the Forbidden City

6 | Saving the Stones — 98
Kang, Heated Brick Platforms

7 | The Timber Frame — 118
Calligraphy in the Garden

8 | Baked Earth — 138
Roof Guardians

9 | Palaces of Gold and Jade — 160
Painted Decoration

10 | Tiger Skins and Bamboo Shoots — 182
The Interior Decoration of the Studio of Esteemed Excellence

11 | A Museum of Chinese Architecture — 196
A Contemporary Space Inside the Garden
Alexander Beels, *China Heritage Fund*

Afterword — 208
Michael Petzet, *President, International Council on Monuments and Sites*

Glossary — 210
Ming and Qing Reigns — 214
Acknowledgements and Sources — 215
Illustrations — 219
Index — 220

Preface

Ronnie Chan, *Founder and Chairman, China Heritage Fund*

When the idea of China Heritage Fund was first conceived, I wanted to do restoration projects as far away from Beijing as possible: things are always complicated at the political center. But when the possibility of restoring the Garden of the Palace of Established Happiness was brought to my attention, I recognized its uniqueness immediately. This book, like the film being produced, documents the restoration of that Garden in the Forbidden City.

From the beginning, I was convinced that the process of restoration was as important as the product. This emphasis on the process made our decade-long endeavor much more difficult, but the result, in terms of the knowledge acquired and retained as well as the physical product, is more pleasing and valuable.

Let me cite a few examples. Overseas experts were brought in to train local craftsmen on restoration work. These artisans gained invaluable experience that will be useful in future restoration endeavors. Our friends at the Palace Museum originally thought that the donors would simply hand them the money. Instead, China Heritage Fund brought in a quantity surveyor to certify the quantity and quality of work before a penny was disbursed. I demanded a detailed construction contract on a par with those conforming to international standards. To the credit of the Museum directors, they eventually accepted these novel ideas, though often after much persuasion by my staff. They later expressed their appreciation of our insistence, having recognized the value of the suggestions.

What made all that possible was a strong sense of mission shared by the State Administration of Cultural Heritage (SACH), the Palace Museum and China Heritage Fund. My colleagues and I at the Fund have labored harmoniously alongside successive generations of Museum directors and deputy directors as well as frontline workers.

The project could not have been so successful if it were not for my former Personal Assistant at Hang Lung Properties, Miss Happy Harun. For the past seven years she has been the on-site Project Director of China Heritage Fund. A Stanford University-trained geologist turned banker, Happy came to work for me fifteen years ago, handling my charitable activities among other duties. When she volunteered for the Garden restoration, I was skeptical at first, but appointing her to the job may well have been the single most important decision I made for the project.

Under the eaves of the Pavilion of Prolonged Spring.

Preface

Although born and raised in Hong Kong, Happy studied French instead of Chinese in high school. When she started full time on the Garden, her written Chinese was weak and spoken Mandarin poor. But the discovery of her 'Chineseness', coupled with an intense love for the work, fired her eagerness to learn as quickly as she could from those around her. In the process, Happy has found her life's mission and has become something of an expert on traditional Chinese construction. I am delighted for her and indebted to her as well. The Palace Museum and China Heritage Fund are now embarking on the next joint project which is even more challenging — rebuilding the Hall of Rectitude. This structure, built in 1627 toward the waning years of the Ming dynasty, was lost in the same 1923 fire that destroyed the Garden of the Palace of Established Happiness. Happy's knowledge and enthusiasm will once again be called upon for the second restoration project.

I would also like to thank a number of Chinese government officials whose help was crucial. Madam Wang Limei of SACH helped launch the project. She introduced me to Mr Zhang Deqin, the first of several leaders of SACH whose unwavering support was indispensable, and to Mr Jin Hongkui, now a Deputy Director of the Palace Museum. Mr Zhang Wenbin, former Director of SACH, Mr Pei Huanlu, former Deputy Director of the Museum, as well as its present Director Mr Zheng Xinmiao, have all contributed much.

In May 1999, at the signing of the restoration contract in the presence of Mr Sun Jiazheng, China's Minister of Culture, I stated that the destruction of a nation's cultural heritage reflects the country's decline and turmoil, but its restoration is a sure sign of the country's rise and prosperity. It is thus apt that, after twenty-six years of economic opening and reform, which have brought peace and prosperity unknown to the Chinese people for two centuries, we should witness the completion of this historic Garden.

The Garden project, as the only newly constructed group of 'ancient' buildings within the Forbidden City, is an illustration of modernity in antiquity and antiquity in modernity. The best of Western technology is represented in the Garden. This too is a sign of the times, when finally East and West are learning to work together in harmony. After all, the Forbidden City is a cultural heritage site not only of the Chinese people but of all mankind.

Foreword

Zheng Xinmiao, *Director, Palace Museum, Beijing*

Deserted and in ruins since the devastating fire of June 27, 1923, the Garden of the Palace of Established Happiness has been restored and will be unveiled by the eightieth anniversary of the founding of the Palace Museum.

Approved by the State Council, sponsored by China Heritage Fund, and co-managed by the Palace Museum and China Heritage Fund, the restoration has been a collaborative effort. The empty ground where the original Garden stood, and the incompleteness of the Forbidden City that it represented, had long been a matter of deep regret. Now the last missing piece in what was otherwise the largest and best-preserved architectural monument in China has been put back in its place.

A restoration is not an opportunity to ring the changes or engage in new designs. It should be, as far as possible, a faithful replication of the original. Such replication, using the traditional tools, processes and materials, and on a site where only the foundations and stone pedestals survived, would test the skills of the most experienced craftsman. But all those involved played their part, putting their heart and soul into the project and striving to produce work of the highest quality. It is clear from the outcome that the combination of ingenuity, exertion and dedication has been unequivocally successful.

Built by Emperor Qianlong from 1742, the Garden is the second largest in the Forbidden City. As we know from contemporary memorials and later studies, Qianlong interested himself in the design and construction, and greatly valued the Garden's charm and seclusion. Not only did he keep many of the treasures of his art and antiquities collection there, he also composed poems about virtually every pavilion in the Garden. Some of those poems help to conjure up the beautiful prospects that he enjoyed from the verandahs and windows: the peonies at the Pavilion of Prolonged Spring and the plum blossom outside the Pavilion of Tranquil Ease, for example, and the bamboo swaying beside the Lodge of Viridian Jade, not to mention other scenic delights such as the Garden's appearance after spring rains or a fall of snow in winter.

A decision was made right at the beginning of the project to document the whole process of restoration, which has obvious and significant implications for the conservation of Qing-dynasty architecture as a whole. This book, researched alongside the reconstruction, makes for an invaluable supplementary record, providing vivid detail on the work in stone, wood, tiles and paint, as well as selected transcripts of interviews with many of the participants. It is also a means by which knowledge of traditional imperial architecture may be disseminated to the wider world, forming one link in the continuing discourse between the Palace Museum, a World Heritage site since 1987, and the international cultural community. Through its pages, the historical Garden and the Garden in its newly-restored guise spring tangibly and resplendently to the reader's eye.

The Belvedere of Abundant Greenery, with the Pavilion of the Rain of Flowers in the distance.

The Forbidden City
紫禁城

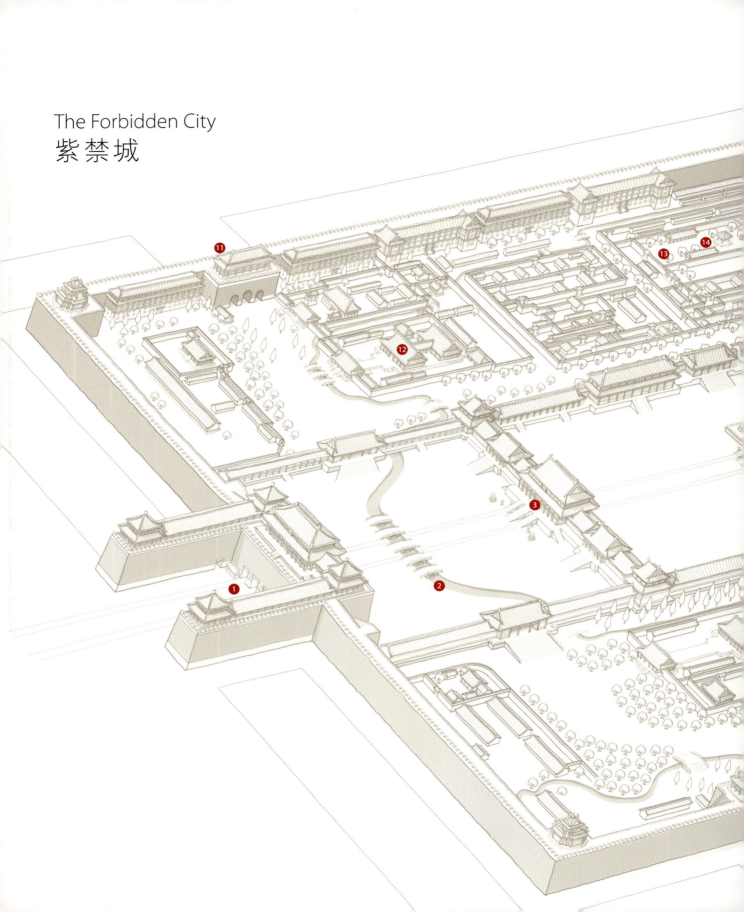

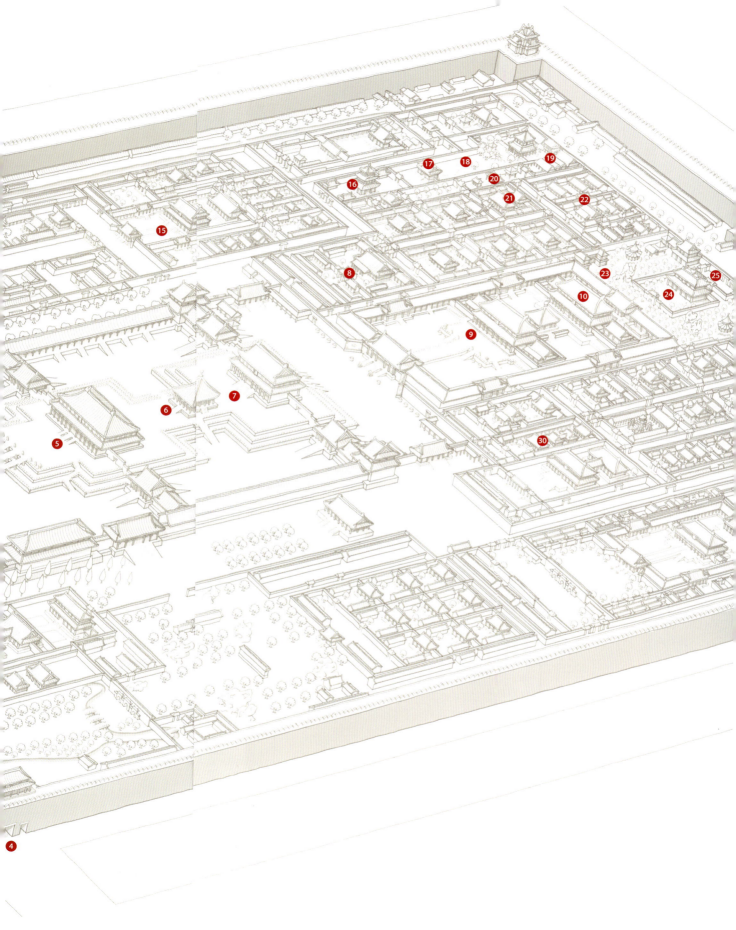

1 | The Fire

1 | The Fire

It was late on Tuesday, June 26, 1923. Earlier in the day, the whole sky had been filled with a drenching rain, but now a breeze was blowing and the air was clear and cool. The Forbidden City, its gates barred against the outside world since dusk, was silent. 'Draw the bolts, lock up, careful with the lanterns!' the eunuchs closing the massive doors had cried, a perfunctory warning uttered so often that they no longer thought of it as a reminder to guard against fire.

1 | The Fire

(Pages 14-15) The desolate Garden site, before restoration work began: the footprint of the square Pavilion of Prolonged Spring is clearly delineated by its stone terrace and column plinths.

No light illuminated Jianfu gong, the Palace of Established Happiness, in the northwest quarter of the Forbidden City, for it was no longer lived in, and used mainly for storage. There was no sound save the sough of its garden's ancient trees. All was quiet and dark — until midnight, when an eerie light started to glow in the farthest corner of the garden, where the Studio of Esteemed Excellence stood. The light seemed to emanate from the inner chamber known as Derixin, 'Virtue Renewed Daily', after the inscription on the plaque over its entrance.

become monks held services in them, assembling at regular intervals throughout the day and night to light incense and intone the sacred texts. It was a eunuch-lama, Ma Lailu, on the point of changing shift, who discovered the fire.

The Studio of Esteemed Excellence was now ablaze, with sheets of flame billowing out of its casements and running along the interconnected galleries. Shocked though he was, Ma Lailu had enough self-possession to alert the Office of Eunuch Affairs. Within minutes of the office

(Right) The Garden after the fire.

On the other side of the southern wall of the Garden of the Palace of Established Happiness, monks were saying their prayers in the Hall of Rectitude, a temple and repository of sutras, Buddha statues and a magnificent golden pagoda thirteen feet high. The Qing emperors were punctilious in their religious observances and had three buildings in this part of the Forbidden City designated as shrines to the deities of Tibetan Buddhism — the Hall of Rectitude, the Hall of Precious Prosperity and the Pavilion of the Rain of Flowers. Palace eunuchs who had

raising the alarm, eunuchs were converging on the site to salvage what they could. But most of them, a Beijing newspaper was to remark caustically two days later, were so petrified that they did little more, besides saving a few possessions, than stand on the sidelines looking 'moronic or drunk'. Succumbing finally to agitation and fright, Ma Lailu passed out.

Away from the Forbidden City, Tatiana and Joseph Carson of the British Legation were dancing on the roof garden of the Grand Hotel de Pékin when a red glare lit up the night sky to the north. They were momentarily transfixed by the sight; then, without further hesitation, they went directly downstairs to try and find the scene of the fire. They were joined by another secretary from the legation, Mr Gascoigne, and Tatiana's sister, Irene Staheyeff.

'We got into a rickshaw and set off to have a look,' Irene Staheyeff wrote to her mother in Shanghai two days later. The streets were crowded, for other rickshaws, cars and many pedestrians, seemingly bent on the same purpose, were hurrying toward the northern entrance of the Forbidden City. All stopped dead at the Gate of Divine Prowess. Irene Staheyeff's letter continued: 'Three times we tried to get through the gates, and three times we were escorted back, as not only Europeans but Chinese, with the exception of the mandarins, are not allowed in.' Meanwhile, swarming in front of the gate and raising a racket loud enough to assail the steadiest of nerves, were firemen from the Inner City brigade, the Italian Legation guard 'with their water wagon', members of the city police, army and Palace Guard, and people from the neighborhood. But even as black rolls of smoke rose skyward behind them, the Palace guards claimed they had no instructions from their officer and refused to open the gate.

Inside the Palace, Shao Ying, comptroller of Neiwufu (the Imperial Household Department), was frantically trying to find Puyi. Although he had been dethroned, Puyi was still living like an emperor in his make-believe court at the rear of the Forbidden City. By the time Shao Ying ran him to ground in one of the western palaces, it was 1:20 am, more than an hour since the fire had begun. Dynastic regulations prohibited outsiders from entering the Forbidden City without a specific imperial edict giving gracious permission. All the same, Puyi only allowed a side gate to be opened for the firemen and the gathering crowd. Of the four approaches into the Forbidden City, this gate on the eastern wall, nearly a mile from the entrance to the Garden, provided the farthest and most circuitous route to the fire.

Afterward, witnesses would speak of towering pillars of fire as high as thirty feet from the ground . . .

At 2:50 am, as the clanking fire engines plunged in, Mr Gascoigne, Miss Staheyeff and the Carsons found themselves swept along until they, too, were hurrying toward the Garden of the Palace of Established Happiness. There Shao Ying was directing rescue operations in the midst of confusion and havoc, a sight both incongruous and pitiful. Eunuchs were running to and fro, with no semblance of organization, randomly retrieving pieces of furniture and decoration from the pavilions. By now the fire was well entrenched, devouring columns, walls, rafters, beams — indeed everything but the stone terraces and foundations. Afterward, witnesses would speak of towering pillars of fire as high as thirty feet from the ground, flames that left

1 | The Fire

(Left) Shao Ying, comptroller of the Imperial Household Department.

(Right) Puyi in his court robes.

behind a desolate jumble of sparks, smoke, charred wood and ash.

The firemen from the Italian Legation, assisted by M. Riva, an Italian ex-flying officer, were competent and dogged. But the odds were stacked against them. An appeal to the U.S. Legation had gone unanswered, as Irene Staheyeff complained in her letter: 'You know, Mama, these Americans are the pits. We rang them four times, from the hotel and the Palace, asking their help as they are the only ones with a fire brigade — and the swine never came.' Worse, the Forbidden City had no running water. Until the hoses could draw from the wells and the moat, some immediate way of bringing water needed to be devised. Besides, it was summer, and the water level in the moat was low. More time elapsed while a command to raise the sluicegates controlling the flow of an underground stream was carried out. Meanwhile, what water there was got passed in buckets, and soon Tatiana Carson had placed herself in the human chain of water carriers. Years later, in the politically correct autobiography Puyi would write under the eye of his Communist masters, she was to make a brief appearance as a rather overbearing foreigner:

> When the fire was being fought the place was full of foreigners and Chinese, residents of the palace and outsiders, all coming and going hither and thither. It can be easily imagined that they were not only concerned with extinguishing the fire, but the Forbidden City expressed its gratitude to all of them. One foreign lady who came to watch the excitement started quarrelling with a Chinese fireman and actually hit her opponent on the nose with her fan. Later she showed me her bloodstained fan as evidence of her courage and I wrote a poem on it as a mark of my gratitude.

'One is very sorry for the little emperor; he stood there surrounded by his relatives all the time and just watched.'

To one eyewitness on the night, Puyi appeared merely pathetic: 'One is very sorry for the little emperor,' Irene Staheyeff wrote, 'he stood there surrounded by his relatives all the time and just watched.'

Still, he had the presence of mind to order refreshments to sustain the firefighters, and tea, beer, biscuits, cake, fruit were brought. As the night wore on, however, it became apparent that the firemen's efforts were to little avail. It was so hot that they could only stand back against the walls and throw water around the edges of the conflagration. There was no hope that the fire could be quenched; the most that could be done was to contain it. Fortunately the wind had dropped. Even so, the fire had spread over the wall to the Hall of Rectitude and laid that to waste. The air was thick with flaky ash that sieved down, floated between the smoldering pavilions and drifted onto the scorching, cracked stones.

Summoned by a messenger, Puyi's English tutor Reginald Johnston arrived just before dawn. He recounted the scene in his book, *Twilight in the Forbidden City*:

> I found the emperor and empress standing on a heap of charred wood, sadly contemplating the spectacle. Several of the princes had already arrived, and the officers of the Nei Wu Fu were fussily doing their best to instruct the well-disciplined Italian firemen in the art of how not to extinguish fires.
>
> The flames were still raging when I arrived. Just after I had reached the emperor I was astonished to see three Europeans — one of them a lady — all in evening dress that at an earlier hour had been immaculate, smilingly emerging from clouds of smoke. The first impression I received from their appearance was that their dress clothes would never again be fit to wear. The second was that all three were personally known to me. They were Mr Gascoigne and Mr Carson of the British Legation staff, and Mrs Carson. After I had presented them to the emperor and empress, who at once thanked them for the zeal and courage they had shown in helping to fight the fire, they told me they had seen the fire from the roof garden of the Grand Hotel de Pékin and had at once driven to the Forbidden City. Baffled at first in their attempts to pass the guards they had succeeded in making their way through the gates by mingling with the Italian firemen.

It was not until 7 am that the burning subsided and only wisps of smoke were left, like low-hanging clouds, over the dying throes of the fire. By then the Garden of the Palace of Established Happiness was an annihilated landscape of gaunt, blackened hulks of buildings and smoking rubble.

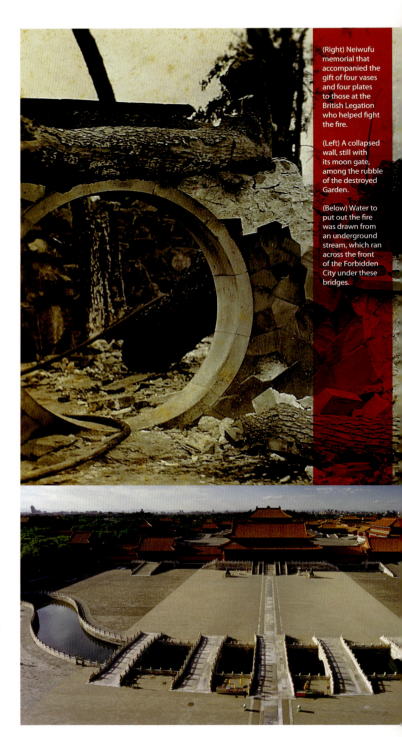

(Right) Neiwufu memorial that accompanied the gift of four vases and four plates to those at the British Legation who helped fight the fire.

(Left) A collapsed wall, still with its moon gate, among the rubble of the destroyed Garden.

(Below) Water to put out the fire was drawn from an underground stream, which ran across the front of the Forbidden City under these bridges.

1 | The Fire

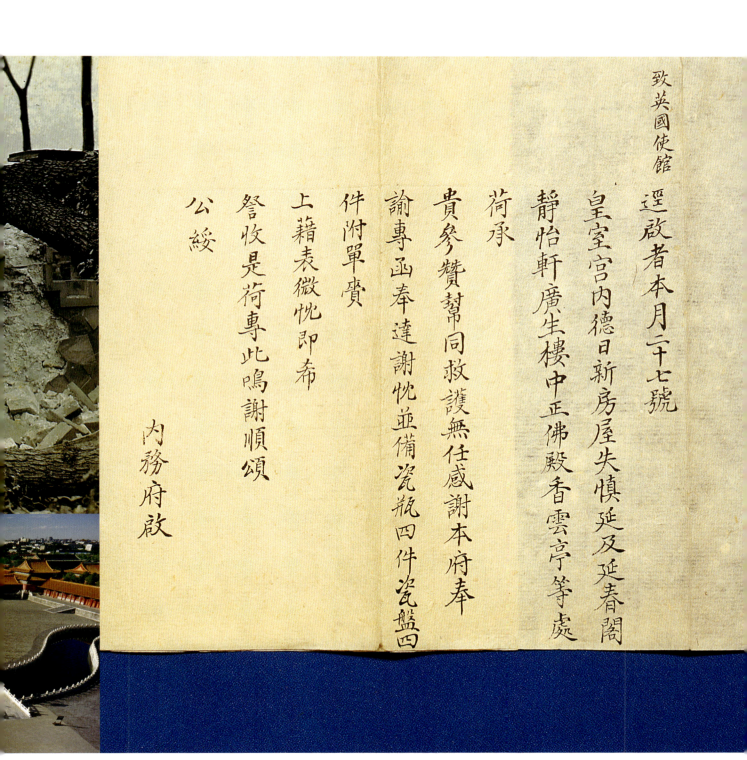

致英國使館

逕啟者本月二十七號皇室宮內德日新房屋失慎延及延春閣靜怡軒廣生樓中正佛殿香雲亭等處荷承貴參贊幫同救護無任感謝本府奉諭專函奉達謝忱並備瓷瓶四件瓷盤四件附單贄上藉表微忱即希詧收是荷專此鳴謝順頌

公綏

內務府啟

A Vase and a Dish

Transcending the barriers of time and distance, two mementos of the 1923 fire have ended up in London. One graces a private house and the other a museum dedicated to Chinese ceramics.

The first is an oxblood vase in the possession of Tatiana Browning, the daughter of Tatiana Carson (née Staheyeff).

The Staheyeff family were White Russians who had fled the Red Terror and settled in Shanghai. In the summer of 1921 young Tatiana Staheyeff became governess and companion to Lucy, the daughter of Sir Beilby Alston, the British ambassador to Peking. Being not much older than her charge Lucy (also known as Loody), Tatiana fitted into her new milieu very quickly, especially as life seemed an endless round of amusing engagements. She regularly wrote about it to her mother in Shanghai:

> We have lessons in the morning. Lunch is usually en famille and their guests, unless something is very official. As the weather is beginning to get very warm, we usually have a rest after lunch and then can play tennis, sightsee, walk or pay calls on Loody's friends. We drove to the Temple of Heaven yesterday. It is beautiful, all white marble, blue sky and many trees in the Park, surrounding it.

There were also picnics in the Western Hills, days at the races, shopping from Chinese merchants who 'came to the drawing room' to show embroideries and porcelain, dinners at the various legations, dancing at the Hotel de Pékin where Tatiana once essayed 'a Valse, but did not try the foxtrots.' In fact, life was so full, and she received so many invitations, that

I shall have to have a few evening dresses for the winter season. You will be pleased to know that your daughter is admired & gets complimented on her toilettes.

Joseph Baldwin Carson, Second Secretary of the British Legation, admired more than her toilette. By the summer of 1923 he had married Tatiana and was dancing with her himself. Something of her energy and her ability to think for herself, which he must have discerned, was revealed on the night of the fire, as this report in the *North China Daily News* of June 27, 1923 attests:

> The Emperor's Thanks
> An interesting sequel to the fire in the Ex-Emperor's Palace occurred on Sunday, when the thanks of the Emperor were formally tendered to four members of the foreign community who played a conspicuous part in the work of fighting the flames. The three Ministers of the Household sent their representatives with a card of greeting, and a letter from the Master of the Household stating that he had been commanded by the Emperor to thank Mr and Mrs J. B. Carson and Mr Gascoyne [sic] of the British Legation, and Miss Irene Staheyeff, Mrs Carson's sister, for the help they rendered in saving the Palaces. As a token of his gratitude, the Emperor presented each with a vase of sang de boeuf porcelain and a piece of 'blue and white' from the Imperial collection, each piece bearing the Emperor's seal. These gifts were sent in appreciation of an arduous and plucky night's work in which all the recipients, having been admitted to the scene of the fire, by their coolness and initiative inspired the panic-stricken attendants to make an organized attack upon the flames. Mrs Carson in particular earned the praise of her companions and the personal thanks of the Emperor for the pluck and steadiness she displayed.

A Ru ware dish that survived the fire was bought by a collector and is now in the Percival David Foundation of Chinese Art at the University of London. A 'shallow dish with rounded sides and slightly everted rim, standing on a low, splayed foot', it dates from the early twelfth century, a high point in the history of Chinese pottery. Glazed and covered with a fine crackle, the dish would have been grayish-blue in color when first produced. It is inscribed 'by the order of the emperor Qianlong in the summer of *yihai* year' on the base. 'Ru' derives from Ruzhou, site of an imperial kiln making green ware during the Northern Song dynasty (960–1126). The '*yihai* year' reference dates the inscription to 1779.

Tatiana Staheyeff (right) with Lucy Alston in Beijing.

Sir Percival David was born in Bombay in 1892. He attended the universities of Bombay and Cambridge and was set on a career in law until, spurred by a growing interest in oriental art, he applied himself to studying Chinese instead. He made his first journey to China and gained his first sight of the Forbidden City's treasures in 1924.

The imperial collection was a vast one, its luster only slightly diminished by the depredations of foreign troops at the Garden of Perfect Brightness in 1860 and in Beijing in 1900. But the imperial house itself was no less rapacious when Palace coffers needed replenishing. In 1901 the dowager empress Cixi (1835–1908) borrowed money from the Salt Industry Bank, putting up selected antiques, including porcelain, as collateral. Some forty pieces of these were eventually sold to Sir Percival by the bank. At least twice after his abdication — in 1922 and 1924 — Puyi took bank loans secured on gold plate and gold ornaments from the Imperial Palace. In one case, the gold was not redeemed but 'sold' to the lender, the Hongkong and Shanghai Banking Corporation.

Thus, through sale, theft and looting, a great many pieces from the Forbidden City gradually fell into private hands. Relics salvaged from the 1923 fire also resurfaced and were offered for sale by Beijing antique dealers: the Ru dish, said to be Sir Percival's first acquisition in 1924, was one. Its original grayish-blue glaze is now mostly opaque gray with pink smudges. It has been suggested that the dish might have been placed close to bronze vessels and the pink tones were caused by hot copper burning onto the dish in the intense heat of the fire.

2 | Qianlong Builds a Garden

2 | Qianlong Builds a Garden

Colors fade from the pavilions' painted columns,
Birdsong floats by like notes from distant flutes.
With such secluded charms before one's eyes,
Why seek vistas of gorgeous mansions afar?
Birds wing through trees, shaking the blur of blossom-red,
Orchids and lilac shimmer in the haze.
As dewdrops drench the rockeries at night,
To Lushan's falls my dreams take flight.

2 | Qianlong Builds a Garden

(Pages 24-25) Painting of Emperor Qianlong in a garden, admiring peacocks; believed to have been mounted on a wall, the painting shows the cut-out of a doorway.

(Right) Qianlong's poem 'Summer's Day at the Palace of Established Happiness'.

In 1742, when Hongli, the Qianlong emperor (r. 1736–95), had been seven years on the throne, he gave orders for a new palace and garden to be built inside the Forbidden City. The garden was the first of several he would build in his lifetime. He named the group of new structures Jianfu gong and Jianfu gong huayuan — the Palace and Garden of Established Happiness — and it became his most cherished retreat.

The Forbidden City, also known as the Imperial Palace, was a complex of stately halls and smaller internal palaces, some of them no more than a building or two set within a grid of inner walls. Built in the early fifteenth century during the reign of the Ming emperor Yongle (r. 1403–24), it was taken over by the Manchus when they conquered China in 1644 and founded the Qing dynasty. Qianlong, the fourth Manchu ruler to ascend the Chinese throne, had the whole of the Forbidden City to live in, and it was already much too vast for him and his consorts. Besides, he had at his disposal a summer palace on the outskirts of the city, not to mention several hunting parks farther afield. Elaborate excursions to those parks were regular occurrences in the imperial calendar, taking him away from the Forbidden City for long periods at a time. He hardly needed to build anew.

But he had his reasons. First of all, the new Palace and Garden were to be an oasis of serenity, a beautiful place in which to amuse himself and rest from the cares of office. He implied as much in several poems he wrote on the theme of 'A Summer's Day at the Palace of Established Happiness', including the one quoted above. Years later, he justified his passion for garden-building this way:

> An emperor or king, when he has time before holding an audience or attending to the affairs of state, should have extensive grounds to stroll in, and lovely vistas to enjoy. If he has such a place, he will be able to cultivate his mind and refine his emotions; otherwise, he may take pleasure in trivial things and that will only sap his energies and willpower.

In a prose poem written toward the end of his reign, he cast a backward glance to the oppressive heat of his first two summers as emperor. Twenty-seven months after the death of his father, while he was in official mourning, Qianlong lived in the Hall of Mental Cultivation, which had no garden. He was then young and robust enough, he said, to endure the stuffiness of its partitioned chambers, but he could foresee a time when he would yearn for cooler surroundings. A more refreshing milieu tempered by trees, open galleries and promenades was the answer.

His favorite place in the Garden of the Palace of Established Happiness was to be the Pavilion of Tranquil Ease. Several poems were composed there; the provenance of the pavilion's name is clear from one of them:

> Voices from the town bemoan the unusual heat,
> Enclosed by walls of red, unlike a house with a garden,
> The palace is sweltering.
> Only in the Pavilion of Tranquil Ease can one seek the crisp, cool air.
> Once, in the quiet delicious cool, I did convene
> A meeting to talk about religion and poetry.
> But indulgence in such tranquility can only be rare
> When one bears the joys and sorrows of all under heaven.

Ever anxious to deflect accusations of self-indulgence, though, Qianlong also claimed a filial motive. Anticipating his mother's old age, when she might ail and become infirm, he thought that a palace garden would be a fitting place of convalescence for her. And when the inevitable time came for him to mourn her demise, would a garden not be just as recuperative for him? Perhaps Qianlong protested his filial piety too often, but he was in fact an exemplary and solicitous son, even if the Palace of Established Happiness was never

to fulfil its morbid purpose, much to his later regret. Instead, he spent the mourning period for his mother in the Garden of Perfect Brightness.

Filial affection apart, there was also the precedent set by Qianlong's father, Yongzheng (r. 1723–35). When Yongzheng became emperor, the mansion he had lived in outside the Forbidden City was deemed too exalted for commoners to occupy. It was subsequently dedicated to a higher purpose and consecrated as a temple, a use considered more in keeping with Yongzheng's imperial status. By the time it was Qianlong's

View from the Pavilion of Tranquil Ease toward the Gate of Preserving Integrity.

turn, fawning ministers were clamoring that he should follow his august father's example, and so the tradition came about that when a prince of the blood was elevated to the throne, all the buildings associated with him rose in rank too. An obvious way to raise a building's status was to improve or rebuild. Never one for half measures, Qianlong had no hesitation in knocking down existing buildings and starting afresh. What mattered was that the replacement structures should be a proper and enduring index of his consequence. Before his long reign was over, he would build and refurbish several more gardens and parks, most lavishly at the Garden of Perfect Brightness, his father's summer palace.

In these projects Qianlong betrayed his penchant for conveying imperial prestige through architectural monuments. That was but one measure, however. A great monarch must also evince a palpable interest in such civilized pursuits as scholarship and an appreciation of the arts. Qianlong was energetic in cultivating that perception of himself. He had been well trained, avidly copying the paintings and calligraphy of old masters while in his teens, and it was his proud claim that before ascending the throne he had 'thoroughly got by heart the six classics and the various histories'.

In these projects Qianlong betrayed his penchant for conveying imperial prestige through architectural monuments.

His schooling had been strictly conventional except in one respect: he was educated at court. Born in his father's house in 1711, Hongli was one royal prince among several and genealogically the fourth son of the future Yongzheng. But at ten he was singled out by his grandfather, Emperor Kangxi (r. 1662–1722), and summoned to the Forbidden City. This was a rare honor, for Kangxi had more than 120 other grandsons, and it marked Hongli out very early as a prince with an exceptional destiny. The story goes that Kangxi passed the throne to his fourth son, Hongli's father and the future Yongzheng, on condition that Hongli would be named heir-apparent to succeed in turn.

(Left) Qianlong in a garden: dressed in the robes of a scholar, he is engaged in one of his literary pursuits, perhaps writing a poem.

In the event, the old emperor and his favorite grandson had little time together, for Kangxi died within a year of Hongli's move to the Forbidden City. Nevertheless, there had been encounters enough for Kangxi to leave a strong impression on Hongli's young mind. Once, at a family gathering in the Garden of Perfect Brightness, Hongli was flattered when, after reciting from the classics to the assembled company, Kangxi was generous with his praises and offered to take the boy under his wing. On another occasion, they visited the hunting park at Rehe together; there Hongli not only witnessed Kangxi's skill as a horseman and archer, but saw that he was equally adept at literary pursuits, reading history and practicing calligraphy. In time Hongli's own study of history was to be even more assiduous and extensive.

When Hongli became the Qianlong emperor, he tried harder than his father and grandfather to portray himself as a scholar and aesthete. What better setting could he contrive to foster this image than a garden, a quiet place in which to ponder, give vent to poetry and express his appreciation of nature with impromptu paintings of foliage and flowers? As palaces were to wealth and power, so gardens were to intellectual and aesthetic accomplishments. Qianlong is shown in at least one painting, writing brush in hand, posed in a rustic studio and framed by rock and bamboo. He makes references in his poems as well to 'the constant companionship of books and paintings', and to 'the felicity from books and a *qin*' [Chinese zither]. A garden with a *jiashan* ('artificial mountain'), a piled-up collection of rocks and boulders, also evoked the peak-top habitation of immortals, a mystical world to which the earthbound Taoist or Buddhist aspired. Nothing if not conscientious about his spiritual responsibilities, Qianlong made three pilgrimages to the sacred mountain of Wutai shan during the building of the Palace and Garden of Established Happiness. His poems were sprinkled with references to mountains and immortals.

The site Qianlong chose for his new Palace and Garden was near his former living quarters. Running in close parallel with the north wall of the Forbidden City, there were five residential complexes on the east and five on the west. In contrast to most other halls and palaces, these complexes were prosaically named — First Eastern Abodes, Second Western Abodes, and so on. When he moved to the Forbidden City from his father's house, Hongli had initially lived in the Palace of Nurturing Joy, where his schoolroom was also located. Just before his sixteenth birthday, his wedding took place. This auspicious event was celebrated at the Second Western Abodes, which then became his official quarters: 'I moved from the Palace of Nurturing Joy to the Second Western Abodes upon my marriage in the fifth year of Yongzheng's reign,' he was to recall in an imperial edict. Eight years later he succeeded his father as emperor and the Second Western Abodes gained promotion, too. Yongzheng had started the tradition of upgrading his former residence on becoming emperor. Now, his ministers urged, it was Qianlong's turn to be so honored. Thus, refurbished and renamed the Palace of Multiple

(Right) Hongli preparing to shoot a deer. Following in his grandfather's footsteps, Hongli had hunted since he was a boy.

The Palace of Established Happiness

(Left) A collection of ancient texts, published with imperial permission in 1905, includes drawings of the processes of construction. A comparison with the photographs taken at the Garden site shows that the very same crafts and building activities were employed in the restoration.

(Right) Original Qing-dynasty *tangyang* for a complex at the Garden of Perfect Brightness.

Splendors, the Second Western Abodes would never again be lived in by a mere prince. The buildings on either side of it were converted into respectively a theater and a kitchen. These changes were, however, only the beginning of Qianlong's architectural spree. Within a few years, he would order the demolition of the Fourth and Fifth Western Abodes to clear a space in which to build the Palace and Garden of Established Happiness. The narrow site was, however, less than ideal. Making the best of things, he appropriated the passageway to its west and the side of a courtyard next to it, to create a greater expanse for the garden.

Architecture did not exist as a profession in imperial China, and design was largely the work of builders. Apprenticed to their fathers or masters from an early age, these artisans knew all the structural characteristics of a traditional building and could have erected one without ground plans, scale drawings or written instructions. Yet they had help of a sort. 'The architecture of China,' the architect and architectural historian Liang Sicheng (1901–72) wrote, 'is as old as Chinese civilization', and over that long history it had evolved into a set of variations on a formula, with a building's structural characteristics becoming increasingly standardized. In 1103 Li Jie (c. 1060–1110), an official engaged in construction under the Song emperor Huizong (r. 1100–25), published his *Treatise on Architectural Methods*, a manual covering every aspect of design and technology from a building's foundations to its ornamented roof tiles. This was succeeded by other books, notably *Structural Regulations* issued in 1734 during the Qing. Styles changed between those two dates, but the fundamentals remained the same. All that a builder needed to do, apart from reflecting current practice in certain details, was comply with what was prescribed in such pattern books.

The basic paradigm was set, so it comes as no surprise to find that architectural drawings for the Palace and Garden of Established Happiness have not survived: perhaps few existed in the first place. Such drawings would have been, in any case, closer to artists' illustrations than the plans familiar to builders today. (Significantly, ground plans are not mentioned in *Treatise on*

Architectural Methods and *Structural Regulations*.) There is, however, a relevant statement in a memorial submitted on the fifth day of the twelfth month in the sixth year of the Qianlong reign. It said that the new buildings would be constructed 'according to the *tangyang*'. A *tangyang* was a scale model made of pinewood, papier-mâché or sorghum stalks; the assembled components were fixed with a water-based glue, and a flatiron was then used to press them together. In the Qing court, the management of construction fell within the extensive reach of the Imperial Household Department, which was nevertheless required to submit memorials and await the emperor's decree on every practical issue, from the need to replace tiles on a pavilion roof to the estimated expenditure, however trivial the amount. Any arrangement to start new building works would have also involved the treasury, which calculated the costs of materials, and the model-making room, which took charge of designs. For a large project like the Palace and Garden of Established Happiness, there would have been innumerable memorials, perhaps a handful of drawings and, most useful of all, several *tangyang*.

Imperial Household officials set about the new project with commendable forethought. Besides overseeing the demolition of the Fourth and Fifth Western Abodes and clearing the site, they issued orders for materials to be put in hand. The same memorial recommended the immediate purchase of *qingbaishi*, a greenish-white marble, even though construction would not start until the following spring; but extraction was already proceeding at the quarry and supplies were readily available. A keen eye was kept on expenditure: one Fan Yubin, given responsibility for providing the Garden's plants, was enjoined to be economical in accordance with regulations, while intact tiles taken down from the demolished buildings were to be reclaimed. The submission went on:

> It is as well to lay in bricks and lime in quantities and stockpile them in the vicinity of the construction site. To avoid delay to the construction while awaiting allocation of funds, please advance 50,000 taels* of silver against future expenditure, exact accounts of which will be rendered when costs are ascertained . . . Your servant humbly awaits Your Majesty's instructions on where to draw the aforementioned 50,000 taels.

The silver was duly handed over by the treasury, which continued to release funds as the pavilions and galleries of the Palace and Garden rose in stages over the next nine years. By the time it was finished, the nearly 44,000-square-foot Garden was crammed with buildings — buildings which could be lived in throughout the year, not just in summer.

Echoing the orientation of the Forbidden City's most important buildings along the meridian line, the main structures of the new Palace and Garden faced south. All the buildings were given propitious, even whimsical, names. There were essentially two groups of them. Along one axis was the Palace of Established Happiness, which consisted of a gate on the south; the Hall of Controlling Time; the palace building itself; and an elegant, square open-sided structure named appropriately the Belvedere of Favorable Breezes. Bearing in mind the eventual demise of his mother, Qianlong saw to it that tiles of blue — the color of mourning — were used to roof the Palace of Established Happiness, rather than the customary yellow on the other palace buildings of the Forbidden City. Deep blue tiles with a fringe of turquoise ones were also laid on the roof of the Belvedere of Favorable Breezes.

A short flight of steps led up to the Gate of Preserving Integrity. The Garden lay through this gate. Straight ahead was the Pavilion of Tranquil Ease and, completing this group along the same axis, the Tower of Illuminating Wisdom. Although the large partitioned Pavilion of Tranquil Ease properly belonged to the Garden, it contained the imperial bedchamber and was thus as much a part of the Palace as the Garden. Squeezed between the pavilion and the back wall was the Tower of Illuminating

2 | Qianlong Builds a Garden

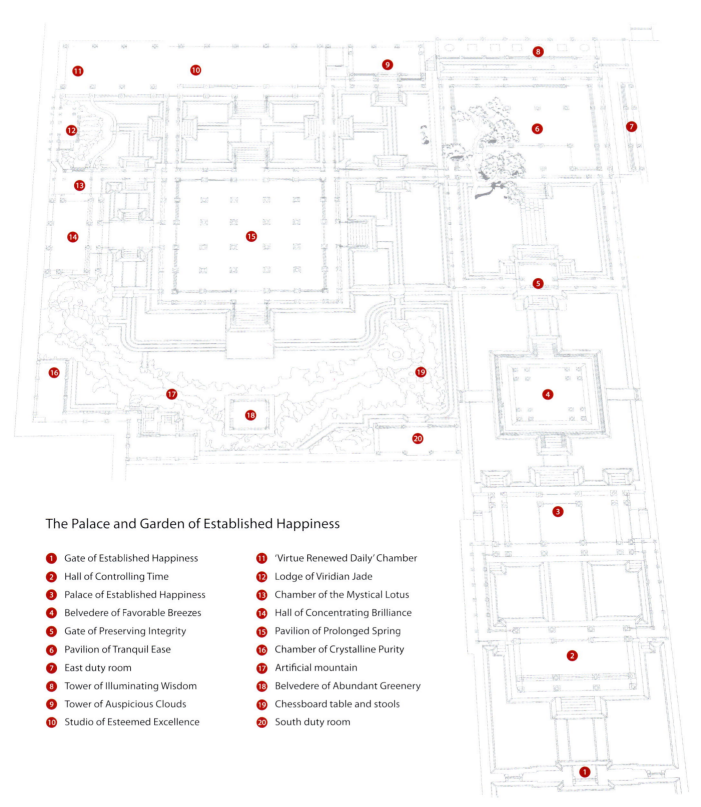

The Palace and Garden of Established Happiness

1. Gate of Established Happiness
2. Hall of Controlling Time
3. Palace of Established Happiness
4. Belvedere of Favorable Breezes
5. Gate of Preserving Integrity
6. Pavilion of Tranquil Ease
7. East duty room
8. Tower of Illuminating Wisdom
9. Tower of Auspicious Clouds
10. Studio of Esteemed Excellence
11. 'Virtue Renewed Daily' Chamber
12. Lodge of Viridian Jade
13. Chamber of the Mystical Lotus
14. Hall of Concentrating Brilliance
15. Pavilion of Prolonged Spring
16. Chamber of Crystalline Purity
17. Artificial mountain
18. Belvedere of Abundant Greenery
19. Chessboard table and stools
20. South duty room

Wisdom, a narrow, compact space which served as a Buddhist shrine. It shared a staircase with the Tower of Auspicious Clouds, which lay at right angles to the axis. To the west was a tiny enclosure, most probably a utility room for the washing and storage of chamber pots.

A second cluster of buildings took up most of the remaining space. Occupying the northwest corner of the Garden was the rectangular Studio of Esteemed Excellence. Continuing counterclockwise, smaller buildings abutted the west wall: the Lodge of Viridian Jade, the Chamber of the Mystical Lotus, the Hall of Concentrating Brilliance and the Chamber of Crystalline Purity. The name of the last building, another Buddhist shrine, was an allusion to a poem which compared the transparency of a pure heart with a jade flask. All these buildings were shallow from front to back, yet there was no sense that they were there purely to relieve the large expanse of high, blank walls. A rockery — artificial mountain — skirted the southern boundary of the Garden. Atop it was the Belvedere of Abundant Greenery. And in the center of the Garden stood the Pavilion of Prolonged Spring, crowned by an impressive finial. This pavilion was a multi-storied, five-bay square edifice to which all the other buildings were peripheral.

So closely pressed together were these structures that, to anyone accustomed to sweeping lawns and flower beds, it is hard to think of this space as a garden at all. A Chinese garden, however, is unlike a Western garden: it is more about architecture than horticulture. Imperial gardens were more architectural than most, and differed even from the famous gardens of the literati in the temperate Yangtze valley. Though nestled among private apartments and utterly removed from public gaze, gardens in the Forbidden City were still designed to express pomp and grandeur. There could be no rustic cottage, wattle fence or plain whitewashed wall. There would be no meandering stream or graceful humpback bridge. With little attempt to imitate natural landscape, the style of this Garden represented the triumph of convention over spontaneity: with its straight lines and right angles, it had a regimented quality about it.

Qianlong . . . was to write of dark pools of shade cast by juniper and pine, of fragrant plum blossom in season and of drifts of silvery snow against the vermilion walls.

The builders of the Garden nevertheless strived for a sense of informality. All the structures were different in size, height and shape. A symmetrical ground plan, so conspicuous a feature of the Forbidden City's outer court, was eschewed. Instead, the builders mapped an irregular layout for the Garden and filled it with architectural variety, even if this variety was more evident in the buildings' designations than their structural aspects. From the multi-storied *lou* (tower) through to the *zhai* (studio), buildings in the Garden ran the whole gamut of *dian*, *tang* (both of which might be translated as 'hall'), *ge*, *xuan* (pavilion), *guan* (lodge) and *ting* (usually small open-sided kiosks, gazebos or belvederes) — every type is represented in the Garden of the Palace of Established Happiness. But the buildings themselves shared

2 | Qianlong Builds a Garden

One of a pair of hanging scrolls by Dong Bangda, commissioned by Qianlong to mark his acquisition of the treasured 'Four Beauties', which were kept in the Pavilion of Tranquil Ease.

the unchanging basic architectural attributes of a timber skeleton and projecting tiled roofs.

Other contrivances were cunningly deployed to give the Garden an air of being more extensive and complex than it was: the partitioning of space, for example. Wedged between the buildings and converging on the Pavilion of Prolonged Spring, a maze of bridges and covered walkways in every direction divided the Garden into separate, secluded enclaves. The enclaves were in fact six sunken courtyards, each overlooked by a building and reached by steps leading down from it. Such contrasts — high and low, open and closed — added to the illusion of depth and space. Qianlong was so pleased with the outcome that he celebrated it in reams of verse and descriptive prose: he was to write of dark pools of shade cast by juniper and pine, of fragrant plum blossom in season and of drifts of silvery snow against the vermilion walls. He also extolled the fine view from a window of the Lodge of Viridian Jade, the welcome coolness of the Pavilion of Tranquil Ease and the brighter hues of peonies after rain. It was no wonder that he chose these pavilions to store the best of his art collection — scrolls painted by old masters to roll out and admire, sensuous jade carvings for holding up to the light to catch their color and translucence, richly glazed porcelain from the ceramics capital Jingdezhen. The Garden was as much the setting for Qianlong's treasures as it was a place of relaxation.

* *a Chinese monetary unit equal to the value of a certain weight (a tael) of standard silver.*

The Palace of Established Happiness

The *Admonitions* Scroll

Mounting pictures and making caskets for the storage of precious curios were all in a day's work for the Imperial Household Department. Such tasks were noted, for example, on the twenty-fifth of the fifth month in the twenty-third year of the Qianlong reign. Afterward, the record said, a eunuch was told to place the lines of Buddhist sutras written in the imperial hand together with a flower painting on *Xuan* paper by Zou Yigui (1686–1774) in the 'Reunion of Four Beauties' ('*Si mei ju*').

The 'Four Beauties' were a set of antique scrolls, the jewels of Qianlong's collection. They were entitled respectively *Admonitions of the Instructress to the Court Ladies*, *Xiao and Xiang Rivers*, *Shu River* and *Nine Songs*. Kept in caskets in the Pavilion of Tranquil Ease, the scrolls gave their collective name to the chamber in which they were housed. The characters '*Si mei ju*' on the chamber's inscribed plaque are thought to be in Qianlong's own hand.

Of the four 'beauties', the most treasured was the *Admonitions* scroll, a work of ink and color on silk. Attributed to the fourth-century master Gu Kaizhi (c.344–c.406), this is a narrative painting illustrating a poem composed about a century earlier by a courtier, Zhang Hua (232–300). The poem's themes are concerned with ideal feminine virtues and the proper conduct of empresses, consorts and imperial concubines. They were also a veiled critique of a ruthless and encroaching empress of the Western Jin (265–316). Appropriating the emperor's authority, Empress Jia had flouted the Confucian code of womanly behavior and hazarded the stability of the dynasty. The admonitions are presented in the scroll as scenarios or morality tales featuring delicately-painted figures of men and women. If

(Above and below) Scenes from the *Admonitions* scroll.

The *Admonitions* Scroll

the admonitions had been heeded by Empress Jia, her life might not have ended in forced suicide after she was toppled in a palace coup.

Actually there are two versions of Qianlong's *Admonitions* scroll, one now in London's British Museum and the other in the Palace Museum in Beijing. Although it is known that neither is original, the attribution to Gu Kaizhi has persisted. The work in the British Museum, painted by an unknown artist between the fifth and sixth centuries, consists of nine of the original twelve scenarios, the first three as well as the text of the fourth having been lost long ago. The copy in the Palace Museum, dated to the twelfth century, is intact.

The 'Four Beauties' were a set of antique scrolls, the jewels of Qianlong's collection.

In China, connoisseurs would traditionally express their admiration for a work of art and pride in owning it by imprinting their seals or writing eulogistic inscriptions either on the painting itself or on its mount. During its passage from one collector to another, the *Admonitions* scroll gathered an accretion of such marks. This had necessitated remounting and extending the length of the scroll by the addition of end-panels. In the case of the British Museum *Admonitions* scroll, what scholars call its 'colophons panel' is almost as long as the painting itself. A patchy history of the painting's ownership has been pieced together by reference to the colophons panel and other documents.

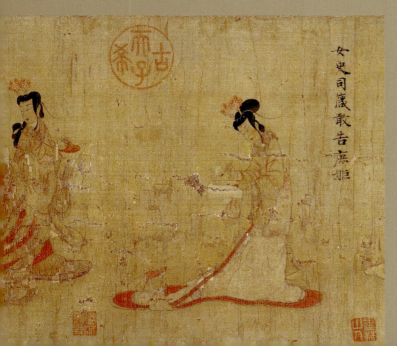

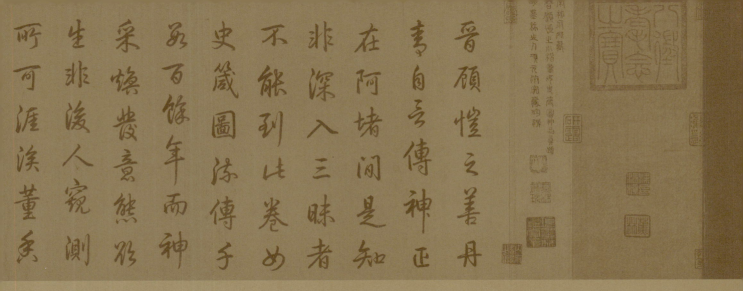

The Palace of Established Happiness

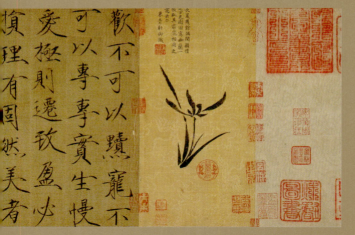

We know that the painting was once in the possession of Huizong, an emperor of the Northern Song. One of his great-grandsons might have held it for a time. It could have passed to the Mongols, for Khubilai Khan completed his conquest of China in 1279, but there was no mention of it in a catalog of confiscated imperial art drawn up by the newly-established Yuan dynasty (1279–1368). Nor was the painting listed in any of the inventories or catalogs produced during the early to middle Ming. Not until the middle fifteenth century did it re-surface: a seal from this period has been identified as that of a high court official. From then on there were frequent changes of ownership but the scroll probably remained in private hands. It came to rest for a while in the 1560s with a scholar-official and connoisseur, Gu Congyi, but moved on again when acquired by an assiduous collector, Xiang Yuanbian. A renowned calligrapher and literati painter, Dong Qichang (1555–1636), commented on this masterpiece while it was in Xiang's possession. Dong particularly mentioned the *Admonitions* and three landscape paintings by the famous Northern Song-dynasty painter Li Gonglin (c.1041–1106) as 'pre-eminent' among the scrolls that had previously belonged to Gu Congyi.

We hear of the *Admonitions* scroll once more at the start of the period with which we are most concerned — the Qianlong era. Some time before its acquisition by Qianlong, the owner of the scroll had been a Korean salt merchant, An Qi. When An Qi died, it returned to the imperial collection. Qianlong had it remounted in 1746, adding a title-piece and, on the end-panel, a painting of a single orchid. He commissioned the artist

(Above and left) Orchid painted by Emperor Qianlong on a panel of the scroll. The calligraphy to its left is believed to be by the Jin emperor Zhangzong.

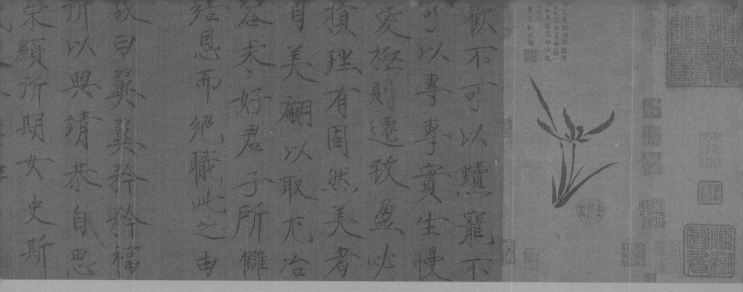

The *Admonitions* Scroll

Zou Yigui to provide a painting-colophon, and appended his own colophon. A translation of this colophon reads:

> Gu Kaizhi of the Jin dynasty was skilful at painting in colour. He said himself that the power to express a man's soul in a portrait depended entirely on the pupils of the eyes; and he knew that without entering deeply into samadhi this power could not be attained. This scroll, illustrating the *Admonitions of the Instructress*, has been handed down for more than a thousand years. Yet the radiance of genius shines forth from it; every expression and attitude is full of life; an art not to be measured by the compasses and plumb-lines of later men. Dong Qichang says in his inscription on Li Gonglin's picture of the *Rivers Xiao and Xiang*: 'Mr Secretary Gu [Gu Congyi] was the owner of four famous scrolls, and in enumerating them he mentions this one first'. This is true! This picture had always been kept in the Imperial Library, but subsequently, having acquired the *Shu River*, *Nine Songs* and *Xiao-Xiang* scrolls by Li Gonglin, I had it shifted to the Jingyi Pavilion of the Jianfu Palace, so that together they might correspond exactly to the famous group mentioned in Dong's note. The inscription says: 'The Four Beauties are brought together to express profound admiration'. Deeply impressed by the unexpected reunion of these ancient and classical treasures, I have hastily scribbled these words, to show that I regard this scroll as 'a sword reunited with its fellow'. Written by the Emperor in the Jingyi Pavilion [Pavilion of Tranquil Ease], five days before the summer solstice of the year *bingyin* [1746] in the reign of Qianlong.

The scroll stayed in the imperial collection until it fell into the hands of a Captain Clarence Johnson in the turmoil of the Boxer rebellion in 1900. Units of Captain Clarence Johnson's regiment, the Bengal Lancers, were among the allied troops sent by Western powers to put down the Boxers. Returning to London in 1902, Johnson asked the British Museum for a valuation of the jade toggle on the scroll — or so the story goes. He eventually sold the scroll to the museum for £25.

The survival of the *Admonitions* scroll through the vicissitudes of history, together with the iconic status it has acquired, is nothing short of a miracle. To re-examine the painting and its 'biography', to study the way it was considered and viewed, some twenty art historians assembled in London in June 2001. The papers delivered at this colloquy were later published in two books. The extract below, from Shane McCausland's *First Masterpiece of Chinese Painting: The Admonitions Scroll*, describes what the painting meant to the Qianlong emperor.

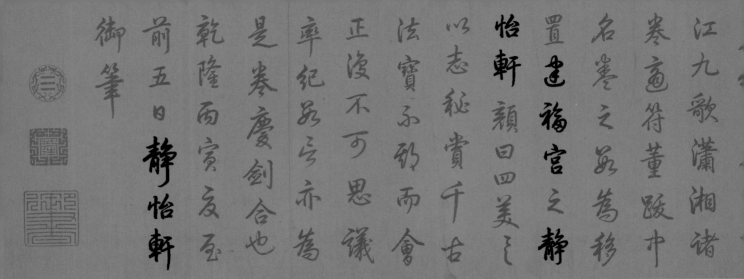

The Palace of Established Happiness

A contemporary of imperial rulers including Frederick the Great of Prussia (r. 1740–86), George II of England (r. 1727–60), and Louis XV of France (r. 1715–74), the Qianlong emperor was also their rival. It would be well worth considering what the equivalent of the *Admonitions* scroll might have been in collections of these European monarchs — a treasure like the Bayeux tapestry, perhaps, in the case of Louis XV? The emperor Qianlong competed with these rulers to be patron of the greatest men of learning and artists of the day. He also maintained a vice-like grip over his Chinese dominion, and was masterly in his use of learning and the arts to stabilize Manchu rule.

When the Qianlong emperor had the *Admonitions* remounted, we assume he included everything that had been mounted with it previously, but he also made a number of significant changes and additions. These included a new patterned blue-brocade outer protective wrapper (frontispiece) on which he attached a buff label inscribed in his own calligraphy with the legend,

> The 'Admonitions of the Instructress to the Court Ladies' painted by Gu Kaizhi, including his calligraphic inscriptions; genuine traces. A trinket [work of art] of the Inner Palace. Divine Category.

This wrapper matched that placed around the handscroll containing the *Xiao and Xiang Rivers* painting in Tokyo National Museum, which, as we will see below, was part of the same set of four most treasured paintings in his collection . . .

A major addition to the scroll is a colophon the Qianlong emperor prepared for it at the Pavilion of Tranquil Ease (Jingyixuan) 'five days before midsummer' in the year 1746, at the time of its remounting in the palace works department. This is the last section of the 'colophons panel'. In this essay written in middle sized running-script calligraphy, he crows over having just acquired what he considered his four most important paintings: the *Admonitions*, together with three he believed to be by the late Northern Song master Li Gonglin, *Xiao and Xiang Rivers* now in Tokyo National Museum, *Shu River* in the Freer-Sackler collection in Washington DC, and *Nine Songs* now in the Palace Museum, Beijing. (None is today believed to be by Li Gonglin.) Overjoyed at having reunited four scrolls that had been owned by Gu Congyi and praised by Dong Qichang, he celebrated what he called the Reunion of Four Beauties by having all four scrolls housed in his residential quarter, the Pavilion of Tranquil Ease, where they would be at his disposal. To celebrate the Reunion, Qianlong also commanded the scholar-official Dong Bangda (1699–1769) to paint a pair of hanging scrolls entitled *Reunion of Four Beauties*. In them, the emperor is seen in the Pavilion of Tranquil Ease relaxing and looking at a scroll. The building has been transported away from the Forbidden City to the more atmospheric surroundings of a mountain retreat.

(Above) A section of the colophons panel of the *Admonitions* scroll showing references to the Palace of Established Happiness (Jianfu gong) and Pavilion of Tranquil Ease (Jingyi xuan). (Right) Scenes from the *Admonitions* scroll.

晉顧愷之善丹
青自云傳神正
在阿堵間是知
非深入三昧者
不能到此卷丒
史箴圖深傳于
玅百餘年而神
采煥發意態然笏
生非後人窺測
所可涯涘董其
光跋李伯時瀟
湘圖云碩中舍
所藏名卷弖四
以此為第一信哉
是圖向貯御書

The *Admonitions* Scroll

The emperor even set aside a corner of this quarter to house and provide space to study these four self-improving works. In so doing, Qianlong restored to the imperial collection one of the early functions of paintings on furnishings: using portraits of historical figures to serve as models for the sovereign to avoid or emulate.

Calling the *Admonitions* scroll one of his Four Beauties was a masterly stroke by which he identified art collecting with enlightened leadership and politics, for the term Four Beauties also referred to the traditional four accomplishments of the virtuous ruler, 'ruling, tranquilizing, manifesting, and glorifying'. When we look at the other three of the Four Beauties, it also becomes clear how he had them outfitted and mounted as a set. He used the same blue brocade for the outer wrappers, he wrote them all title-pieces and colophons, and sketched his own paintings on them, and also commanded four scholar-official painters to provide painting-colophons for them . . .

Including various seals impressed after his painting and inscriptions, the Qianlong emperor stamped in all some several dozen seals on the *Admonitions* scroll and the painting itself in the course of his long reign (1736–95). We know he imposed a cap on the number of imperial seals that could be impressed on paintings, but it is also likely, since he kept the Four Beauties in his private quarters, that he viewed the scroll frequently. In fact, a study of what seals he stamped, where and when would be worthy of another book. One of his seals . . . for instance celebrates his being the father of five generations of his family, and another . . . his eightieth birthday. It is almost as if he attributed these blessings to his possession of the *Admonitions* scroll.

When the Qianlong emperor acquired the *Admonitions* scroll he wrote that he had received 'a divine omen from antiquity'. In short, for him, possessing this object corroborated his mandate to rule China, as well as the conservative political ideology by which he governed.

3 | The Garden in Twilight

3 | The Garden in Twilight

The final years of Qianlong's reign are often described by historians as a turning point in imperial power — from zenith to a protracted decline or, in the Chinese phrase, *sheng ji er shuai*. Certainly, by the last quarter of the eighteenth century, the glorious record of the Qing dynasty had begun to be tarnished by economic troubles and failures of policy. Military campaigns in the frontier areas had been expensive and not uniformly successful; corruption among high officials was on the increase; and revolts — an infallible sign of loss of confidence in the ruling dynasty — broke out over many parts of the empire.

(Pages 44-45) The Garden before restoration.

(Below) One of a set of twenty illustrations painted on paper of famous scenic spots in the Garden of Perfect Brightness.

Above all, the huge growth of population following an era of relative peace and prosperity was intensifying strains on arable land, which had expanded not nearly as rapidly as the number of mouths needing to be fed. Without a sound fiscal system, the government's financial resources were steadily weakening. Qianlong's extravagance and, as he aged, his susceptibility to his court favorite, Heshen, only hastened the decline of dynastic fortune.

Qianlong spent massively on the summer resort at Rehe (now Chengde) outside the Great Wall, and Yuanming yuan or the Garden of Perfect Brightness northwest of Beijing. Rehe, created by Kangxi and encompassing a complex of palaces, lakes and parks, was famous for thirty-six specially designated beauty spots. Qianlong doubled the number of beauty spots and added eight imposing temples, one a copy of the Potala Palace in Lhasa. The Garden of Perfect Brightness, which had belonged to his father, Emperor Yongzheng, lay next to another summer palace and park built by his grandfather, Emperor Kangxi, at the end of the seventeenth century. Kangxi enjoyed the spacious parks of his summer palaces where he could ride under the open sky and roam in the wilds: he was more nostalgic than either his son or grandson for such customary Manchu pursuits as hunting. More temperate, too, when it came to luxuries, Kangxi kept expenditure on those pleasures within bounds. Not so Qianlong, under whom the Garden of Perfect Brightness attained the height of magnificence.

By then this splendid summer palace had in fact become three parks in one, enclosing as it did the original Garden of Perfect Brightness, which Qianlong completed in 1744, the Garden of Everlasting Spring, added in 1751, and the Garden of Gorgeous Spring, laid out twenty years later. Thus, by absorbing gardens to its east and south, the Garden of Perfect Brightness was expanded into an enormous pleasure park that was twelve miles in circumference at its fullest extent.

Dotted among its artificial lakes, islands and man-made hills were thousands of palace buildings, pavilions and gardens with rocks and bridges, all carefully sited to furnish picturesque views. Recalling vistas gleaned on his tours to the Yangtze valley, Qianlong designed settings for pavilions that displayed close affinities with southern landscapes. The most striking feature of the Garden of Perfect Brightness was, however, Qianlong's extraordinary baroque folly, the group of 'Western palaces' erected against the north wall of the Garden of Everlasting Spring. For this he called upon the ingenuity of the European artists resident at his court, particularly Giuseppe Castiglione (1688–1766), who had probably broached the idea of building such a complex in the first place. Once Qianlong had seen the Jesuit artist's pictures of European palaces, what could be more natural than that he should want similar buildings reproduced in his own park?

> '... later generations should not dispense with this garden to build another, thereby draining the resources of the people yet again.'

It was 1747, three years after the completion of the Garden of Perfect Brightness and five years since the commencement of work on the Palace of Established Happiness. Qianlong was ready for a new project, and something in a Western style piqued his fancy. Castiglione began by designing a glasshouse and a maze; then, with the help of Father Michel Benoist (1715–74), another missionary at court, he added a series of floridly-ornamented halls set in Italianate gardens featuring pools and mechanical fountains around which twelve finely-carved animal-figure sculptures spouted jets of water at set times.

The only architecture left after the sack of the Garden of Perfect Brightness by allied forces in 1860 would be the ruins of these Western palaces, built not of wood, as usual in traditional Chinese construction, but mainly in stone and brick, and so were less easily destroyed by fire when the garden was torched. Ironically, relics of broken masonry from those buildings modeled on European palaces would

later be seen as a symbol of China's subjugation by Western powers. They lie near the more recently erected National Humiliation Wall, a reminder of China's decadence and helplessness in the second half of the nineteenth century but also a spur to Chinese patriotism today.

To Qianlong in a sentimental mood, the allure of gardens was irresistible. He was nevertheless conscious of their moral significance, at least of the temptation to excess and extravagance that they presented. In a collection of prose writing on the Garden of Perfect Brightness, he praised its beauty: 'protected by heaven and blessed by the earth', here was a resort worthy of an emperor. However, he also included this warning: 'later generations should not dispense with this garden to build another, thereby draining the resources of the people yet again. Instead they should follow the example of diligence and thriftiness set by my imperial father.' But in a gloss to a poem about the

3 | The Garden in Twilight

(Left) Pavilion Over a Pond seen through the trees in the Garden of the Palace of Compassion and Tranquility.

(Right) A pavilion in Qianlong's Garden sheltering a 'cup-floating stream', site of a poetry rhyming game.

Garden of Everlasting Spring, he forgot himself so far as to say, 'It had long been a cherished wish of mine that should I be so fortunate as to attain the age of eighty-five, having reigned for sixty years, I would retire from ruling. That was why I embellished this garden to the east of the Garden of Perfect Brightness, so that I could then pass the rest of my days in carefree leisure.' For all his advocacy of thriftiness, there was clearly one rule for the reigning monarch and quite another for his descendants. His protestations sound even more hollow if we recall that the Garden of Everlasting Spring was completed in 1751, when he was only forty years old and nowhere close to retirement.

Qianlong did not let up on his construction projects and, in another example of advance planning, embarked on building the Palace of Tranquil Longevity in the northeastern quarter of the Forbidden City in 1772. This was to be for his use in retirement, although he was never to live in it, just as he was never to give up his sovereign powers upon abdication. Thirty-five years earlier he had ascended the throne in a mood of optimism and confidence, praying to heaven that he might rule as wisely and benevolently as his grandfather Kangxi. As he was then only twenty-five years old, his other wish — to be granted a reign as long as Kangxi's — did not seem unreasonable. But out of filial respect, he vowed to rule no longer than his grandfather's sixty years. Thus it was that in 1796, on New Year's Day by the lunar calendar, he ceremoniously passed the throne to his fifteenth son, who became the Jiaqing emperor (r. 1796–1820). Later that day, the abdication proclamation was read to the populace from the high platform of Tiananmen, the Gate of Heavenly Peace.

Because the Palace of Tranquil Longevity was to be for his retirement, Qianlong saw to it that a garden was included in the plans. There are no allusions in his writings to this garden's design; we do know, however, that a part of it was closely modeled on the Garden of the Palace of Established Happiness, which seems to signify his high degree of satisfaction with the prototype.

The Forbidden City now had four gardens. Two were built by Qianlong, as we saw. In fact, so closely was the Garden of the Palace of Tranquil Longevity identified with its creator that it is now known simply as 'Qianlong's Garden'. And once this garden had risen on the east, it was only a matter of time before the Garden of the Palace of Established Happiness was called the 'West Garden'. The other two gardens had been laid out earlier in the Ming dynasty. The Imperial Garden just inside the north gate had existed since the Palace was built by the Ming emperor Yongle in 1420. Some of the architecture within it was added later, and its massive artificial mountain, complete with a water-spouting gargoyle, was built by the Ming emperor Wanli (r. 1573–1620) on the site of a demolished pavilion in 1583. It is the Forbidden City's largest garden. Symmetry clearly rules here, for the central pavilion, the Hall of Imperial Peace, sitting squarely on the meridian line, is balanced on right and left by four pavilions, two of them straddling ponds. Another Ming creation, the garden attached to the Palace of Compassion and Tranquility, lies to the west of the great ceremonial halls. This garden was designated for the use of dowager empresses and consorts, who must have found it both a solace and a respite from the suffocating constraints of court life. The least crowded of the gardens in the Forbidden City, it is graced by a variety of ancient trees including lacebark pine, gingko and the Chinese parasol tree (*Firmiana simplex*). Peeping above those trees is the yellow-tiled pyramid roof of the charming Pavilion Over a Pond, which sits on a bridge over a shallow expanse of water enclosed by white marble balustrades.

Bird's eye view of the Garden of the Palace of Compassion and Tranquility. The Pavilion Over a Pond is the small building in front with a pyramidal roof.

It was at the Garden of Perfect Brightness that the impressive presents brought by Lord Macartney's embassy to Qianlong in 1793 were laid out, and at Rehe that the British party was finally ushered into the presence of the eighty-three-year-old emperor.

By the late eighteenth century considerable contact between Britain and China had developed through trade, but not only did the Qing government confine the traffic to

the southern port of Guangzhou, it imposed numerous other restrictions on the foreigners' freedom of movement as well. Qianlong's foreign policy sprang from a conviction of the power and affluence of China, long used to treating her neighboring countries as tributary states. His relations with more distant foreigners were based on exclusion, for such 'barbarians' were regarded as troublesome and best kept at arm's length. Lord Macartney's mission, on the other hand, was mounted precisely to attempt to forge a closer relationship with Qianlong's empire. It hoped to do this through negotiating a treaty that would allow a diplomatic presence in Beijing and place commerce on a more favorable footing. Qianlong, on the other hand, had no interest in those objectives, and sent Macartney away empty-handed. But that encounter was to be the first link in a long chain of events which eventually brought Western gunboats to the very ports of China, with disastrous consequences for the Chinese empire.

Neither Qianlong nor his heir Jiaqing had any intimation of the coming upheaval. It fell to Jiaqing's successor, Daoguang (r. 1821–50), to face the devastating challenge to China's seclusion by the outside world. Over the next half century, beaten in a series of clashes with Western powers, China was forced into granting territorial concessions to Britain, France, Germany, Russia and Japan. The Qing was further weakened by a series of internal revolts, notably the extensive Taiping rebellion that raged in the south from 1850 to 1864. In 1894–95 a war with Japan over the buffer zone of Korea ended in a humiliating defeat for China and the cession of Taiwan to Japanese rule. A surge of nationalistic feelings was aroused as a result of this, increasing in the next decade with the failed 1898 reform movement and the Boxer uprising and its aftermath. These signs of collapse filled scholars and officials alternately with despair and hope: they despaired of China's patently hapless and antiquated regime, but hoped that ideas borrowed from the more materially-advanced West could solve her problems. It was a time of great intellectual ferment as concerned Chinese searched for viable ways to modernize their country. There were those who championed a conservative approach, based on the slogan 'Chinese learning for substance, Western learning for function'; and others among the Han Chinese who blamed the Manchus for their reactionary rule and pressed for more radical reforms. From 1906 onward, several uprisings were launched by would-be reformers and revolutionaries who made the overthrow of the Qing dynasty the focus of their political program. By the time Puyi ascended the throne as the Xuantong emperor in 1908, popular demand had obliged the Qing to concede a phased introduction of constitutionalism. But the court, though under heavy pressure, was not really prepared to relinquish power to the people. Very soon afterward, the matter would be taken out of its hands.

In the three years or so of the Xuantong reign (1909–11), the age-old and utterly predictable routines of the Imperial Palace continued as before, although formal audiences and rituals were conducted on the emperor's behalf since he was a child at the time. Acting in his name were his father Prince Chun as Regent, and his 'foster mothers' — the widows of the two previous emperors. It was the widow of the Guangxu emperor (r. 1875–1908), dowager empress Longyu, who submitted to the demands for Puyi's abdication. Puyi was then five years old.

Anti-Manchu sentiment and republican activism gained momentum under the revolutionary leader, Sun Yat-sen. A turning point in Sun's movement came in October 1911, when a revolutionary group initiated a revolt in Wuchang, one of the three cities that made up the massive metropolis of Wuhan. Faced with this crisis, a desperate Qing government fell back on the most authoritative army leader of the day, Yuan Shikai (1859–1916). Yuan had enjoyed a successful military career before his appointment as governor-

general of the Hebei region in 1901. There he played a crucial role in building up the modern Beiyang (Northern) army, the most effective of the imperial forces. In 1909 he fell into political disfavor and was forced into retirement.

Then came news of the Wuchang revolt. For help in mustering a forceful military defense, the Qing court summoned Yuan out of retirement, recognizing that he still commanded the loyalty of many officers in the Beiyang army. Yuan was the only person, the court believed, capable of quelling the revolutionaries and saving the dynasty. Yuan told the Qing government that he was prepared to return, but only on his own terms. Once those terms were accepted, he acted decisively to stop the revolutionaries' advance from the south. His next step was to switch loyalties: he thought that if he could persuade the emperor to renounce the throne, the revolutionaries would ask him to form a provisional republican government and head it as its president. A politician as well as a soldier, Yuan was adroit at playing opposing sides off against each other.

Decades later Puyi, writing about his

(Left) The military leader, Yuan Shikai, who hoped to inaugurate a new dynasty with himself as emperor.

abdication, recalled a strange audience in the Hall of Mental Cultivation. On one side sat the dowager empress Longyu; kneeling on a red cushion before her was a portly old man. They were both crying. Puyi did not realize then that he had come upon this emotional scene just after a memorial urging his abdication was presented; nor was he aware that the weeping old man was Yuan Shikai. In fact Yuan was not as despondent as he affected to be, for the wretched fate of the Qing was of less concern to him than his own future.

There was nothing the Qing house could do but compromise, and on February 12, 1912 Longyu duly issued an edict on behalf of Puyi proclaiming his abdication. On that day, the 268-year reign of the Qing dynasty, indeed the two-millennia-old empire, came to an end: 'the sun of the Manchu dynasty had set,' Reginald Johnston recorded, 'and the vast regions over which the ten monarchs of its line had ruled, not always inefficiently or unwisely, for nearly three hundred years, entered upon a night of darkness and storm.'

Puyi, Longyu and four dowager consorts remained in the Forbidden City. They were allowed to do so by the 'Articles of Favorable Treatment of the Great Qing Emperor after his Abdication' offered by the new Republican government. The terms of this settlement were quite generous — at least in theory. Besides continued temporary residence in the rear half of the Forbidden City (before moving to the Summer Palace at some future, unspecified, date), Puyi was permitted to retain his 'title of dignity' and his private properties. The Republican government undertook to treat him with the same courtesy as that accorded to a foreign sovereign. He could keep all his employees, servants and bodyguards: the only stipulation was that no more eunuchs were to be engaged. His protection would continue to be ensured by the Palace Guard whose strength and emoluments would remain as before even though it was to be incorporated into the Republican army. For the upkeep of his household, the government undertook to provide an annual stipend of four million taels (four million silver dollars after the reform of

(Right) Dowager empress Longyu with attendants around the chess table on the artificial mountain in the Garden of the Palace of Established Happiness.

the currency). Finally, not only would the late emperor Guangxu's unfinished mausoleum be completed according to plan and at the Republic's expense, but all the ancestral temples and imperial tombs, and the traditional sacrificial rites associated with them, would be maintained in perpetuity.

'... at a time when China was called a republic and mankind had advanced into the twentieth century I was still living the life of an emperor, breathing the dust of the nineteenth century.'

That was how the 'little court' (*xiao chaoting*) came into being. Within it, Puyi was still known by his reign title, Xuantong. As Reginald Johnston put it, 'the light of day seemed unwilling to withdraw itself entirely from the halls and palaces of the Forbidden City, and the sunset was followed there ... by a lingering twilight.' It was in this twilight world, Puyi said in his autobiography, 'that I was to spend the most absurd childhood possible ... I call it absurd because at a time when China was called a republic and mankind had advanced into the twentieth century I was still living the life of an emperor, breathing the dust of the nineteenth century.'

Breathing the dust of the nineteenth century included learning the classics. Like Qianlong, Puyi took his lessons in the Palace of Nurturing Joy, a narrow study on the eastern side of the Forbidden City, while his living quarters were probably in the Hall of Mental Cultivation. At this stage of his life, the people

Puyi (on the plinth to the far right) and Reginald Johnston (sitting, left) in the Imperial Garden.

closest to him were his tutors. Not that he was a conscientious pupil: in fact, he was so apathetic that when he was eight, his brother Pujie and a couple of cousins were brought to the imperial schoolroom to keep him company and to make his lessons more interesting.

Outside of the Palace walls, the infant Republic took its first steps toward developing a political system to replace the one overthrown. There would be a constitution and the basic institutions of government — a president, a cabinet and a parliament. Enshrining such principles as equality, freedom and the rule of law, the draft constitution provided for national elections and, until those took place, a provisional president. Sun Yat-sen was elected to the provisional presidency by delegates at Nanjing about a month before Puyi's abdication. But since the fate of the new nation was still in the hands of those with military power, a deal was made so that as soon as Puyi officially renounced the throne, Sun Yat-sen yielded to the more commanding Yuan Shikai, who became the first president of China.

National elections took place toward the end of 1912, when Sun Yat-sen's recently formed Nationalist Party, with its base in Nanjing, won a resounding victory. This was a setback for Yuan but, in no mood to test the Nationalist Party's strength in parliament, he moved promptly to consolidate his power, resorting to bribery and assassination to gain his ends. He had seized the upper hand by the time the elected delegates gathered in Beijing the following spring. Further flexing his military muscle, he appointed his own men to posts in the first cabinet. In mid-1913 he sacked the Nationalist governors of Jiangxi, Anhui and Guangdong provinces and by the autumn his troops had captured Nanjing. Sun, his vision of the Republic in tatters, fled China to Japan.

Less than a year later, Yuan succeeded in promulgating a new constitution which more or less allowed him to hold the presidency for life and to nominate his own successor. This made him a virtual dictator; his secret ambition, though, was nothing less than to become emperor. Adept at manipulating his supporters, he arranged for provincial representatives to submit one petition after another calling for him to ascend the throne. After a show of reluctance, Yuan agreed, proclaiming that a new dynasty, to be called Hongxian, would begin its reign in 1916. Before then, he would hold a ceremony in keeping with his imminent imperial elevation. Thus it was that on the day of the winter solstice of 1915, Yuan, riding in an armored car, led an entourage to the Altar of Heaven to sacrifice to the supreme deity, as many an emperor had done before him.

But in the country there was bitter hostility to his monarchist ploy. When several southern provinces refused to recognize his claim and declared independence, Yuan had to concede that plans for his enthronement must be shelved. Shortly afterward, he suddenly fell ill and died — of shame, anger and disappointment, it was said.

No sooner had Yuan died than the loyalists — and there were many, it seemed — began plotting a restoration under Zhang Xun

(1854–1923). General Zhang Xun served under Yuan but had never made a secret of his abiding allegiance to the Qing. Because he and his men still wore the Manchu-style queue as a mark of their loyalty, he was known as the 'pigtailed general'. They argued that the Republic was a failure and people still preferred rule by a sovereign; they just did not want Yuan Shikai to be that sovereign. Reviving the Manchu dynasty, on the other hand, would gain wide support — so they assumed.

Moments after Zhang Xun announced the restoration in July 1917, dragon flags were to be seen all over Beijing. However, the flags were to disappear just as quickly. Five days after Puyi had nominally resumed his throne an airplane came swooping over the Forbidden City, dropping three bombs which caused little damage but wounded a eunuch. This was the army's signal that the Republic was not going to countenance the loyalists' political challenge, pathetic as that challenge was. It was all over in twelve days: as the pigtailed general fled to the protection of the Dutch Legation, the restoration fizzled out.

The conspiracy was not held against Puyi; in fact he was treated gently by the President, Xu Shichang, who urged only a change in his education. It would be useful, the President suggested, for the boy to be occasionally removed from the tutelage of his Chinese teachers and given some lessons in modern political institutions. In March 1919 Reginald Fleming Johnston (1874–1938), a member of the British colonial service who had completed postings in Hong Kong and Weihaiwei, was seconded to the 'little court' to teach Puyi something of the history and culture of the Western world, including the English language. A statement by the Republican authorities implied that Puyi's youth and inexperience lay behind the misguided attempt to resurrect the empire.

If Puyi's monarchist dreams were dashed, republican hopes proved difficult to sustain as well. After the death of Yuan Shikai, China plunged into about a dozen years of civil strife and chaos that came to be known as the 'warlord period'. No-one had mastery of the political situation for very long; there were, instead, nine changes of government, fourteen different presidents, twenty-four cabinet reshuffles and twenty-one premiers. Most of the time, the government's authority did not extend very far beyond the capital, Beijing, for with the breakdown of centralized control, political power was increasingly appropriated by military leaders in the areas under their command. Some of those militarists or warlords became a law unto themselves.

It was in the nature of warlords to fight. Some fought their neighbors over territory, others out of vainglory, while a handful believed that they

(Left) A young Reginald Johnston in Weihaiwei.

(Right) Puyi in the courtyard of the Hall of Mental Cultiviation.

could bring about reform by force. Every now and then one or two of them would subscribe to a vague attempt to achieve national unification. Often, warlords banded together into cliques to wage war on each other. Their alliances were constantly shifting, though, so that at any one time the political scene would appear to be a bewildering confusion of plots and counterplots, and feud upon feud. As usual, the brunt of this disorder fell upon the ordinary people, who were squeezed for taxes to maintain armies, robbed of food to feed the troops, or simply pressed into service as laborers or cannon fodder. The wars made life a misery for the mass of the population.

A Painting and a Photograph

Two images of the destroyed Garden are extant. The earlier is *Peace for the New Year* (*Tai cu shi he*), a hanging scroll by the Qing court painter, Ding Guanpeng, in the collection of the Palace Museum in Taiwan. Its composition contrasts the activities at court with the life of commoners in the bustling streets nearby. In the foreground is a part of the Garden of the Palace of Established Happiness, each pavilion crowned with a different style of roof. Lanterns hanging from the eaves of the Pavilion of Prolonged Spring and the Tower of Auspicious Clouds give the scene a festive air. Beyond the wall is a lively panorama of the boulevard and street below Prospect Hill, thronged with the people of the town. There are pedestrians and riders, shopkeepers and farmers, fortune-tellers and actors. Banners swing from shops and taverns. A carriage is trundling toward a temporary stage on which theatricals are in progress. Wisps of low clouds delineate the separation between court and town, although the dedicatory poem in Emperor Qianlong's calligraphy at the top of the painting suggests that on this day, the seventh day of the new year, there is oneness and harmony as the spring light of propitiousness casts a rosy glow over burgeoning life.

Qianlong evidently admired the artist. Ding Guanpeng's birth and death dates are not known, but from the colophons on his paintings it is clear that he was active between 1735 and 1768. His work is characterized by a lavish use of color: he was, after all, a court painter, required by his imperial patron to be both academic and decorative. His application of perspective and shading suggests that he had absorbed some techniques from Western painters. At the same time, *Peace for the New Year* also demonstrates a Chinese style of architectural representation known as 'ruled-line painting'. The essential tools for this technique are a ruler and a length of bamboo or the barrel of a paint-brush, which is split halfway. With the paint-brush inserted in the split barrel, the artist is able to move the brush along the edge of his ruler and simultaneously keep control over the tension he applies. In this way he can draw straight lines of equal thickness, rather like a modern draftsman using a stylograph.

A Painting and a Photograph

Peace for the New Year by Ding Guanpeng, with the Pavilion of Prolonged Spring in the foreground.

The second image is a photograph by Osvald Sirén published in his two-volume work, *The Imperial Palaces of Peking*. In his preface to the book, Sirén wrote:

> The present work is a fruit of my stay in Peking during 1922, when I had special facilities to study and photograph the most important parts of the Imperial Palaces in and around the capital. I worked with the official permission of the Ministry of the Interior in the nationalized section of the Purple Forbidden City, and with the assistance of a special representative of the President of the Republic in the Sea Palaces [imperial park west and northwest of the Forbidden City landscaped with artificial lakes and pavilions] — now utilized as residences and offices of the President — and I also had the good fortune of visiting, under the personal guidance of the ex-Emperor, many inner quarters of the Forbidden City which then still were reserved as residences of the Imperial family, and where very few outsiders, be they native or foreigners, have ever set their foot. I was thus able to collect a large photographic material, partly of buildings which never before have been reproduced, and there can be little doubt, that this material will prove more and more valuable as years pass by and the buildings fall into decay or are destroyed by fire or voluntary desecration.

Sirén could not have known just how valuable

one of his architectural photographs would turn out to be for the restorers of the Garden of the Palace of Established Happiness. Plate 96 in volume two is of a two-story pavilion with a low, patterned wall adjacent to it. The simple caption gives the name of the pavilion in Chinese and in a romanized form, 'Yang Sing Tchai' (Studio of Character Cultivation).

There is indeed a Studio of Character Cultivation in the Forbidden City — in the southwest quarter of the Imperial Garden — but it is nothing like the pavilion in Sirén's photograph. His caption is wrong, for the building is in fact the Pavilion of Prolonged Spring, the dominant structure in the Garden of the Palace of Established Happiness. Despite the small lapse, his collection of beautifully printed collotypes (there are 274 of them), together with the historical text which accompanies it, was to become a standard work.

Many more reference books were published by Sirén, most of them in English. In 1924 there

(Far left) Osvald Sirén's photograph of the Pavilion of Prolonged Spring, taken in 1922.

(Left and right) The rebuilt Pavilion, shot from the same angle, in 2003 and 2006.

was a study of Chinese sculpture from the fifth to the fourteenth centuries; this was followed by a monumental history of Chinese art in four volumes, a history of Chinese painting in two volumes, and *Chinese Painting: Leading Masters and Principles* in seven volumes. He was an indefatigable academic who was particularly successful at acquiring source material that would be inaccessible to most other scholars; gaining the unique opportunity to record some of the archaic architecture of Beijing in 1922 was but one example of his tenacity.

The huge scope of his scholarship on China's cultural and artistic achievements is all the more astonishing when it is recalled that his specialty at Stockholm University, where he began teaching in 1908, was the Italian trecento. Quite why he transferred his interest to Chinese art is not on record; he was apparently as reserved about himself as about his personal taste in art. His practice of art history was based more on documentation, illustration, synthesis and elucidation than on criticism and subjective valuations.

Osvald Sirén was born in Helsinki in 1879. His professorship at Stockholm University was followed by an appointment to the National Museum in Stockholm, where he was Keeper of Painting and Sculpture from 1928 until his retirement in 1945. He died in 1966.

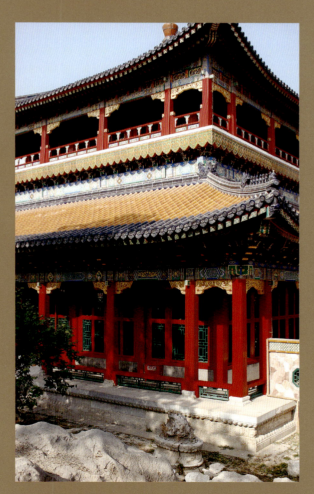

……均儲於內宮內電燈房亦在該殿內易……演電影之用此次如何起火實不知情……太監等所供情形則電燈線或與該火警……以資印證相應函請貴處查照飭傳該……於本月八日下午二時到廳候訊實為公……

4 | What Caused the Fire?

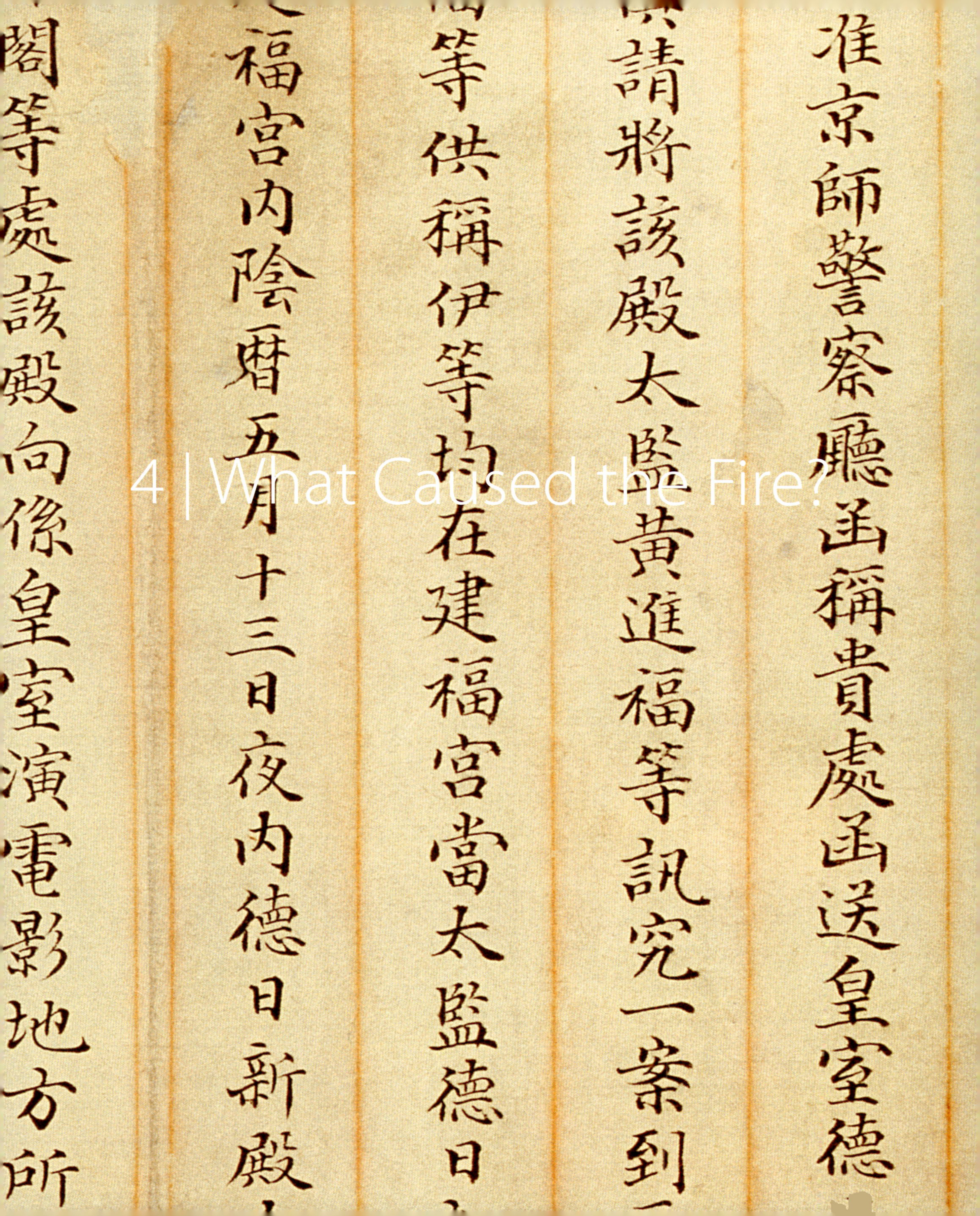

准京師警察廳函稱貴處函送皇室德

供請將該殿太監黃進福等訊究一案到

等供稱伊等均在建福宮當太監德日

福宮內陰曆五月十三日夜內德日新殿

閣等處該殿向係皇室演電影地方所

4 | What Caused the Fire?

With Zou Ailian, Tang Yinian *and* Yang Yongzhan, *First Historical Archives of China*

Writing after the devastation on the night of June 26, 1923, Puyi said 'The cause of the fire is as impenetrable a mystery as the amount of damage it did.' All the same, he laid the blame squarely on eunuchs in the Palace. He had no doubt that many of them were venal; they had been flagrantly stealing from him for a long time, he thought; it would be the work of a moment to remove, while cleaning, a snuff bottle in jade, say, or a Song-dynasty scroll, and spirit it out of the Forbidden City. Reginald Johnston fueled his suspicions, reporting rumors that the many new antique shops which had opened near the Palace were run by eunuchs and members of the Imperial Household or their relatives.

4 | What Caused the Fire?

(Pages 62-63) The memorial from the Office of the Palace Guard to the Imperial Household.

Not surprisingly, Puyi jumped to the conclusion that the fire was started to demolish evidence of the plunder of one of the best-stocked storehouses of treasures in the Forbidden City. He did not, however, launch a thorough investigation, a reflection perhaps of his sad apathy, or his fear that the eunuchs might murder him. What he did do — in a gesture as impulsive as it was foolhardy — was to expel the whole lot of them from the Forbidden City.

'The cause of the fire is as impenetrable a mystery as the amount of damage it did.'

In so doing, Puyi clearly overlooked the fact that he was totally reliant on servants to maintain his living quarters and all his possessions, the very weight of which must have contributed to the oppressive atmosphere of his still considerable court. He had about a thousand eunuchs, and even though the household was now confined to the rear half of the Forbidden City, there was work enough for them. Quite a few looked after the furniture, paintings, books, bronzes, porcelain and myriads of curios that filled each building, inhabited or not. They were supposed to maintain an inventory and, on the face of it, their record-keeping was meticulous: each piece of furniture, each article or ornament, was given a mark or a number. This number, the exact position of a piece (whether on a table or in a display case, for example), the chamber or hall in which it was kept — all those details were meant to be entered in a register by some lowly eunuch. Every now and then a broken piece would be temporarily removed for repair, and that too would be documented. Just as carefully noted were the punishments meted out to careless eunuchs. We hear of thirty lashes for Xu Jinxi in 1851, for accidentally knocking over and smashing a porcelain 'beeswax' *xi* (a washer for writing brushes) while dusting, and the deduction of a month's wages for the eunuch in charge. A year later Xu Jinxi was in trouble again. A gloss in the furnishings list of the Pavilion of Prolonged Spring tells us that he slipped and tumbled when walking upstairs, breaking the yellow wine-jar he was carrying. For this mishap he was given twenty lashes.

It would have been eunuchs who compiled the inventory of the hundred or so items of furnishings in the Pavilion of Tranquil Ease in June 1914, among which were:

(Right) The same memorial.

The Palace of Established Happiness

(This page and far right) To evoke the range of treasures lost in the fire, this page and the next show a representative selection of ornaments and relics from the Palace Museum's current collection. (From left, first row) This jade *bi*, used during rituals in the Zhou dynasty, had belonged to Emperor Qianlong; a flower vase of green jade in the shape of a cabbage; pumpkin-shaped container in silver with gilded floral decoration. (From left, second row) Hairdressing case with combs; elaborately-wrought silver wine vessel; a *baishijian*: this carved red lacquer casket with trays stored writing brushes. (From left, third row) Buddha figure, gilded and studded with pearls; double enamel vase; jeweled potted landscape depicting the fabled abode of the immortals. (Far right) Baskets of fruit in semi-precious stones make up a wall decoration.

> Lacquered wooden four-leaf folding screen decorated with woven floss tapestry of a landscape, partially damaged
> Winged throne seat in hardwood inlaid with jade carving of dragon playing with pearl, pieces of inlay in one wing missing
> Winged chair in hardwood inlaid with marble, marble cracked
> Pair of clocks on small gold-plated bronze stand (a later note: used as emperor's gift on the thirteenth day of the ninth month in the ninth year of the Xuantong era)

It is not too fanciful to see in these few lines a hint of faded grandeur: some of the imperial possessions were simply falling to bits, and there was no longer the will or the resources to repair or renew them. Still, this inventory and other voluminous records preserved the illusion of immutability. More than a century earlier, Qianlong had decreed that nothing in the Forbidden City, not even a blade of grass, must be lost. Long afterward the fiction was kept up that everything was accounted for: were those lists not proof that all was present if not intact? The trouble was, many more of the treasures of the Forbidden City appeared on no list at all. Puyi said as much himself:

> I had been told by my tutors that the treasures of the Ching [Qing] palace were world-famous and that the antiques, calligraphy and paintings alone were amazing both for their quantity and value. Apart from what had been looted by foreign troops in 1860 and 1900, nearly all of the collections that had been amassed by the Ming and Ching Dynasties were still in the palace. Most of these objects were uncatalogued and even those that were catalogued had not been checked so that nobody knew what or how much had been lost. This made things very easy for thieves.

Looking back on it today it all seems to have been an orgy of looting. The looters included everyone from the highest to the humblest; anybody who had the chance to steal did so without the least anxiety. The techniques varied: some people forced locks and stole secretly, while others used legal methods and stole in broad daylight. The former method was the one favoured by most of the eunuchs, while the officials used the latter: they mortgaged pieces, sold them openly, borrowed them 'for appraisal' and asked for them as presents.

But the most sophisticated method, he admitted, was the one whereby he used his brother Pujie as his agent. He would pretend that he was granting Pujie an antique ornament, for instance, or a priceless painting, in gratitude for a service

rendered. His brother would take the article out of the Forbidden City to keep for Puyi or to sell for cash. The proceeds were to constitute Puyi's 'running away fund' — to England, he thought, where he would embark on a course of study. This idea took root shortly after he came under the influence of Reginald Johnston.

The Englishman had given Puyi an inkling of life in the outside world and was to exercise, in the five and a half years he remained as tutor, a great deal of control over the management

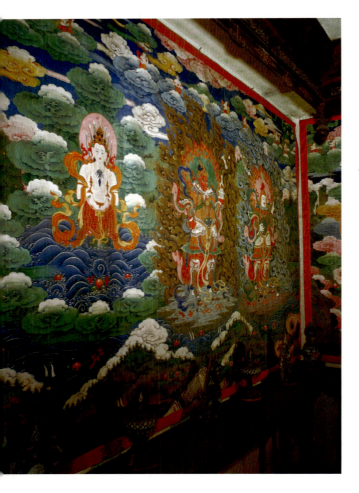

(Left and right) Murals, figurines and ritual objects in the Sanctuary of Buddhist Essence, the matching building to the Tower of Illuminating Wisdom. Also a Buddhist shrine, the Tower of Illuminating Wisdom would have been just as richly furnished before it was destroyed by the fire.

of the court. He was particularly horrified by the corruption of the Imperial Household Department, which had 'a stranglehold' on everything that went on in the Palace. He compared it to 'a vampire draining the life-blood of the dynasty' and blamed it for hastening the Qing dynasty to its demise. In charge of all Palace affairs, from construction and maintenance, security, rituals, daily supplies, tribute and finance to the multitude of servants, the department had ample opportunities to be self-serving. Its accounts for 1915 (or the seventh year of the Xuantong era, because it clung to the customs of imperial times and continued to date memorials by the year of a reign) put the court's expenditure at 2,640,000 taels; of this a significant part must have been diverted into private pockets. In 1924 the department spent 5 million silver dollars in the new currency.

Johnston was certain that the Imperial Household staff was robbing the Palace treasury blind, as were the eunuchs, who took their orders from the department. With all this peculation, it was hardly surprising that the court's finances were in dire straits; no one cared to regulate its expenses or practice economy. And when the Republican government did not always pay the annual stipend promised under the Articles in time or in full, the only recourse was quietly to sell off pieces from the imperial collection to cover the shortfalls. In 1922 the Imperial Household Department invited antique dealers to the Forbidden City to bid for the privilege of auctioning off 138 relics in jade, agate, crystal and enamel; seventy-one items set with gemstones including cat's-eye, ruby, sapphire and amber; sixty-four vases and plates in gold; and 101 items of household utensils in gold-plated silver such as tea caddies, bowls and ewers, as well as censers and seals. Within a year the court was in hock to the Beijing branch of the Hongkong and Shanghai Banking Corporation, and soon after that a loan of 800,000 silver dollars was drawn from the Salt Industry Bank against the security of 365 articles in jade, 200 in porcelain, twenty-three in enamel and twenty-eight in red lacquer.

Proceeds from the auctions of 1922 would have defrayed part of the cost of Puyi's wedding, which took place that year. But, as he tells it, no sooner was it over than 'all the pearls and jade in the empress's crown were stolen and replaced by fakes'. This incident only added to Puyi's unease about continuing to live in the Forbidden City. He felt exploited, hemmed in and, given Beijing's tangled politics, in personal danger. The idea of going abroad now appeared even more attractive, and soon, with Johnston's encouragement, secret preparations were made to effect his escape.

His plan was foiled by his father, Prince Chun, and the Imperial Household. In his frustration, Puyi turned once again to Johnston, who advised him to concentrate on re-organizing the court instead: the rampant theft and embezzlement had gone on long enough. But to discover what was missing, Puyi needed to have an inventory made of his possessions, so one day, with apparent suddenness, he announced that he would look into some of the empty rooms and palaces which had been turned over to storage.

The Palace and Garden of Established Happiness were on his list for inspection. When the eunuchs opened up one of the storerooms, Puyi saw that its doors

> were thickly plastered with strips of sealing-paper and had clearly not been opened for decades, and inside were a number of large chests. It turned out that the very valuable collection of antiques and scrolls they contained were Emperor Chien Lung's [Qianlong's] favourite pieces and that they had been put away after his death. The discovery of all this treasure made me wonder how much wealth I really had.

Soon after checking the contents of those buildings, Puyi recalled in his autobiography, the chests and a great deal besides were lost to the fire that erupted on that warm June night in 1923. Later, Puyi said, as he had 'wanted to find a stretch of empty land for a tennis court where Johnston could teach me to play tennis, a game he said that all the English aristocrats played', he ordered a part of the ruined site to be leveled. Puyi also rode his bicycle in the grounds and built a snowman there one winter.

Such childish pleasures were to be transient, however. In another flare-up of warlord conflict, one general, Feng Yuxiang (1882–1948), staged a *coup d'état*, dismissing the President and forming a new cabinet. On November 5, 1924 Feng's troops presented Puyi with a revised version of the Articles of Favorable Treatment which demanded the imperial family's immediate evacuation of the Forbidden City. That day, Puyi and a pitifully small entourage passed out of the Gate of Divine Prowess to an uncertain future.

With their departure the 500-year occupation of the Forbidden City by emperors of the Ming and Qing dynasties was brought to an end. Johnston was saddened by it, describing that same November day as 'the date on which the twilight that had lingered in the Forbidden City [since the abdication] . . . at last deepened into night.'

After three-quarters of a century, Puyi's conjectures about theft and arson had acquired something like the ring of fact. But was it still possible, if there were the purpose and the means, to unearth the truth? Today, in the First Historical Archives of China, some 400,000 documents, collectively known as the 'Puyi archives', remain largely unexamined and only broadly cataloged. Would a rummage through those archives yield up papers dealing with the fire? Commissioned by China Heritage Fund, researchers in the Historical Archives made such a search in 2002.

Most of the documents in the First Historical Archives have been passed down from the Ming and Qing dynasties. Those from the Republican period are housed in the Second Historical Archives in Nanjing, with one exception: records of the 'little court', which lasted until 1924, are kept together with those of the Xuantong reign (1908–12) and remain with the First Historical Archives. It could be reasonably assumed, therefore, that anything related to the fire would be found in the 'Puyi archives' in Beijing.

The trawl yielded 147 documents. These include detailed lists of food and beverages consumed by the firefighters and others who helped with the clearing up and salvage work in the six to seven weeks following the fire. Officials of the Imperial Household, who presumably directed operations, were generously wined and dined: the lists tell of lunches, teas, dinners and late-night snacks, the total bill amounting to 307 silver dollars for the ten days that they were involved. Over the same period, bottles of wine, cigarettes, tinned foods, meat and vegetables, paraffin for lamps, fruit, tea and cakes were bought for the guards, soldiers and officers — an astonishingly large number of them — who supervised the clearance. Copies were also kept of the letters of thanks from the Imperial Household on behalf of Puyi, notably one to the Italian Legation and another to the British. The letters were accompanied by gifts of money, porcelain, bolts of silk and bottles of wine to their recipients. The four members of the British Legation — Mr and Mrs Carson, Miss Irene Staheyeff, and Mr Gascoigne, although they were not individually named — were each presented with a porcelain vase and a plate.

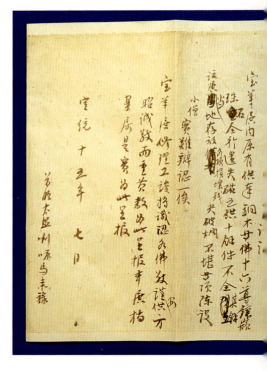

Ma Lailu's draft memorial giving a somewhat incoherent account of the fire.

Several clippings of articles published in Beijing newspapers were also found with the draft letters and memorials. Judging from the reportage, the accusing finger was even then pointing at corrupt eunuchs, careful though the newspapers were to hedge their stories with words like 'unverified' and 'unconfirmed'. Eunuchs were easy targets. One sensational

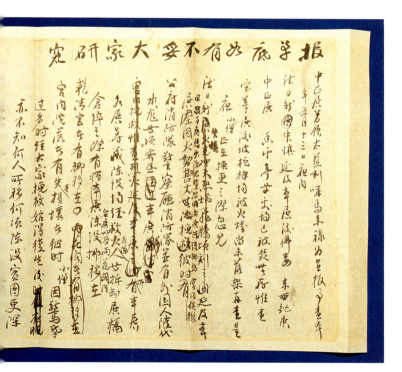

account in the newspaper *Shuntian shibao* on July 2, 1923 claimed that eunuchs who had helped themselves to gold ornaments raked up from the ashes of the fire were searched and beheaded the same day. Other newspapers ran equally dramatic reports, prompting the city police to publish statements in the press to refute the stories. There were sensible editorials too. The fire, said one in the daily, *Minguo ribao*, was a sad reminder that a museum to conserve and display the nation's art treasures was now an urgent priority.

Not only the eunuchs but others who worked for the 'little court' came in for censure. One Palace guard interviewed by the press said, 'The fire started long before anyone outside knew about it. Probably much more could have been salvaged if the alarm was raised earlier. The Palace Guard is a pretty nominal set-up. There's nobody here ordinarily, so when this fire happened, not a soul was around to help.'

Disappointingly, no internal report on the fire was found in the archives. There was only one memorial in draft from Ma Lailu, the eunuch-lama in charge of the Hall of Rectitude to the south of the Garden. Dating the night of the fire by the lunar calendar, the draft (with crossed-out words shown in brackets) gave this account:

> On the night of the thirteenth day of the fifth month, Derixin caught fire. The fire spread to and burnt down the adjacent buildings and the Hall of Rectitude. However, the girders and purlins of the Hall of Precious Prosperity, though scorched, remained in place.
>
> I was just going on duty when I saw the fire in Derixin (the blaze soared to the heavens). It spread to this hall [the Hall of Rectitude] (the fire was so fierce that it was impossible to put it out). At that time, on the orders of the Office of Eunuch Affairs, various buildings were being emptied of their contents. Soon the public fire brigade, the police fire brigade, and some foreigners with hoses arrived and came to (passed) this hall (proceeding to the rescue; however, the fire was spreading to this hall by that time). With the help of the firefighters, the furnishings of this and other halls were stripped, and in everyone's hastiness, the contents of (this) the halls as well as the Pavilion of the Rain of Flowers were moved either to the Palace of Earthly Tranquility, or to the courtyards of the (Pavilion

of the Rain of Flowers, some to the) inner palaces, while some were dropped and damaged in the scramble. Then I fainted from the shock, and it was some time before I was brought round. It was very late at night, my mind was confused and everything was a blur.

Across the top of the memorial was written: 'Draft of report: to be discussed by all if anything is considered inappropriate'.

It is a less than consistent account, and in nothing is the inconsistency greater than in the way Ma Lailu described the progress of the fire. Evidently starting in Derixin, a chamber of the Studio of Esteemed Excellence, the fire engulfed adjacent buildings and 'spread' to the Hall of Rectitude, despite an impeding brick wall and artificial mountain in its path. There could be no doubt, however, that once it had taken hold, the fire would not be quenched quickly — for the simple reason that little water was to hand. Encircled by the rocks of the artificial mountain at the southern edge of the Garden was a well, but it must have been a less bountiful source than the moat outside the Gate of Divine Prowess, which was some distance from the scene of the fire. Away toward the west of Beijing, Jade Spring Mountain feeds a stream which flows into the northwest segment of the moat. From the moat the stream runs beneath the Forbidden City wall along culverts until it resurfaces as the Golden River, the bow-shaped waterway that cuts across the vast courtyard in front of the Gate of Supreme Harmony. It then traces a meandering course before finally flowing out of the Forbidden City under the southern wall. As luck would have it, however, the water level in the moat was low that day, so said Shao Ying and other members of the Imperial Household in a draft letter, dated the twenty-eighth of the fifth month, to the chief of the city's military command:

> Regarding the fire in the Palace ... your captain and soldiers arrived to put it out, only to find that the volume of water in the moat at the Gate of Divine Prowess was insufficient, so great was the blaze. The order was therefore given to lift the sluice gates and increase the flow ...

One result of the fire was a revived interest in improving the Palace's water supply, as another Imperial Household document makes plain:

> The issue of connecting the Palace to the mains has been under consideration for some time, and an appointment was made today with workmen to look into how the pipes might be laid. Once the network and measurements have been ascertained, the matter will be taken further with the water supply company concerned.

A statement by another eunuch, Huang Jinfu, cast an altogether different light on the cause of the fire. His account was contained in a letter from the Office of the Palace Guard to the Imperial Household. Now that China was a republic, the house of Qing no longer had authority to deal with the misdemeanors of its servants. Like everyone else, eunuchs suspected

Damage wreaked by the fire: (left) broken masonry; (right) a section of the derelict Garden 75 years after the fire.

of wrongdoing would be sent by the Palace Guard to be disciplined by the police and the judicial authorities. This letter made it clear that police and official opinion on the fire was coming down on the side of an accidental rather than a deliberate cause.

From the Office of the Palace Guard, twelfth year of the Republic, July 11:

As requested by the city police, the inquiry into the fire at Derixin and further interrogation of Huang Jinfu are to be passed to police headquarters. Huang's deposition is as follows: he is the eunuch assigned to the Palace of Established Happiness, of which the chamber Derixin is a part. On the night of the thirteenth in the fifth month by the lunar calendar, Derixin caught fire and other buildings such as the Pavilion of Prolonged Spring burnt down. That chamber had been used for viewing films, and not only rolls of films but also equipment were stored in it. The electric-lighting room was also in this building, with thick wires leading from it to run the film projector. How the fire started remains unknown, but based on the eunuch's testimony, a connection between the electric wires and the fire seems likely. All this needs to be investigated and confirmed. In the meantime, please ask the person in charge of the electric supply to present himself at police headquarters at two o'clock on the eighth [sic] of this month, to help the police with the inquiry.

Here then, is a more plausible, if also more mundane, explanation. Electricity came to the Forbidden City in 1889 with the installation of a generator in the grounds of the park west of the Palace walls, and 'electric-lighting room' could well have been a homespun term for a transformer. Puyi presumably enjoyed the occasional screening of moving pictures. Celluloid is highly flammable, and a short circuit or a leaking of electrical current caused by faulty wiring could be a potential fire hazard which a fall of rain would only aggravate. Lu Guanli, head of the government electricity board, said as much to Shao Ying when he urged the Imperial Household comptroller to consider acquiring fire insurance for the Forbidden City: 'Quite apart from the fact that the wiring in the Palace has been left unchecked for many years, there was a downpour the evening before last. As with the accident in the deputy presidential palace in Nanjing several years ago, sparks from defective electrical equipment might well have triggered the fire.' Lu also sounded a warning: the firm supplying power to the Palace was badly managed if not downright corrupt, or so he had heard, and this was all the more reason for caution to be exercised. Shao Ying was indeed preoccupied by the danger of electricity, so much so that he resolved to impose a power cut in the Forbidden City. A draft letter from the comptroller to Lu found in the archives, however, attributed the exigency of a power cut not to the risk of fire but to an embarrassing lack of money. It is not known if the supply was actually suspended and if money on electricity bills was thereby saved.

'...as the damage had been done... the less said about it... the better for all concerned.'

Nor do we know the outcome of the interrogations of Ma Lailu and Huang Jinfu, although we may suppose that it was probably inconclusive. For all Puyi's insistence on the eunuchs' culpability, there is no record in the archives of any order to punish them. According to Johnston,

> A few of the eunuchs attached for duty to the destroyed buildings, and also the men in charge of the electric-lighting of the Forbidden City, were placed under arrest. Several were dismissed, but it was not long before some of them, at least, were reinstated. No satisfactory explanation was ever vouchsafed as to why no fire-alarm had been raised till it was too late to save the flaming buildings and their precious contents. The attitude of the Nei Wu Fu seemed to be that as the damage had been done

and could not be remedied, the less said about it, and the sooner it was forgotten, the better for all concerned.

That the Imperial Household officials and the eunuchs, fearful of being blamed, had firmly closed ranks is only to be expected. Their unwillingness to take responsibility for the calamity, a habitual wish to appear circumspect — these are also understandable reactions. Yet a tinge of spuriousness still lingers over Ma Lailu's report, and one wonders what there was to conceal. Question marks hang over, for example, his claim that the fire originated in the Studio of Esteemed Excellence. Where was he at the time? If he had just arrived for duty at the Hall of Rectitude, how could he have seen across a wall and an artificial mountain to the very back of the Garden, some eighty yards away?

He was also vague on how the fire spread to the Hall of Rectitude. It is true that the wall between this and the Garden was, at a little over eight feet high, not likely to stop the fire entirely in its tracks. Nevertheless, the hall was still some distance from the nearest structures in the Garden — almost fifty feet from the Belvedere of Abundant Greenery, and some eighty feet from the Pavilion of Prolonged Spring. For the fire to travel from those structures to the hall, a pretty strong northerly wind needed to be blowing. But as every Beijing citizen knows, the second half of June is high summer, and a particular feature of the weather during this season is the prevalence of a southeasterly wind, especially at night. Only during stormy weather would the wind come from another direction. When the fire started, the rain had ceased and so had, one assumes, any wind from the north or northwest. Writing to her mother, Irene

Looking south across the site of the Hall of Rectitude toward the Pavilion of the Rain of Flowers.

Staheyeff had said: 'Luckily there was no wind, otherwise all would have perished.' Under such conditions, it is hard to see how the flames could have leapt across to the Hall of Rectitude. And even if the wind had not dropped, the puzzle is why the buildings in its path — the Belvedere of Favorable Breezes, the Palace of Established Happiness and the Hall of Controlling Time, all lying to the south or southeast of the blaze — were untouched. Not only did those buildings escape intact, but so did the utility room tucked in the corner between the artificial mountain and the separating wall.

Ma Lailu's narration seems deliberately imprecise on the sequence of events. To the remark about the arrival of the fire brigades, he had originally added 'the fire was spreading to this hall by that time', which would have been a little before three o'clock in the morning. But the sentence was scored through. At what time, then, did the Hall of Rectitude catch fire? How? Did the eunuchs, who were asked to discuss Ma's draft before a fair copy was written out, muddy his report on purpose? These are questions which plant suspicion in one's mind, and perhaps the mystery is not how the fire started in the Studio of Esteemed Excellence, but whether its escalation to the Hall of Rectitude was also accidental.

The Palace of Established Happiness

How Much Was Lost?

With Tang Yinian, *First Historical Archives of China*, *and* Yuan Hongqi, *Palace Museum*

Puyi knew no more about the extent of damage wrought by the fire than he did of the existence of the chests of treasures put away after Qianlong's death. Afterward, all he received from the Imperial Household was a 'muddled' inventory which listed the losses as: 2,665 gold Buddha figures, 1,157 paintings and works of calligraphy, 435 antiques and several tens of thousands of ancient books. Heaven knows, he says in his autobiography, how the department managed to conjure up those figures. He thought that an inventory of what was salvaged from the ashes would provide a better clue. There were, of course, no traces of paintings, calligraphy or ancient porcelain in the rubble but there was a great deal of gold, silver, copper and tin. The gold merchants of Peking were invited by the Household Department to submit tenders and one of them bought the right to dispose of the ashes for 500,000 dollars; he picked out over 17,000 taels* of gold from them. When he had taken what he wanted the Department packed the rest into sacks and distributed them to its personnel. One Department official later told me that four gold altars one foot in height and diameter that his uncle gave to the Yung Ho Kung Temple and the Cypress Grove Temple in Peking were all made of gold extracted from some of these sacks of ashes.

Actually Puyi's recollections were nothing if not flawed, for the Imperial Household submitted quite a different account, the draft of which reads:

Niches filled with Buddha figures and (next two pages) enamel dagoba in the Sanctuary of Buddhist Essence. Judging from the report of gold, silver and other metals salvaged from the fire, its twin building, the Tower of Illuminating Wisdom, also had many dagobas and Buddha figures.

How Much Was Lost?

This memorial reports on the completion of salvage work after the fire on the thirteenth day of the fifth month . . .

The ash and debris were sifted for metallic remnants from melted Buddha figures, scripture tablets and other bronze and tin objects and collected into 508 sacks. Pieces of gilded bronze and damaged jade were gathered and filled forty-three chests. Officials have subjected these to closer inspection. Those objects that have not melted and might be repaired have been set aside . . . they include forty-nine items that are intact . . .

According to a note at the end, the original memorial was submitted to Puyi on the fifth day of the seventh month in the fifteenth year of the Xuantong era, and kept by him for review. To accompany the memorial, there was a detailed list of the forty-nine items retrieved, among them a green jade loop-handled bowl with an incised design of lotus petals; a pair of peaches carved in white jade; a jade ewer carved with a pattern of sunflowers; jade figures of animals, fish and fantastic creatures; a white jade brush washer in the shape of a tiger; carved miniature mountains in white and green jade; large and small jade discs or *bi*; and several bottles and other vessels.

'The ash and debris were sifted for metallic remnants . . . and collected into 508 sacks.'

About two and a half months later, the contents of the 508 sacks were sieved again, an exercise which yielded substantial quantities of gold and silver from objects wrecked by the fire, with the former weighing in at 2,409 taels and the latter at 11,287 taels. On top of all that, fragments of gold, gold mixed with sand and gold dust were also recovered. It is no wonder that dealers in precious metals and jewelry were summoned from the city to bid for the disposal of the still valuable scrap.

So much for gold, silver and jade. To gain an idea of what had perished, we can hunt among the archives from another time — the Guangxu period (1875–1908), for example. From the inventories of furnishings in the Pavilion of Prolonged Spring, the Studio of Esteemed Excellence and the Pavilion of Tranquil Ease alone, we count more than 10,000 objects ranging from furniture of precious hardwoods to bronzes, jades, ceramics, lacquerware, musical instruments, books, scrolls of painting and calligraphy, and clocks and watches. There were ritual vessels from the Shang and Zhou dynasties (c.1500 BC to 221 BC), paintings from the Jin (265–420) and Tang (618–906), porcelain from the Tang and Song (960–1279), not to mention Buddha figures both ancient and contemporary.

Guangxu, and Puyi after him, were heirs to a collection amassed by their ancestor Qianlong. Where the arts were concerned, the distinguishing trait of Qianlong's reign was not creativity but patronage: there was substantial imperial acquisition on the one hand, and an expansion of decorative crafts and artisan production on the other. Qianlong collected every kind of *objet d'art* and artifact, his eclectic taste drawing from the past as well as from different cultural traditions, whether Manchu, Mongolian, Tibetan or European. Of course he also built on the collections of previous emperors. During the Ming, as a result of refinement in techniques, carved

lacquer, porcelain, painted enamel and cloisonné became increasingly prized. While vast quantities of porcelain were acquired for practical uses, most of the objects served no other purpose than as decoration. Qianlong certainly amassed them all, as well as carvings on bamboo, wood and ivory. Curios were sourced from various parts of the empire but were also crafted in the Palace workshops which increased from thirty-eight to forty-one during his reign. Qianlong, it is said, took a personal interest in those workshops. Nothing was manufactured either, without designs being submitted first for imperial approval, and neither effort nor expense was spared to produce ever more exquisite pieces for the emperor's gratification.

The antiques and artifacts were displayed in a variety of cabinets and shelf units, but even greater quantities were stored, and for treasures that were taken out only occasionally and admired, special caskets — large and small — were made. The caskets were themselves fashioned from beautiful materials and finely decorated — lacquered wood inlaid with mother-of-pearl, for example, or red sandalwood carved with archaic motifs. They were called *baishijian* — 'hundred assorted pieces' — for when it came to the likes of snuff bottles or archers' thumb rings in jade, up to a hundred or more could indeed be kept in one casket. Each bottle or ring would be wrapped in a square of silk or brocade before being laid on a tray, drawer or shelf inside. Whether stored in *baishijian* or put on display, Qianlong's magnificent collection was scattered among the places he frequented, both within the Forbidden City and at his villas at Rehe and the Garden of Perfect Brightness. There can be no doubt that countless treasures from this collection were lost in the fire of 1923, for nowhere boasted a greater abundance of antiques, paintings and curios than the Palace and Garden of Established Happiness.

* *both a monetary unit and a unit of weight that once had varying values but was later fixed at roughly 1.333 ounces. thus 17,000 taels weighed nearly 1,420 pounds.*

5 | China Heritage Fund

(Pages 80-81) The Garden restoration's project managers, scaffolders, masons, tilers, carpenters and painters.
(Right) China Heritage Fund logo.

5 | China Heritage Fund

Osvald Sirén photographed the Forbidden City at arguably its most desolate and unforgettable. Puyi and his 'little court' still lived at the rear, it is true, but the outer courts and ceremonial buildings were deserted and silent. That emptiness endowed those buildings with a solemn beauty which would not be seen again, for within three years the fallen Palace had been opened to the public.

ChinaHeritageFund
中国文物保护基金会

On October 10, 1925 the Forbidden City was inaugurated as the Palace Museum. Such a crowd of visitors turned up on the day that traffic in the center of the city was practically brought to a standstill. But it was not an auspicious beginning. Transforming a palace into a museum was not the work of a moment, and the directors struggled to bring order out of the chaos left by the departed court. There were, for a start, more than a million antiquities, paintings, books, relics, statues, imperial robes and furniture to catalog and maintain, not to mention the 178 acres of grounds within the walls. The neglect of years was everywhere evident in the decay and deterioration of the buildings and their surroundings.

> There were ... more than a million antiquities, paintings, books, relics, statues, imperial robes and furniture to catalog and maintain ...

The directors' problems were compounded by the convoluted political situation in Beijing and the rest of the country. Then, as later, their tenure depended on patronage, and less than a year after the inauguration, a change of government resulted in the removal of the incumbents and the installation of new directors. Soon these, too, were replaced. In 1933 the director appointed by the Republican government in Nanjing, Yi Peiji, was harried out of office by allegations of corruption. His accusers claimed that he had purloined antiquities from the Museum and sold them.

No less than it had been for Qianlong, the imperial collection that was now in the custody of the Republican government represented a focus of power and status. For its keepers, those early years cast a long shadow, as their sense of a sacred charge was now mingled with elements of insecurity and mistrust. The dread of losing the collection was particularly acute through the years of political instability. Heroic efforts were made to save the treasures ahead of the Japanese attack on Beijing in 1933, when they were packed up and sent south to Shanghai and onward to the southwestern provinces for protection and concealment. Some of the best and most priceless of the collection never returned to Beijing, but were taken to Taiwan by Generalissimo Chiang Kai-shek and his retreating troops in 1949.

A heightened sense of the collection's vulnerability was inherited by the Communist government which took over in 1949. Though hampered by limited means, those responsible tried hard to provide safer storage for what was left of the treasures. They also faced the daunting challenge of reversing the Forbidden City's physical deterioration over the previous decades. Some of the most unstinting participants in this restoration exercise were demobilized soldiers from the People's Liberation Army. From those beginnings the tradition grew of recruiting trustworthy army officers to the Museum staff; the practice may also have something to do with the pervading compulsion to remain watchful against further loss and theft.

Pei Huanlu joined the Palace Museum from the army in 1991. His life, he says, could be divided into three phases:

> I was born to a peasant family in 1941 in Shanxi. Until I was 20, I led the life of a student. I was given training in coalmining but I joined the army instead and spent the next thirty years working my way up the ranks. I saw action in Vietnam, where I was posted for a year and a half. My time as a soldier turned out to be the best years of my life.
>
> In 1991 I came to the Palace Museum. Why? Well, I was always interested in history, and the job offered a chance to learn more of it. In any case, you can't stay in the army forever. At the time, the Ministry of Culture was looking in the army for people who'd been in collective leadership positions, who'd undertaken political and ideological work, and who'd been secretary of a Party committee. I fit the bill, so I applied. My position at the Palace Museum is deputy director and Party committee secretary.

Between 1991 and 2002 the Palace Museum had several deputy directors but no director. The director before 1991 was Zhang Zhongpei, a scholar and archeologist who, during the turmoil in the summer of 1989, made no secret of his sympathy for the students in Tiananmen Square. While not relieved of his duties until 1991, Zhang was nevertheless inactive in museum administration after June 4, 1989. He was not, according to Pei, a man who shirked responsibility.

Director Pei was put in charge of security, administration and architectural conservation. He found himself unable to reconcile the work of conservation with the budget at his disposal.

Around the time he joined the Palace Museum, China's central government increased its annual funding for the preservation of historical relics from 80 million to 130 million yuan, 'but there are just too many relics requiring preservation. Heritage sites — and I'm only talking about those above ground — number 350,000. Obviously the budget is not enough. Local authorities generally have allocations as well, but they too fall far short of needs.' As for the Palace Museum, maintenance alone cost more than the

annual disbursement of 8 million yuan. There was no thought of soliciting support from other sources. It was only later that the importance of private endowments became clear to Pei: 'We couldn't expect the central government to conjure up more money. That's why we must look to corporations and individuals abroad for donations to strengthen our conservation efforts.'

In 1993 a foreign film company gained permission to shoot a documentary in the

Forbidden City for broadcast on Discovery, a television channel in the United States. Its London-based director was accompanied by his associate producer Caroline Courtauld, a writer and film producer then living in Hong Kong. Another key participant, who was to become critical to the founding of China Heritage Fund, was Diane Woo. An émigrée from Shanghai, Diane Woo has lived in New York since 1959 and travels frequently to China as a consultant to Americans investing in businesses there. The documentary group also had the crucial backing of Wang Limei, the official at China's State Administration of Cultural Heritage (SACH) responsible for foreign liaison.

Preparing for the ground-breaking ceremony.

In talking, thinking and planning the documentary's premiere in Beijing in 1995, the producers touched on the possibility of raising a fund for conservation work on the Forbidden City. It seemed to them entirely appropriate that such a fund should be launched at the premiere, an event that was to be attended by many guests with a strong interest in China. 'By coincidence,' Director Pei recalls, 'the completion of that documentary was going to be in the same year as the Palace Museum's seventieth anniversary. Discovery Channel wished to participate in our celebrations by inviting leading figures from America, Britain and Hong Kong to Beijing. However, when the proposal was submitted to the State Administration of Cultural Heritage, for various reasons there was little support for it.'

Plans for the premiere might have collapsed, but Caroline Courtauld did not abandon the idea of a conservation fund. That summer, back in Hong Kong, and accompanied by Diane Woo, she broached it with Ronnie Chan, scion of a Hong Kong family and Chairman of Hang Lung Group. Then in his mid-forties, Chan had been educated in Hong Kong and at the University of Southern California.

The Hang Lung Group consists of two publicly-traded companies engaged in real estate development and investment in Hong Kong and mainland China. On the private business side, Ronnie Chan co-founded the Morningside group, which owns and manages companies active in Asia, Europe and North America. He has served on the governing boards of a number of international educational and cultural bodies such as the World Economic Forum, the East-West Center, and the University of Southern California. He currently serves as a Vice Chairman of the Asia Society and as Chairman of its Hong Kong Center.

'Caroline Courtauld brought the topic to my attention,' Ronnie Chan recalls, 'I'd never thought of doing cultural heritage restoration, but when I heard about the project I thought it was very worthwhile.' A meeting with Wang Limei in Hong Kong when she was in transit between New York and Beijing confirmed this impression. Ronnie Chan decided to take some soundings, 'to speak to a few friends' as he put it, about getting some money together, having already resolved that his family foundation would put in an amount to get the ball rolling. One of the friends he spoke to was M. R. 'Hank' Greenberg of American International Group (AIG), chairman of The Starr Foundation.

In 1919 Cornelius Vander Starr established his first insurance venture in Shanghai; it grew into the American International Group. When he died in 1968, he left his estate to the Foundation, which in 2004 had assets of U.S.$3.5 billion. In 1994 The Starr Foundation had set a precedent in philanthropy by purchasing from a private European collector ten bronze window panels looted from a pavilion in the Summer Palace during the Boxer rebellion, and offering them to China. This was the first time that a foreign organization had donated missing antiquities back to China. As it happened, the Garden restoration project fell right into one of the Foundation's current program areas — that of making grants to large cultural institutions such as museums. According to Ronnie Chan, Hank Greenberg promised his support soon after hearing about China Heritage Fund.

This was the first time that a foreign organization had donated missing antiquities back to China.

But the current of feeling on the Chinese side needed to be gauged before plunging in, and it was agreed that Caroline Courtauld would fly up to Beijing with Chan to meet the director of SACH. In 1994 the director was Zhang Deqin; with Wang Limei as the intermediary, an appointment was made for lunch at a restaurant in Wangfujing, downtown Beijing. Ronnie Chan told Zhang Deqin that he would try to raise some money 'mainly from Hong Kong Chinese but I would also approach friends of China from the outside world. And I told him about my discussion with Hank. Zhang was right away very touched, visibly touched.' It transpired that Zhang had been directly involved in the reception of The Starr Foundation's gift, so naturally he was delighted at this fresh evidence of interest: 'Yes, for centuries foreigners only plundered cultural relics from us. The first person to return anything to us was Hank Greenberg of AIG.' There was no question that Zhang would not be supportive of both the China Heritage Fund project and its sponsors.

A target for this sponsorship soon presented itself. Pei Huanlu remembers taking Ronnie

Chan to the site of the Garden of the Palace of Established Happiness in the summer of 1995. There had been another candidate for the largesse — the Pavilion of the Rain of Flowers, at the time desperately in need of some attention and repair — 'But the Garden,' said Pei, 'was a much larger and more meaningful project. To restore it had been our aspiration since the 1950s. After looking round the site, Mr Chan asked us to come up with a reconstruction design and estimate.'

(Right) The Pavilion of Prolonged Spring under scaffolding; in the foreground is a model of the same building.

(Left) On site, from left to right: Pei Huanlu, the foreman behind him, Ronnie Chan and Li Yongge.

Back in Hong Kong, Ronnie Chan proceeded to incorporate China Heritage Fund as a non-profit organization. To lend gravitas, Dr Quo-wei Lee was asked to be a co-founder. Dr Q. W. (as he is generally known), formerly chairman of Hang Seng Bank in Hong Kong, had served on the Executive and Legislative Councils there and was an active and highly respected leader of the community. He is a well-known collector and connoisseur of Chinese art. As Chan tells it,

> I never intended to ask Dr Q.W. for money, but one day he happened to be in my office. As I walked him to the elevator, he said, 'Oh, how much money are you expecting?' Well, when you ask your friends to support a cause, it's customary for each one to donate the same amount — 'a portion', you would call it. Dr Q.W. asked me what the portion was. I said I didn't know yet. And then, without my soliciting, he volunteered to give me some money — sizeable money. Obviously Dr Q.W. is a very generous man; he understands the arts and culture of China, and he was my father's close friend and an 'uncle' to me. So when he volunteered, what could I say except 'Thanks a lot, that's wonderful'?
>
> I serve on the board of a British company, and it's my practice not to ask companies on whose boards I serve to donate money unless I am convinced that it's good for the company business-wise. And let's face it, companies give money not just out of the goodness of their hearts but also to further their corporate goals — which is fine, a good thing to do, for corporations to participate in projects that are good for society and good for themselves. So I got Standard Chartered Bank to donate some money knowing that this project will receive a lot of attention.

What Ronnie Chan had not appreciated until his lunch with Zhang Deqin was a startling fact: up to that point the Palace Museum had never had financial sponsorship on such a large scale from any source except the central government. Setting such a precedent, as China Heritage

Fund was proposing to do, would require nothing less than the approval of the State Council.

The application process proved very lengthy and difficult. Just before Christmas 1995, Ronnie Chan was confiding his worries to Diane Woo: 'I am somewhat concerned that China Heritage Fund may lose some momentum.' One stumbling block, according to Wang Limei, was an imminent change of guard at SACH, where Zhang Deqin was about to make way for a new director, although no announcement on his successor would be made for months. Government by its nature is cautious and ponderous, and the workings of bureaucracy, especially at the top, tend to be opaque anywhere, not just in China. Various explanations for the delay suggested themselves: it was possible for China Heritage Fund to have the blessing of a high-ranking Chinese leader and yet be stalled by officials at the lower levels; or there might have been regulatory constraints in accepting donations. Whatever the reason, the project quite simply 'got stuck' — for nearly

The Palace of Established Happiness

88

More examples from the ancient texts on construction: in the photographs, workers on the Garden restoration replicate the same crafts of tiling, joinery and stone-carving.

three years. Never summoned to Beijing to present his proposal or provide details about the Fund's participants, Ronnie Chan thought that delay unfortunate: he felt that he could have raised more money if the initial burst of enthusiasm had not seeped away. But the delay had one positive outcome. In 1999 a late benefactor to the project came in the form of a leading software company in the U.S., Computer Associates International, whose founder and chairman, Charles Wang, is a personal friend of Ronnie Chan. It seemed particularly apt that Wang should support the Garden restoration project, for though he had migrated to New York from Shanghai, his family originally hailed from China's renowned garden city of Suzhou.

In traditional Chinese construction, 'architecture' is even less differentiated from artisanship ...

With such encouraging commitments, Chan took steps to establish a tax-exempt organization, Friends of China Heritage Fund, in the United States. Simpson Thacher & Bartlett, an American law firm with an office in Hong Kong, agreed to provide *pro bono* work to set it up. The board was to consist of Barbara Bush, the former first lady; Barber Conable, a former congressman and president of the World Bank; Ronnie Chan; and Diane Woo, who consented to be secretary.

Pei gave the task of design and estimate to Shi Zhimin, then deputy head of the Palace Museum's department of traditional architecture. In Western terms, 'architecture' means the art and science of designing and constructing buildings, while 'architects' are thought of as practitioners who have undergone years of study and training in universities or professional institutes. Neither the profession nor the discipline emerged in China until the arrival of Western architects in the late nineteenth century. In traditional Chinese construction, 'architecture' is even less differentiated from artisanship, and the 'architect' is frequently a former builder who deploys his experience and technical know-how in design work. Shi Zhimin is, like others in his field within the Palace Museum, not professionally qualified, although to all intents and purposes he works as a designer of buildings. He trained on the job, beginning with a stint in the Palace Museum construction team and gaining promotion to the department of traditional architecture in 1988. His first forecast of the cost of the Garden restoration turned out to be too conservative. Pei recalls: 'The initial estimate reflected our modest expectations of the donation, and when he came again in 1996 Mr Chan said as much. So we went back to the drawing board to work out a more realistic figure.'

Vague even as a preliminary plan, the document produced by the department of traditional architecture in December 1996 expended more words on the history of the Garden than the breakdown of estimated costs. It reads as if its authors had little belief in the restoration becoming a tangible reality, but were going through the exercise because they were told to do so. Nor is the plan accompanied by

drawings. After rehearsing the story of the fire, it outlines the basis of restoration, describing what was extant and proposing a two-phase reconstruction. At present, it reports, no main structures are left save a small three-bay building in the southeast corner. Nevertheless, most of the foundation stones and column bases remain, and from the footprint they define it is clear that there are conspicuous similarities in layout and design to a part of the garden attached to the Palace of Tranquil Longevity. Commonly known as Qianlong's Garden, this was constructed over a period of time from 1772, thirty years after the Palace and Garden of Established Happiness. That the earlier garden served as a model for the later one is, in any case, confirmed by documentary evidence.

A first phase of the reconstruction would include restoring all structures and the artificial mountain as well as establishing plantings around them. Then, if more funds were forthcoming, a second phase to encompass the interior decoration could be embarked upon. Ballpark figures for the former were given: Rmb 2 million for the foundations, Rmb 20 million for the structures, Rmb 5 million to paint and gild them, Rmb 1 million for the artificial mountain and Rmb 800,000 for the plantings. With smaller sums for site clearance and other necessary tasks, the total was a moderate Rmb30 million.
In the expectation that State Council approval would eventually be forthcoming, China Heritage Fund's office in Hong Kong proceeded with reviewing the restoration proposals and budgets. There was a flurry of activity in early 1997 as several key decisions were reached. One important step was getting Happy Harun involved. Daughter of a Shanghainese mother and a Jakarta-born Hakka father, Happy was born and raised in Hong Kong. Her father, with business interests in Indonesia, had changed the family name from Qiu to Harun as a result of policies, introduced in the Sukarno era, which aimed at assimilating ethnic Chinese into the indigenous society. Happy had been a student

(Left) Bird's eye view of Qianlong's Garden.

(Right) Happy Harun and Zhang Jinian, project manager for the Palace Museum, in an informal discussion.

in the United States since her teens, earning a Bachelor's as well as a Master's degree in applied earth sciences from Stanford University. She later tried her wings working for an oil company in Texas. Back in Hong Kong, she was laughingly called *gweimui* — 'foreign girl' — by her Cantonese friends on account of her American mindset and manner. When the management of the China Heritage Fund restoration fell into her lap, she had already been employed as Ronnie Chan's personal assistant for several years, looking after projects in Hong Kong and, for a time, in Shanghai. It happened in the most casual way, she remembers, during a business trip to Shanghai. As Chan talked about the restoration in the Forbidden City, he turned to her and asked, 'Why don't you take care of it for me?'

One of her 'caretaking' responsibilities, as she saw it, would be 'to recruit the right people for the project, including a professional site manager.' But when no suitable candidate for site management materialized, she offered to take on the role herself. Ronnie Chan had reservations about her ability to handle the job, and for her part, Happy was unaware that she was going to be thrown in at the deep end. In 1997 she was only in her thirties. The first to admit that she had no experience of construction management and heritage conservation, nor indeed much of working in China, she confesses to being completely 'ignorant of the scope, of the complexities of the project ... When I told a good friend about it, the first thing she said was "It's a good thing you're not afraid of scale, then." I didn't have a clue what she was talking about.'

Language was to prove a huge stumbling block. For Cantonese-speaking Happy, wrestling with the northern Chinese dialect, *putonghua*, wasn't just a case of altering the intonation and cadence of the spoken words; she found that it also involved learning a new vocabulary. 'That was the biggest challenge ... for me, to express an idea in my poor *putonghua* became very tortuous.' Of course there was always the option of communicating by writing words down, but to someone more used to typing out English on a computer, that was both impractical and laborious. This initial linguistic inadequacy would often come between her and her colleagues at the Palace Museum. But perhaps what her colleagues found most mystifying was her practice of modern management techniques.

Happy claims that she didn't know she had a system of management: 'I just exercised common sense, doing what I thought was best and in the interests of the project.' Her approach was to 'take one step at a time — how else can you do anything?' Impatient by nature, she learnt to bide her time, awaiting developments and postponing decisions 'because you need to in China'. Some of her colleagues at the Palace Museum,

(Left) Not exactly a palace: China Heritage Fund's office in the Forbidden City. Happy Harun and Zhang Shengtong working at the table.

though, were more struck by her confidence and toughness. One later dubbed her a *nüqiangren* ('powerful woman') — strong, not one to suffer fools gladly, and very adept at mustering allies from near and far.

Those allies would include, she hoped, specialists both from within China's cultural establishment and from conservation organizations working internationally. Directors in the Palace Museum have always deferred to the 'old experts', an informal group of specialists whose long years of toiling in their individual fields of research have given them inviolable authority to pontificate on historical, aesthetic and conservation matters. One of its most eminent members is Luo Zhewen, a native of Sichuan who in 1940 entered the Institute for Research in Chinese Architecture and came under the influence of its luminary, Liang Sicheng. Since then Luo has been associated with Tsinghua University and the Ministry of Culture, and published widely on such subjects as ancient pagodas, the Great Wall and imperial tombs. Luo and other experts were now brought in to advise on the Garden project.

'It is as if, on this tiny 4,000-square-metre site, the vast country that once tried to destroy its own past is at last rediscovering it.'

A significant decision made by Happy in 1997 was to recruit the British conservation architect John Sanday as a consultant on stonework. Trained at the University of Bristol, Sanday cut his teeth at Donald Insall Associates, the architectural firm which was to be closely involved in the restoration of Windsor Castle after the devastating fire of 1992. But much of Sanday's conservation work has taken place in Asia. By chance his career began in Nepal: 'I just happened to be in the office one day when the post arrived, and there was a letter from UNESCO asking if Donald knew anybody who would take on the job of preparing an inventory of the historic buildings in the Kathmandu valley.' He volunteered to spend a month there, but, 'as they say in Nepal, you come for a month and you stay a lifetime.' His first project in Kathmandu — an ambitious one which took UNESCO by surprise — was the Hanuman Dhoka, the old royal palace. He has since worked for the Getty Foundation, designing 'the whole process of a grant program', and the World Monuments Fund, for which he is Field Director of a project at Angkor in Cambodia.

In theory China Heritage Fund was now ready to disburse the funds and make a start on its first project just as soon as the State Council gave its approval. As far as anyone knew, the application papers were still moving, though at a snail's pace — from the Palace Museum to the Beijing municipal government, then to the State Administration of Cultural Heritage, which in turn waited to submit a report to the State Council. In the spring of 1999 the green light was finally given. At this point nobody on the Chinese side thought much beyond receiving the money and putting it to use.

On May 24, 1999 a memorandum of understanding was signed with China Cultural Property Promotion Association, an arm of SACH. It confirmed the extent of the project and the responsibilities of the parties concerned. Dividing the work into six (later four) phases, the memorandum stated that the total budget covered only the structures in the Garden and their exterior decoration. The Palace Museum, which had its own department of traditional architecture as well as a restoration and construction division, would be named as the main contractor; SACH, the national body responsible for all heritage sites in China, was to set and maintain standards of quality. As the donor, China Heritage Fund assigned to itself the task of ensuring the proper use of funds. A report of the signing sent over the newswires of Associated Press included a hopeful sound bite from John Sanday, who said that the Garden would be restored using traditional crafts and materials. Master craftsmen could be brought out of retirement to teach apprentices about traditional building techniques, he added, and this would help preserve ancient skills that were in danger of being lost. In another news story published some months later, a reporter for Britain's *Daily Telegraph* wrote: 'It is as if, on this tiny 4,000-square-metre site, the vast country that once tried to destroy its own past is at last rediscovering it.'

It would be another year before a construction contract was signed — a year in which differences in cultures and expectations were played out. In March 2000 Happy was

(Far right) Ronnie Chan and Happy Harun.

telling Diane Woo: 'As to Gugong [the Palace Museum], we are still in negotiation with them on the contract. As expected, the construction contract they have in mind is a seven-page document that is more an agreement for donation than a real construction contract. The challenge is for us to convince them about the importance of a proper contract, and on how to proceed with site control and management ... The more I work with them, the more I realize they really have been operating within a closed, self-contained environment all this time. They don't report to anybody, and whatever system of checks and balances they have applied all these years is definitely inadequate for this project.'

'We could have a series of checks, but at some point we'll just have to close our eyes and dive in.'

The point of 'a proper contract', besides giving protection to both sides, was of course its fine print, spelling out specifications and guidelines with such comprehensiveness and stringency that nobody bound by it would get away with anything remotely slipshod, be that materials or workmanship. As Happy was later to find in the matter of roof tiles, though, it is difficult to legislate against poor craftsmanship, however iron-clad contracts are. Another challenge arose from the dissimilar perceptions of the triangular relationship between China Heritage Fund as donor, the Palace Museum as museum and recipient of the donation, and the Palace Museum as contractor. Happy was later to attribute the problem to the fact that the Palace Museum, which had long been a self-contained organization with little experience of collaborating with outsiders, had simply fallen back on precedent and convention in its dealings with China Heritage Fund, envisaging no continuing role for the donor once the money was paid out. The donor, on the other hand, had every intention of monitoring expenditure and making sure that the job would be done to the best possible standard.

Since there would be no tendering process, as is usual in a commercial construction venture, or an independent surveyor, how was 'the best possible standard' to be gauged? John Sanday suggested forming an *ad hoc* advisory group as another line of control, but he also said, 'We could have a series of checks, but at some point we'll just have to close our eyes and dive in.' Hanging over all this were the issues of trust and expectations. At that juncture, Happy couldn't be certain that the Palace Museum was prepared to, or capable of, meeting her expectations. Li Yongge, head of the Palace Museum's construction division, was to remark later: 'I have been working on repairs to traditional architecture for many years, but during the initial stage of the China Heritage Fund project, I had absolutely no idea as to what was required.' Nevertheless there were those employed on architectural design and restoration who took the view that if they were good enough for the leading museum in China, they were certainly good enough for China Heritage Fund. If that was a somewhat narrow view, it was also perhaps a measure of the effect of long years of isolation from professional dialogs and international conservation practices.

While all this was going on, Happy was becoming frustrated by the lack of progress on the architectural drawings. As it transpired,

Some of the restoration team in 2004.

not Shi Zhimin but another member of the traditional architecture group was assigned to the task by the departmental head. Their attitude appeared to suggest that the buildings would get erected whether the drawings were finished or not. They did not seem familiar with the idea that a project of this kind (or indeed any kind) required proper documentation, an accurate time-scale and a regular flow of communications between those involved. For the China Heritage Fund team, on the other hand, such requirements were only logical: without clear target dates for each phase and a detailed design, no meaningful estimate of labor and material costs could be arrived at. And while there was no question of controlling the design — this was a restoration after all — yet it expected to be confident that even though the need to accommodate minor changes might very well emerge, nevertheless every detail beyond the schematic plans should be anticipated, and no nasty surprises should crop up in the actual construction.

So it became imperative for China Heritage Fund to have its own 'architect' and 'expert', someone with proven expertise on Ming and Qing architecture and, crucially, someone who could check every detail of the drawings when they eventually appeared. A stroke of luck at this point conjured up the very person, Zhang Shengtong.

Conserving the Architecture of the Forbidden City

Before the 1950s, pitifully little was done in the way of conservation, and the Forbidden City's buildings, some already quite derelict by the last years of the Qing dynasty, were showing all the ravages of history. With limited resources, the Republican government made only minor stopgap improvements, such as the laying of a grid of water pipes and the installation of fire extinguishers in 1932.

A five-year plan to put this Palace and monument to order was drawn up during the first years of the People's Republic. Although the trappings of 'feudal society' were now in disgrace, China's new cultural leaders were nevertheless not about to erase the past: they recognized that there was some urgency in restoring and protecting the endangered fabric of its buildings. Zhang Shengtong was one of those recruited to the task:

> I enlisted in the army in 1949 and transferred to the Palace Museum in 1952 to begin work in traditional architecture and restoration. I never received any training — it was a case of learning by doing.
>
> The Palace Museum was then run by the army, as the 'Three-anti' and 'Five-anti' movements were under way and the old staff had been sent off for re-education. Over a thousand people were working in the Palace Museum at that time. Most of those at the supervisory level and above were from the army.
>
> We began by clearing the place. Like removing the ashes of the Garden of the Palace of Established Happiness after the fire, even the piles of rubbish and debris had to be subjected to inspection before disposal, to sift out anything valuable that might have been inadvertently thrown away. Just clearing the weeds sprouting on the roofs was a challenge. In some places the grass had grown pretty high.
>
> So it was all hands to the plow. Those of us in the design section had first to investigate the extent of the damage. With our little hammers, we tapped here and there, thoroughly checking the soundness of the structures. Then we set to with drawings, designs, project planning. In due course these were approved, and then it was the turn of the construction team.
>
> No attention was paid to the Garden of the Palace of Established Happiness, which I finally saw in 1957 — it was a mess! Nobody was even thinking of restoring it: there were simply no resources.

Meanwhile, the waterways around the Forbidden City were dredged, and their embankments strengthened. The repainting of the main buildings along the central axis —the ceremonial halls— proceeded alongside the installation of lightning rods.

The next five-year conservation plan was drawn up to tackle the infrastructure: heating, electrical installations, sewerage disposal and so on. Fifty years after the founding of the People's Republic,

Tiles bound in rope for protection, stacked in a closed part of the Forbidden City. A major overhaul of the Palace is undertaken ahead of the Beijing Olympics in 2008.

attention turned to tidying up the Palace Museum's surroundings and to its exhibition facilities. About half of the Forbidden City was open to the public by the end of this period. But the available resources were never enough: the 160 million yuan allocated over those fifty years was barely sufficient to maintain the areas on display; upkeep of the rest extended only as far as stopping the roofs from leaking and the structures from tumbling down. Even at this minimal level, conservation of the historic buildings, exposed as they are to a rather harsh climate and to the stresses of time, is never less than a formidable struggle.

Economic reform from the early 1980s improved the livelihood of the population but also raised expectations. In the eyes of some visitors today, the Palace Museum seems still to languish in the old ways, remaining somewhat shabby, its facilities sadly outmoded and its exhibition spaces utterly inadequate and devoid of technical conveniences. Others who tramp through have little concept of respecting it as a museum, seeing its halls and pavilions merely as vestiges of a bygone, decadent age. Yet they spare no thought for the fundamental reality of the Forbidden City — that when it was built, only one man, the emperor, was expected to inhabit it. Not least of the dilemmas faced by the Museum's decision-makers is the contrary purpose of needing to treat the buildings very gently on the one hand, and throwing them open as showcases to hordes of tourists on the other.

In a millennial manifesto headed 'New Thoughts, New Orientation, New Program, New Prospects', the Palace Museum placed architecture at the top of its conservation agenda. 'The architecture of the Palace Museum is not only a shell for storing and displaying antiquities; it is a historical monument and a world heritage relic in its own right', the statement acknowledged. By 2008, when Beijing hosts the Olympic Games, the Museum intends to have accomplished repairs and restoration of: road surfaces; Forbidden City walls; decaying structures, notably the Hall of Martial Valor and the Palace of Compassion and Tranquility as well as its garden; internal fixtures such as ceilings, partitions and screen doors; out-of-doors relics in stone and bronze; crumbling foundations to some of the palaces and halls; fire prevention and public safety facilities; and water and electrical infrastructure. In the longer term, it aims to build a state-of-the-art exhibition center, probably underground. The manifesto ends on a buoyant note: 'by 2020, the 600th anniversary of its creation, the Forbidden City will be celebrating not only the glories of its past, but also its present and future.'

6 | Saving the Stones

6 | Saving the Stones

A consensus was reached quickly on how to restore: the Garden would not be returned to its state on the day before the fire, but to its earlier life under Emperor Qianlong. The question was discussed at the first meeting of the Palace Museum's panel of some thirty experts in the fall of 1999, and a comment made by one of them about the last emperor clinched the matter. 'Don't forget,' he said, 'what Puyi did when he took to riding his bicycle there. He had some of the thresholds removed. We would hardly want to replicate this childish act of vandalism.'

(Pages 98-99) This old piece of stone, which had fallen off the side of a terrace, is manhandled off the platform.

(Right) Stonemason working in front of the remains of the Pavilion of Prolonged Spring.

There was no debate about leaving the Garden as a picturesque ruin — that wasn't an option. After all, China Heritage Fund was offering the means for a reconstruction, and those experts had long wanted to replace what had been lost. John Sanday was initially skeptical. He says, often, that he doesn't feel he has the right to reverse the course of history. China Heritage Fund, he thought, should have looked for a project dealing with conservation: 'I didn't fully support the idea of going into the Imperial Palace and recreating something that had long disappeared.' Against this, Happy would argue that 'history is continuous'; in thinking about the complex issue of conservation, she had been particularly struck by a comment in the book *The Future of the Past*: 'The conservation of the past is . . . a peculiarly modern preoccupation, born out of a vain hope that we can freeze time and the vain notion that what we are trying to freeze is the past . . . What we are trying to freeze is actually the present, which offers a highly distorted, fragmentary version of the past.'

Having said that he was not interested in reconstruction, Sanday changed his mind once he saw the stones, although his first sight of the Garden was far from romantic. Left untended for three-quarters of a century, the ground was heaped in dirt and rubble, with abandoned bicycles here and there and even the rusted frame of a bed. But underneath all that was the Garden's architectural footprint in stone. Cracked and eroded though the plinths and terraces were, Sanday could see that they were not so damaged as to be beyond repair. 'There were the remains of stone plinths and platforms, the only evidence that the buildings existed, but now they were actually threatened by a reconstruction.' Seven eroded stone pedestals

also remained where the Tower of Illuminating Wisdom had stood. These could not be anything other than bases for life-size Buddhist sculptures or pagoda-shaped altars, for the building's replica in Qianlong's Garden, the Sanctuary of Buddhist Essence, is still filled with icons of Lamaism, including colorful murals, a statue of Tsong-kha-pa, thousands of Buddha images and six cloisonné dagobas. It is more than likely that the Tower of Illuminating Wisdom was similarly furnished.

John Sanday describes himself as a 'doctor' of historic buildings — mostly those in Asia, where he has been working for thirty years. 'The problems I'm faced with are common to many old buildings in Asia,' he is wont to say. His main interest is masonry: 'The weather in southeast Asia, with recurrent typhoons, is fairly disastrous on materials, particularly stone.' He had no doubt that, with some sensitive attention, most of the Garden's stone remains could be saved. Besides, the exercise could serve as an example of architectural restoration methods adopted by international bodies such as the World Monuments Fund. Privately, he was of the opinion that neither a conservation 'philosophy' nor an integrated approach to conservation procedures was clearly understood or consistently applied in China. To be sure, there is a slew of laws on the protection of cultural relics as well as a set of principles on heritage conservation based on the Venice Charter. Nevertheless, the gap between theory and practice remains disquietingly wide. Sanday says: 'The rather *ad hoc* approach [to conservation] that I observed as a tourist wandering through the Imperial Palace had worried me. There is an enormous need for conservation management planning. I saw for both China Heritage Fund and for myself an opportunity of persuading Chinese bureaucrats and technicians to recognize the difference between conservation and reconstruction.' Part of the planning, as far as Sanday was concerned, was the issue of training, which would begin with involving local craftsmen and end with a restoration that could be maintained by them. In his view, the Garden project could help 'train the minds of the professionals and regenerate the skills of the craftsmen as well as establish standards in architectural conservation. The Imperial Palace is one of the greatest monuments in the world. And you felt that getting a foot in the door and beginning to demonstrate the importance of conservation, training and maintenance might represent a chance to have an impact on the future of historic buildings in China.' Familiar with international conservation practice,

Moving pieces of limestone manually and with the aid of metal rods to lever the heavy load.

he also alerted Happy to the importance of systematically documenting the entire process.

...the gap between theory and practice remains disquietingly wide.

He couldn't wait to get his hands on the stones. Feeling as balked as Happy by the delay in finalizing contracts and budgets, he urged her 'to transcend the bureaucratic maze. The first Tranquil Ease, the Gate of Preserving Integrity and the covered galleries across the Garden. All internal walls, mosaic pathways, garden 'furniture' and trees and plants would fall into phase four.

Work on the stone terrace and column plinths of the Pavilion of Prolonged Spring would come before everything else. From a report by the Palace Museum's own architects, Sanday knew that nothing needed to be done on the foundations. Preliminary tests had revealed that, varying with the loads to be supported, the

day we walk with our overalls on to the site and tackle the stones is the first day that work starts.' At this point, a schedule of building works had already been sketched out. The Pavilion of Prolonged Spring would be restored first. Phase two would be the erection of the structures along the western boundary, together with the artificial mountain and its belvedere. For the third year of construction, the list of planned works comprised the Chamber of Crystalline Purity, the Tower of Auspicious Clouds, the Tower of Illuminating Wisdom, the Pavilion of

depth of the foundations to the buildings in the Garden extended from eight to nearly fifteen feet below ground. Composed of a bedding of tamped earth and backfill retained and capped with brickwork, the foundations were in reasonable condition and generally stable, showing subsidence as a result of surface water seepage only in a few spots.

So Sanday could safely direct his attention to the stonework above ground. 'How much do I know about the architecture of the Imperial Palace?

Well, I'm not a specialist in Chinese architecture but a specialist in materials. My job is to assist China Heritage Fund in the basic principles and procedures of conserving and repairing a historic structure, and that entails the overall planning of the project as well as going into the detailed conservation and repair of the stone bases. In any case I always make a point of learning about the history of a building.' And what he had learnt was that most palatial buildings in China were erected on a platform or terrace of banked-up earth and brick with a facing of dressed limestone slabs. Such terraces could become very high and grand. In the outer court of the Forbidden City, those supporting the ceremonial halls are triple-tiered and edged with carved white marble balustrades. They are approached by stone ramps decorated with spectacular bas-reliefs of dragons chasing flaming pearls against a background of clouds. These ramps were part of the 'Imperial Way', the route traveled by the emperor in his sedan chair as he was carried to and from his audiences at the Hall of Supreme Harmony. In and around this hall, which had the highest status of all the buildings in the land, the stonemason's artistry was lavished on scores of dragons, which are everywhere — noticeably on the baluster caps and in the form of gargoyles for draining rainwater from the open terrace.

In a garden setting, the terraces are lower and plainer but no less finely dressed. They may be of the sort known as *xumizuo*, a reference to the Buddhist peak of Sumeru, the abode of deities. A sumeru base has tiers of stone molded into the undulating double S-shaped contour referred to as *cyma recta* and *cyma reversa* in classical Western architecture. Between the upper and lower curves is a part known as the 'girdle' (*shuyao*), a block of stone carved with friezes of sculpted motifs including flowers, intertwined vines and scrolled clouds. Balustrades surround the terrace, and on their crosspieces are decorative low reliefs, sometimes of lotus petals, another allusion to Buddhism.

Wind and water, not to mention fire, snow and ice, have taken their toll on the sumeru terrace under the Pavilion of Prolonged Spring. Pollution has accelerated what Sanday calls 'structural failure'. On a visit one cold February day in 2000, he saw chunks of broken discolored moldings scattered among weeds around the site. Of the larger blocks still standing, most were cracked or disintegrating, the bas-reliefs on them decaying and wearing away. As he walked round the terrace and scrutinized the stones piece by piece, Sanday noticed that only on the southern

(Below and right) Working on one of the 'girdles' under the Pavilion of Prolonged Spring.

elevation was the damage less than severe, but even there, all the balustrades and coping, as well as the staircase leading up to the terrace, had deteriorated beyond repair. New pieces of stone amounting to some thirteen feet long would have be found to replace a section of the 'girdle' on this side.

(Right) A carved floral scroll in close-up.

He was more optimistic about the column plinths. A cursory inspection showed that all sixty-four remained, though in conditions that ranged from intact if slightly eroded to endangered, so fragmented had some of them become. He decided with mounting excitement that those column plinths would form his first project in the Garden when he returned to Beijing in March.

In March Director Pei suggests a visit to Fangshan, the source of the stone, and Sanday is nothing if not enthusiastic. The district of

Fangshan, less than two hours' drive southwest of Beijing, is studded with quarries. It is the locals' proud boast that back in the fifteenth century Fangshan produced the carved stone ramp which adorns the Imperial Way behind the Hall of Preserving Harmony in the Forbidden City. This monolithic slab, said to weigh as much as 250 tons, was delivered to the Palace one

freezing winter when it could be towed from Fangshan to Emperor Yongle's new capital city along the icy, slippery roads with comparative ease.

Shiwo or Stone Pit Factory in Fangshan is, not to put too fine a point on it, a hole in the ground, a crater scooped out of the flat North China Plain. You can see deposits of the limestone on the crater's vertical face. Along the gently sloping face on the opposite side, men are hauling blocks of stone up to the top with the help of a motorized winch. Though streaked with the reddish soil that lies in piles around, the stone is mostly startlingly white.

Striding round the edge of the open pit and feeling very much in his element, Sanday plies the factory head with questions. Through an interpreter, his host confirms that the factory harvested its stone by slicing from the surface downwards. Several forms of limestone have been excavated from Shiwo and from other quarries in the area, the factory head explains, and the masons differentiate them not by their geological but by their traditional names. 'We tell

The Palace of Established Happiness

106

(Left) Masons preparing to build up a flight of stairs with old and new stone. The triangular slab seen being moved will support the treads. It has been carved with a ribbon motif (far right).

them apart by their appearance,' he says, 'so they are called "China royal white", "greenish-white stone", "speckled stone", "mugwort-leaf green" and so on. The 'greenish-white stone' found at Fangshan is sometimes marked by a coil-like pattern in pale green. Equally distinctive, 'speckled stone' is variegated, exhibiting spots and streaks of color from brown and yellow to pink and purple, and is much prized for use as paving. It was laid, for example, on the floor of the gallery around Pavilion of Prolonged Spring. Smooth, fine-grained and hard, all these types of stone stand up well to weathering.

Fangshan has sent a team of masons with a foreman to work on the Garden project — not an ideal arrangement, in Happy's view. She is concerned about the lack of expertise on stonework within the Palace Museum, which means that there is nobody on the staff available to oversee what the masons are doing. Sanday, disregarding the transient involvement of the team, still has hopes that the masons would be susceptible to his 'learning by doing' exercise. For him, the key to any historic conservation project is the group of craftsmen working on it. Back on site, he asks masons Xu Xuekun, Zhang Jiye and Fan Youliang, already at work dressing slabs of new stone from the Shiwo quarry, 'What do you think should be done with this broken plinth?' They look at him, puzzled. 'Surely,' one can imagine them thinking, 'you dig it up and replace it with a new piece.'

Zhang Shengtong understands this response all too well:

> For years, the thinking behind restoration in the Palace Museum was that if something perishes or rots or is ruined, you replace it. We attach importance to durability but we don't pay enough

attention to what's original. When the department of traditional architecture replaced something, they simply reproduced what was there before. If there was a philosophy of restoration, that was it. Actually the architects hardly needed to be involved; certainly there was little need to produce drawings or precise measurements. Sometimes the artisans took the initiative and made the decisions. With the Garden of the Palace of Established Happiness it's a whole new ball game.

'We attach importance to durability but we don't pay enough attention to what's original.'

Sanday is anxious to demonstrate another approach, one which concedes that, where total authenticity is not a desired or an available option, the best thing with a crumbling structure is to reinforce and secure it in its existing form by discreet and unobtrusive means. Such intervention, which may end up saving only the facade of a structure, could involve the use of unhistorical modern materials and technology. He is insistent, on the other hand, that the result of the intervention should not be disguised, for example by distressing new stone and applying artificial marks of weathering and age. To illustrate all this, he conjures up a videotape of Cambodian workmen in action repairing a broken lintel on a portico at Preah Khan, a Buddhist temple complex built in the late twelfth century, in the ancient Khmer city of Angkor. Under the aegis of the World Monuments Fund, a team of specialists and artisans are wresting the stones with which the temple was built from the ruinous effects of high humidity and the entangling and encroaching vegetation of the jungle. The short film is going to reveal how the principle of 'minimum intervention for maximum protection' could be applied to the stones in the Garden. Sanday has even had the voice-over done in Chinese by an interpreter from one of Angkor's China-sponsored projects, to drive home the point to Xu and others that reinforcing stone is a good example of current conservation practice.

As the video plays, Sanday adds his own commentary:

> How do you begin with a lintel in pieces?

> Well, the first thing is to work out the job of this lintel, which is to support a very heavy weight — in this case about eighteen tons . . . Then you ask yourself what material you can use to substitute or put the strength back into that old piece of stone. One solution is of course to change it for a new piece of stone or, as French archeologists did in the 1950s, put in reinforced concrete supports which at the time was quite a wise thing to do but today, with modern technology, one can find many different ways of consolidating stone. For us the most easily accessible material is stainless steel, which is employed to replace the tensile stress of stone . . .

> Now when you have a piece that's damaged, the easiest way of repairing it is to put in steel because steel has great tensile strength. We also have to take into consideration the problem of shear, which is a lateral deformation of a substance when pressure is exerted on it. My structural engineering colleague at Preah Khan, Dr Predrag Gavrilovic, designed a system whereby we put a cradle of oblique and horizontal stainless steel bars under fractures that were caused mostly by shear. We were then able to reload the lintel, clean up the structure and give this beautiful portico its life again.

What you do with a defective piece of stone, Sanday elaborates, is to cut away the broken

part and fit the gap with a new section. The old and new sections are pinned together with thin stainless steel dowels which act against horizontal movement. Once reassembled correctly, the pieces are bonded together using an epoxy resin thickened to a paste with silica gel powder. Taking about three-quarters of an hour to set, the glue reaches its maximum strength in two to four days depending on the ambient temperature. The setting takes place as a chemical reaction and once complete the material becomes totally inert and is resistant

(Right) Shaping the baluster cap of a balustrade.

(Left) Floral themes are favored for the bas reliefs on the stone terraces.

(Below) The lotus petal motif has Buddhist associations.

to extreme temperatures and weather. Two halves of a split slab of stone can be bonded together in the same way. There is every reason for the same treatment to work in the Garden, Sanday maintains. What's more, this method of repair is not only invisible but also more or less permanent. There's no general formula, though. Where a chunk of stone has spalled off and a new piece is cut to replace it, no attempt will be made to show that it is anything but a pastiche, a blend of old and new.

It is now time to do a trial, and at the Garden site Sanday gets down on his knees to earmark a number of column plinths for repair. As he has brought a clutch of steel pins from Cambodia, all he needs to do is find the right epoxy in Beijing. But tracking down a supplier proves more difficult than expected — which is surprising, since the producer, Swiss chemicals company Sika AG, already has a presence in China where a ready market for its processing materials for sealing, bonding and reinforcing load-bearing structures is found in the booming construction industry. By the next day, however, Sanday has run a can of epoxy to earth. It isn't from Sika, but it may be good enough for the time being.

The experiment begins after lunch. Sanday assembles the equipment as the masons look on. His tools could not be simpler: a power drill to bore holes in the stone for the steel dowels, a bowl to mix the epoxy mortar in, a few spatulas and a syringe fitted with a thick needle for injecting resin into the cracks. He also needs stone dust and clay to fill the larger fissures and to adjust the consistency of the epoxy. The injected adhesive accumulates in a reservoir inside the slab, he explains; being viscous, it will find its way into the internal fractures and consolidate the stone when it sets. Meanwhile the stone dust and clay stop the epoxy from seeping out: 'This is state-of-the-art technology,' Sanday quips, 'using a clod of mother earth!' It doesn't work. By next morning it is clear that the makeshift adhesive has not set under the very low temperatures that prevailed overnight. 'It's too depressing,' says Sanday. 'Unless we get the right material we shall not make progress.'

Meanwhile, Happy is faced with a development that threatens to derail any plans for remedial work on the stone altogether. The Palace Museum's architects have completed their own

survey, which calls for a blanket treatment of the outermost ring of column plinths: 'Their instructions,' she recalls afterward, 'were to replace practically every piece of stone. I didn't feel confident that they had come to this conclusion rationally. The decisions seemed arbitrary enough to suggest to me that the architects had taken the path of least resistance.' As she reflects on the prospects of persuading the architects to do otherwise, she decides that a better use of Sanday's remaining time in Beijing would be for him to conduct a proper analysis of every stone plinth in the Pavilion of Prolonged Spring.

By the time Sanday wrote to Happy from Nepal two months later, his 'right material' — a range of epoxy carrying the brand name 'Sikadur' — had been sourced. He had another piece of good news. His stone analysis now complete, he confirmed that out of the sixty-four column plinths in the Pavilion of Prolonged Spring, only two needed to be replaced. As for the rest, his recommendations for the external plinths ranged from 'remove part of upper section' and 'remove all to base' to 'corner repairs'. He had found the internal plinths in good to excellent condition, their carved decoration only partially eroded and requiring no intervention at all. The commentary in China's own 'Principles for the Conservation of Heritage Sites' was clear on this point: 'Damaged carvings, clay sculptures, mural paintings, rare and valuable decorative paintings, and other artworks must be protected in their existing conditions to guard against deterioration. It is not necessary to restore such works to their original completeness.'

For the masons, it was enough that they had a steady flow of work to keep them in Beijing. One task now completed was the dressing and carving of a foundation stone, but as the Museum officials and invited guests went through the motions on ground-breaking day, May 31, 2000, the masons carried on working. Zhang Jiye chiseled away at a shallow relief of a lotus petal on a plinth, while Fan Youliang rubbed down a sculpted floral frieze on a new slab of stone. They carved by eye, helped by a rough tracing of the design on the stone before they began but otherwise relying merely on their experience and their simple tools of hammer and chisel. An electric sander was used only for finishing and smoothing. Zhang was self-effacing about his craft: 'I grew up with this work being done all around me; you couldn't help but pick up some skill. It wasn't as though I was formally apprenticed to a master mason.'

Later that day, in his speech after the foundation-laying ceremony, Ronnie Chan made the point that the Garden

> encapsulates a period in Chinese history which was quite brilliant. It was the glorious heyday of Qianlong. In retrospect, though, it was also the beginning of dynastic decline. And the Garden, which was razed to the ground in 1923, has been sitting there for more than seventy years. I shouldn't have been given the opportunity to rebuild it. But why hadn't it been rebuilt? The fate of this destroyed Garden is an apt reflection of the tragic and tumultuous history of twentieth-century China. But it is also apt that when China has finally achieved a certain degree of stability and prosperity that somebody should come along to restore this cultural relic.

A repaired column base.

Speaking afterward, Li Yongge, head of the Palace Museum's construction division, promised that the restoration would be 'a work of excellent quality and a model of its kind.' Despite his grandiose words, though, everyone involved realized that the impact of this huge task would be felt in a more pedestrian way — through attrition by a thousand details needing daily if not hourly attention. Happy, increasingly aware of the need to be on the spot when decisions had to be made, was now spending more and more time in Beijing (she was to move out of her hotel into an apartment in the winter of 2001).

'The fate of this destroyed Garden is an apt reflection of the tragic and tumultuous history of twentieth-century China.'

Trouble cropped up within a month of the ground-breaking. It happened quite suddenly, according to Sanday. In fact it had been simmering since the architects submitted their survey, but Sanday had not been monitoring the situation day by day, as Happy had. He had not heard the rumblings of disagreement from the experts who, it seemed, were inclined to the view that repair and conservation of the stones carried more risk than replacement. In June Happy told Sanday that the experts had expressed reservations about his attempt to save some of the stones. 'They generally questioned whether John's proposed methods were sound, and whether epoxy would be reliable,' she explained. By then Sanday knew enough about operations in the Palace Museum to understand that approval from the experts was an essential precondition for any architectural plan or strategy to be adopted. He chose to see their misgivings as a challenge to his whole approach: 'I realized that my neck was on the line, as it were.' His response was to arrange for structural tests to be carried out by engineering laboratories at Beijing's Tsinghua University and 'to organize a meeting, prepare a statement and confront the experts with it.'

As luck would have it, he recalls, the meeting was postponed until the last day of his visit to Beijing. That gave him the breathing space he needed to check the results of Tsinghua's tests and to compose the outlines of his statement. It dawned on him just in time that he should contact his colleague from Cambodia, Dr Predrag Gavrilovic at the Institute of Earthquake Engineering and Engineering Seismology in Skopje, the Republic of Macedonia. 'We set up an e-mail link and sent messages backwards and forwards over two to three days, and he came back with some fantastic facts and figures. I realized that I had the data for a presentation to the committee of experts.' Gavrilovic's report read:

According to European Standards Epoxy has been described as a normal construction material that has a minimum duration of 100 years. This is a standard, which needs no further qualification.

In cases of extreme and aggressive conditions where Epoxy has been considered for works related to structures retaining the sea, laboratory tests have been carried out to ascertain its performance over time and the laboratory scientists are extremely optimistic concerning its characteristics. Their laboratory results have ascertained that under these types of conditions the Epoxy has a minimum life expectancy of 285 years.

In Europe Epoxy Resins have become a standard material for repair. Recent applications have been recorded in Italy: in the 13th-century Cathedral of St Francis of Assisi, which was severely damaged by an earthquake in 1998, and the 11th-century Cathedral of St Mark, in Venice, which is often inundated by sea water. In the UK Epoxy has been used extensively in the structural repair of several cathedrals but in particular the 12th-century York Minster and 10th-century Westminster Abbey.

It is very important that the best-quality materials from reputable companies are used in all cases of repair. If the materials are sub-standard the durability of the repair will be reduced.

If the experts represented a collective force to be reckoned with, Sanday nevertheless hoped that this force would resolve itself into the figure of architectural historian Luo Zhewen. Perhaps Luo, known for his conservationist sympathies, would bring the others to his persuasion. 'I suppose I'd prepared the presentation with him or someone like him in mind,' Sanday acknowledged. Matters then took an unfortunate turn: Luo, as Sanday and Happy discovered to their dismay, had gone out of town before they could contact him.

Between leaving messages for Luo's wife and rounding up the other experts, Happy was desperately running around trying to find equivalent Chinese names for the various technical terms. These were terms that in the

(Left) Stone balustrade being hauled into place.

ordinary course of events she would scarcely have encountered. Her own wry comment afterward was: 'How do you translate into Chinese "epoxy, when set, is neutral"?' In the circumstances she could hardly share Sanday's confidence when he assured her that they were well prepared. In fact, she said, 'I was sweating bullets! However strong John's case might be, it had to be presented in Chinese, and I was the only person available to translate for him.' The irony of the situation was not lost on her: 'Why am I, an outsider, trying to save the stones? What's the logic here? The Palace Museum should be defending the conservation of the stones; instead the onus has fallen on China Heritage Fund.'

John Sanday was not aware of her nervousness about translating his words. On the day, as he remembers it,

> We filed into this enormous room, not quite knowing who was going to be there. Eventually about a dozen people were gathered round the large table in the center of the room, and lo and behold Mr Luo appeared and sat down next to us.
>
> I realized that we had to hold the stage from the beginning and had asked Happy to make certain that I was going to have the audience facing me. I was duly introduced and given the floor.
>
> I said we had two questions to which we wanted answers that day. The first was: should we conserve the whole of the central pavilion terrace? Much to our relief, Mr Luo immediately said, 'Of course!' Given this response, my next question was: how should we undertake its repair and conservation?

Sanday followed this by dealing with the experts' concerns one by one. He had received strong hints, he said, that doubts had been cast on the structural characteristics and durability of epoxy resins. 'Let us then discuss the material first,' he proposed:

> Several different types of epoxy, which is a generic term, are used for this type of adhesive. The level of efficiency of many of these materials may be poor. This can be compounded by not properly observing the method of mixing and application. Your criticisms of epoxy being brittle and prone to discoloration are fully justified in the case of such inferior quality materials.
>
> However, Sika materials have been chosen for use in the Garden project. They are designed for the construction industry and are expected to provide top performance under extreme conditions. The material is more costly as it is made to exacting standards and formulated for use as a structural adhesive in the construction of bridges and roadways as well as for repairing dams.
>
> As for the ageing of epoxy resins, it should be remembered that epoxy is an organic matter which will eventually change its characteristics. Simulated ageing of epoxies under chemical laboratory conditions has given good results, but like all organic materials, including timber, it has a defined life expectancy. From a structural point of view, epoxy can be expected to have a minimum life span of one hundred years with no degradation of its characteristics.

(Right) Wooden columns on repaired column bases.

This was going far beyond anyone's expectations, but there was more. As Sanday moved on to the tests by Tsinghua's engineers, the four specimens they examined were presented: these were an original fragment from the site untouched by the fire; a second piece which had been through the conflagration; a composite sample made up of three pieces of stone glued together; and finally a newly quarried chunk from Fangshan. The tests revealed that little strength had ebbed from the stone purely as a result of the fire. This was more than encouraging. An even better result, Sanday announced, was that all of the stones had proved 'capable of carrying the nine-ton load given as the maximum load expected per column'. And if any doubt still remained, the visible evidence of the third sample was unambiguous. When that composite sample was crushed, typical signs of failure characterized by diagonal fractures appeared; crucially, however, the fractures cut across the glued joints and not a single joint had split open during the tests. This was an utterly convincing demonstration that the epoxy was stronger than the stone. 'It is interesting to note,' Sanday added, 'that in the shear test, the stone fractured not on the line of the epoxy but five millimeters beyond the joint.' The conclusion that emerged from the presentation was clear and irrefutable: the timber columns are more likely to fail and wreak damage to the structure, over time, than any movement caused by the failure of the epoxy.

The meeting had lasted nearly an hour. Sanday remembers very distinctly that

> when the questions had been asked and the voices had died down, I turned to Happy and said, 'Do you realize that we seem to have won this battle?' She looked at me and said, 'Really? Do you think so, John?'

Then we all had lunch and I went off to the airport. Two days later I got an e-mail from Happy. It had finally sunk in and she'd written: 'It's amazing but we have actually won that battle. Thank you very much.'

Masons at work in the Garden: lifting a new piece of stone to replace the broken plinth under the Pavilion of Prolonged Spring; white qingbaishi balustrades are carved on site.

6 | Saving the Stones

115

Kang, Heated Brick Platforms

For Qianlong and members of his court, refuge from the chilly northern winter was provided by chambers known as *nuange* where, reclining on cushions over a heated brick platform under the south window, they could read, eat or take their ease. Such heated platforms or *kang* could be found all over northern China. In a palace or a well-appointed mansion, miniature cabinets and low tables placed on top of the platform would keep knick-knacks, books, spittoons and teacups within reach. By no means were 'warm chambers' found in every pavilion and hall in the Forbidden City, however. They were not installed in the Pavilion of Prolonged Spring, for example, or in other more 'public' buildings visited mainly in the spring and summer months. The Studio of Esteemed Excellence, the Hall of Concentrating Brilliance and the Pavilion of Tranquil Ease, on the other hand, would have been cosy havens judging from the flues found under their broken flooring. The flues are evidence that those buildings had heating under built-in brick platforms and were occupied in winter.

At the Hall of Concentrating Brilliance, the *kang* system consisted of a network of underground flues, two stoke holes for live coals beneath the terrace and a round smoke vent, encircled by a carving of a ribbon-like cloud pattern in the stone, on an external wall. Palace regulations in the Qing dynasty specified the first day of the eleventh month as 'stove-lighting day', when eunuchs would begin feeding burning coal into stoke holes outside the warm chambers of the inner court. All the stoke holes, flues and smoke vents were preserved in the restored Garden.

(Left) In a painting of a winter scene, Qianlong is shown sitting on a *kang*.

(Right) Flues found under the floor of the Hall of Concentrating Brilliance.

Kang, Heated Brick Platforms

7 | The Timber Frame

7 | The Timber Frame

During the early months of 2000 the issues of contract documents, cost estimates and quality management continued to dominate discussions between Happy and the Palace Museum. Happy brooded on the need for an independent surveyor, and looked at various possibilities until Ronnie Chan recruited the help of a Hong Kong firm of chartered quantity surveyors, Levett & Bailey, which agreed to provide free professional services to the project through its branch office in Beijing.

(Pages 118-119) Carpenters working on site.

Another step forward was the formation of a separate advisory group of experts on traditional architecture; its inaugural meeting, convened by Jin Hongkui, deputy director in charge of conservation at the State Administration of Cultural Heritage, took place on February 18. First mooted by John Sanday as 'another line of control', this group was to comprise members of various local offices of SACH (Beijing municipality, Chengde municipality and Hebei province, for example) and to be independent of the Palace Museum. It was one of its members who recommended seventy-one-year-old Zhang Shengtong to Happy.

(Right) A crisscross of columns and beams making up the timber frame of the Pavilion of Tranquil Ease.

A Jiangsu native who has called Shanghai home since 1947, Zhang learnt his trade in the Palace Museum, as we saw. In 1962 he was transferred to Chengde, formerly Rehe, the summer hunting park of emperors Kangxi and Qianlong. To Kangxi's modest resort Qianlong had added eight magnificent temples in the hills to the east. It was the main hall of one of these, the Temple of Universal Peace, that Zhang was recruited to restore. Working on this, he gained 'useful experience and particular knowledge of wooden structures'. He was to stay in Chengde for close to thirty years, except for a break during the Cultural Revolution, when he was sent to work in agriculture, but 'the less said about that the better,' he suggests. In those three decades 'I was involved in more or less all of the Qing buildings in Chengde — in the design and the technical back-up. It was a tremendous way to build up my expertise.'

On retirement in 1991 he decided to go back to Shanghai, but what with one consultancy and another he was not left in idleness for long, and he had kept his hand in. When Happy asked him to participate in the Garden restoration, he said, 'I can't make any long-term commitments, but yes, why don't we give it a try?'

A full set of architectural drawings for the Pavilion of Prolonged Spring, the sole project of the first phase of the reconstruction, was still not ready for review when he arrived in Beijing in the spring of 2000. If there were reasons for the delay, neither he nor Happy was apprised of them. There was, in any case, no uncertainty about the design of the Pavilion: it was to be a hypostyle building of two stories with a mezzanine floor, double-eaved and verandah-encompassed in elevation and topped by a pointed hipped roof. All measurements could be derived from its twin, the Pavilion of Met Expectation in Qianlong's Garden.

Still, a few drawings had been completed, so Zhang was able to make some sort of start immediately. It was just as well that he had a sharp eye for inconsistencies, for he found the drawings rife with errors — discrepancies in measurements, miscalculations and wrong

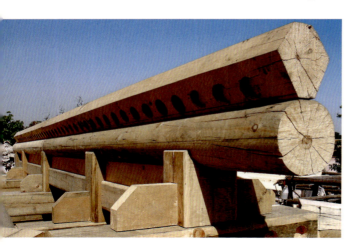

positioning of components in the overall structure. He spent his first weeks on the job marking the blueprints and sending them back for amendments. Inevitably, a confrontational element crept into China Heritage Fund's dealings with the department of traditional architecture, an unfortunate outcome that would only be resolved later that fall by a change of personnel, when responsibility for design was transferred back to Shi Zhimin. Shi had worked on the preliminary restoration plan for the Garden in 1996.

To the untrained eye, the drawings seemed covered with terms which had very little to do with engineering or architecture. Grasping this bewildering nomenclature — the legacy of early craftsmen — comes with long experience, says Zhang, who has all the terms at his fingertips. Don't analogies make things easier to remember? Craftsmen in times past obviously thought so, improvising a string of mnemonics and rhymes when they saw a 'grasshopper's head' in the shape of a certain beam end, a 'tyrant's fist' in the bulbous mass of a corner column capital, a 'cat's face' in the contours of a tile, or a crescent moon in the curve of an arch. It takes time to master this terminology; meanwhile, Zhang suggests, one should approach traditional Chinese architecture by stripping it down to its five 'building blocks'. The first is a podium or terrace of stone, the base for a building. Next is the grid of thick columns of wood which, rising up in rows from the podium, are generally named according to their positions — eaves' columns, corner columns, and so on — with the exception of the 'golden columns' standing at the perimeter of the internal space. Columns take much of the load of the superstructure, not least the roof. In the Pavilion of Prolonged Spring, there were to be thirty-two 'golden columns' at the ground level out of a total of sixty-four columns. Four columns in the center would 'pierce' through the second floor stopping right beneath the third floor. Then there is the 'thunder god column' — not strictly a column but the king post rising to the apex of the pyramidal roof. Thirdly, horizontal beams help to transfer the weight of the roof to the columns. And to secure and stabilize this framework, says Zhang, you have lintels, the fourth 'building block', which connect the columns or support a ceiling. His fifth 'building block' consists of

(Right) It is the fitting together of thousands of separate timber members in the construction that gives traditional Chinese architecture its distinctive flexibility.

(Left) Thick logs destined to be turned into lacquered beams.

7 | The Timber Frame

123

purlins, wooden members under the rafters which carry the thrust of the roof to the lintels and the beams down through the columns to the foundations. All these add up to something immensely daunting in terms of numbers and weight. The Pavilion of Prolonged Spring alone would be composed of more than 7,000 separate timber members, large and small, every single one cut and hand-finished with traditional tools in accordance with Ming-dynasty precedent.

Flexibility, then, is one of the distinctions of a traditional Chinese building.

This interlocking timber frame is fitted together not with glue or nails but by means of mortise-and-tenon joints. (Nails *are* used in construction, but for positioning and pinning only.) The mortise is a cavity or recess cut in a piece of timber to receive a corresponding projection from another piece of timber, called a tenon. Nothing more aptly sums up the Chinese carpenter's art than the mortise-and-tenon joint.

Carpentry is, of course, an ancient craft and the key activity in vernacular as well as imperial architecture, since the principal building material has always been timber. Liang Sicheng found the earliest indication of a timber-framed building in a relief on a bronze vase dating from the Warring States period (475–221 BC). But even as stone and brick replaced wood in other parts of the world, in China the partiality for wood endured well into the twentieth century. Several reasons have been advanced for this There is the obvious economic explanation: to begin with, only vernacular materials were used, and wood was abundant and cheaply obtained

where forests flourished. Moreover, wood is easily worked, a quality especially significant in an agricultural society where a man built his house with his own hands, using basic tools and without recourse to manufactured materials. It is also sturdy, warm and can be beautiful. Another frequently cited advantage — one particularly relevant to a region prone to earthquakes — is a wooden structure's ability to ride out seismic tremors.

Flexibility, then, is one of the distinctions of a traditional Chinese building. A timber frame made up of many separate prefabricated modules can be as easily dismantled as assembled. Walls, not being load-bearing, may be of less substantial materials such as brick and plaster infill; they may also have as many windows and doors as desired. Just as freely, interior space can be divided into rooms by partitions and screens. Liang Sicheng likens the frame to a skeleton, one which 'permits complete freedom in walling and fenestration and, by the simple adjustment of the proportion between walls and openings, renders a house practical and comfortable in any climate from that of tropical Indochina to that

(Left) Assembled *dougong*.

(Right) The Pavilion of Prolonged Spring under scaffolding.

of subarctic Manchuria.' He points out that the Chinese building is a highly 'organic' structure, conceived and born in the remote prehistoric past, maturing into full glory and vigor in the Tang dynasty (seventh and eighth centuries), mellowing with grace and elegance in the Song (eleventh and twelfth centuries) and declining into feebleness and rigidity from the beginning of the Ming (fifteenth century). Throughout those 3000 years, 'the structure has retained its organic qualities, which are due to the ingenious and articulate construction of the timber skeleton where the size, shape and position of every member is determined by structural necessity.'

If there was a decline in aesthetic appeal between the Tang and the Qing, in other respects Chinese architecture altered little over those centuries. Although no timber buildings have survived from the remote past, vulnerable as they were to fire, rot, termites and other pests, evidence gleaned from archeological and literary sources points to a remarkable continuity. This continuity, certainly from the Song dynasty onward, owes something to Li Jie, the first edition of whose *Treatise on Architectural Methods* was issued under the auspices of the Directorate of Construction in 1091. The entire work, published in thirty-four volumes some twelve years later, represented the first systematic attempt to enshrine age-old know-how in a set of written rules. Until then this know-how, gained through centuries of trial and error and largely based on precedent, was the closely-guarded preserve of master craftsmen who passed it down only to their apprentices. Li Jie introduced the *cai*, a standard measurement for woodwork. Based on the dimensions of a timber component used in every building, the *cai* was a proportional measurement for which Li Jie stipulated eight sizes or grades. Thus one grade would be used in designing the timber modules for a palace, another in prefabricating the smaller modules for a merchant's house. From the dimensions of the pre-determined grade flowed the size of every other piece of timber within the building, from column and beam to purlin and rafter, each piece being expressed as a multiple or fraction of the pertinent *cai*. Thus the structural system of the palace and the merchant's house was the same; only the scale

(and certain ornamental and symbolic details) differed. On this basis, the former was simply an exaggerated version of the latter.

Although similar in essentials, however, timber skeletons do vary in the way their roof trusses are assembled. There are three methods, usually characterized as the log-cabin, the column-and-tie and the post-and-beam. The first two need not concern us, since the prevailing system adopted in the Forbidden City was the post-and-beam.

The Palace of Established Happiness

(Left) An early phase of the restoration. (Below) *Dougong* in place.

Imagine a tapering ladder-like structure consisting of two columns horizontally joined across the top by a beam that is in turn surmounted by two short upright posts on which rests a shorter beam or 'rung'. This truss of diminishing rungs terminates with a single post, set in the center of the topmost rung, which holds up the roof ridge itself. Purlins, which are at right angles to the beams and stepped (rather like a staircase with open treads), bear the rafters. Because they are stepped, purlins can carry short rafters to produce the typically curved profile of a traditional roof with its projecting, upswept eaves. Two lateral arrangements of posts and beams joined by purlins and raised on four columns demarcate a 'bay' (*jian*), the unit of measurement used when the dimensions of a traditional building are described. Thus the Pavilion of Prolonged Spring, a square building, is characterized as being five *jian* wide and five *jian* deep. But before the roof comes the columns, the 'spines', as it were, of the skeleton. The columns take the downward and outward forces exerted by the weight of the roof. These forces have to be distributed and kept in balance, and here the carpenter's skill is given full play — in the making of the *dougong*, an architectural feature unique to China.

At its simplest, a *dougong* is a wooden bracket set positioned by means of a tenon on the capital of a column or on a beam between two columns. Invariably found on the exterior of a post-and-beam building, *dougong* may also be arrayed internally. The bracket sets' purpose is to channel the thrust created by the superstructure of a building, including its roof, down through the columns to the foundations. A set may consist of as many as fifty separate but interlocking components. However, it is fundamentally made up of a number of *dou* (each a bearing block, with a groove cut into it, that acts as the base) and *gong* (crossed 'arms' slotted into the groove of the *dou* and curving up in each direction). It is from the height of the cross-section of the *gong* that Li Jie derived his *cai*. The arm that stretches at right angles to the wall of the building, which is called the *huagong*, functions as a cantilever. Successive tiers of *gong* may be fitted together, one on top of the other. A staggered formation, with an upper tier projecting from the tier below, provides stability to overhanging eaves. Additional support for deep eaves may also be furnished by a long timber component placed above the *huagong* and set at a slant; referred to as an *ang*, this consists of one jutting tapered end (called a 'beak') counterbalanced by the pressure exerted by a beam or purlin on its 'tail'. All these components are made by hand, and some of them are carved.

This ingenious bracketing system was developed very early — some scholars say as far back as the second millennium BC — and was certainly widespread by the Han dynasty around 2,000 years ago. Over time, bracketing became increasingly intricate and larger as roofs assumed more complex shapes. Different proportions emerged as a result: during the Song, for instance, the ratio between column height and the pitch of the roof markedly changed; later, the depth of eaves decreased.

With these developments bracket sets became more numerous but diminished in size. By the Ming and the Qing, the pitch of the roof had become steeper, and bracket sets under the eaves eventually did less duty as supports than as decoration.

In the reign of Yongzheng, the Board of Works saw fit to publish its own construction manual, *Structural Regulations*, laying down a new vocabulary and a different set of dimensions. *Doukou*, the groove or mortise of the bearing block, replaced the *cai* as the yardstick. Like the

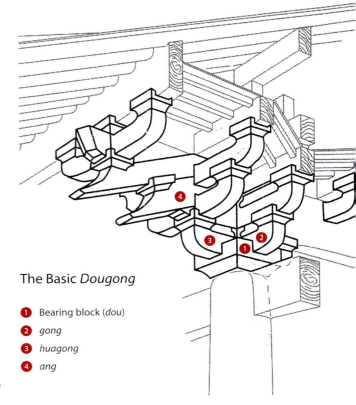

The Basic *Dougong*

1. Bearing block (*dou*)
2. *gong*
3. *huagong*
4. *ang*

cai, it was a relative standard used to express the dimensions of every part of the timber frame. And since the Regulations also specified the diameter and height of the column and the distance between intercolumnar bracket sets as multiples of the *doukou*, it was possible to deduce the length and width of an entire building from this one gauge. In Liang Sicheng's view, this development was a great pity: 'Perhaps it was the uncompromising strictness of the dimensions given in the [*Structural Regulations*] that succeeded in effacing all the suavity and elegance that we find so charming in a building from the period of the [*Treatise on Architectural Methods*].'

One reason for greater regimentation in imperial and official architecture might have been the increasing difficulty of sourcing large trunks of wood. If the felling of mature trees proceeded more rapidly than reforestation, it was no wonder that a shortage began to be felt by the Ming dynasty. When building the Forbidden City in the early fifteenth century, the Yongle emperor had to send to the distant provinces of Sichuan and Yunnan for logs of the hardwood *nanmu*. Transporting them up to the capital involved untold outlays of labor and time. Architecture adapted to these circumstances, evolving features that were less extravagant in

the use of large blocks of timber while retaining the structural system itself.

Nanmu is no longer available in China today and for the reconstruction of the Garden of the Palace of Established Happiness the choices essentially came down to either *liu'an*, a kind of willow, or Korean pine. Li Yongge or one of his men regularly scoured the northeastern provinces of China for suitable wood. During one such mission in Heilongjiang province, Li was surprised by an old couple offering to sell him the logs they had been hoarding for making

their own coffins. 'At least,' he recalls with a smile, 'the timber would have been well seasoned.' He should know, having been a carpenter himself:

> I came to the Palace Museum in 1975, after I was demobilized from the army. I was nineteen. The army would have seen to it that I was assigned to an occupation, but I decided that I'd rather be a driver or a carpenter. Our family roots are in Hebei province but after he came to Beijing my father worked as a carpenter until he moved into a supervisory position. It struck me that a carpenter was not without prospects. Look at Li Ruihan, the carpenter and model worker who studied architecture at night school and eventually became mayor of Tianjin and member of the Politburo Standing Committee! So I looked around and someone helped with an introduction to the construction division in the Palace Museum.
>
> Almost on my first day, I was fortunate in meeting the man who would usher me into the complexities of carpentry. There was no longer the formal procedure of kowtowing to an experienced craftsman to be acknowledged as his apprentice; it was more a matter of just being around Master Zhao while he worked, and showing keenness. I'd chosen carpentry, and in that I was different from my co-workers who were simply put into their jobs without any reference to their aptitude or interest. The old *shifu*, the master craftsmen, appreciated this: they were always happy to teach and mold you if you showed them respect. The other workers thought I was stupid to be so conscientious. One of the *shifu* said to me: 'You don't act like a smart aleck from the city, more like some simple-minded farmer's boy from the countryside.'
>
> In those days there were twenty-eight carpenters divided into two teams. For a while I was a deputy team leader. At twenty-eight years old I was the youngest in the team. I felt a real juvenile, fearful of asserting my authority. And because the head of the team was in poor health, I often found myself dealing with schedules, staff, architectural drawings, estimates and costs. That gained me valuable administrative experience. In a dramatic turn of events at the beginning of 1985, I was

(Left) A *dougong* has a staggered formation, with projecting pieces to help provide balance.

(Far right) Carpenter working on the roof of the Pavilion of Tranquil Ease; in the background is the Pavilion of Prolonged Spring.

summoned to a meeting with the directors of the Palace Museum and told that I was to become deputy head of the construction division. I hadn't progressed up the ranks — hadn't even been a section head — and here I was, transformed from a worker to a cadre overnight. Talk about 'reaching heaven in a single step'!

Li was implying that he had enjoyed a meteoric rise in his career. 'I am not surprised at all,' Happy says. 'Every institution should be so lucky as to have a Li Yongge. He is open-minded, dependable and not afraid of taking risks. This combination of qualities would be rare anywhere in the world, it is all the more so in a relatively closed society like China's. Mr Li is the linchpin of our entire project. Heck, he's the linchpin of my sanity. Without him to help me navigate the nuances and pitfalls of this giant bureaucracy called "Gugong", the project would be dead without us even knowing we'd all been killed. On a personal level, it's a great honor for me to be his colleague and friend. If it sounds as if I am gushing with compliments, that's because I *am* gushing with compliments. Did I mention that he also has a fabulous sense of humor?'

As a former carpenter, Li was all too aware of the need to stockpile timber well before the start of construction. Newly felled *liu'an* or pine would be too wet and still liable to shrink and crack, so the wood for the Garden structures had to be allowed to dry over a long time before priming. In the event Korean pine was selected for the project, and by the late spring of 2000 the lumber yard under the northern wall of the Forbidden City had become a hive of activity, with workmen operating mechanical and hand saws, marking timber with the aid of ink-box and plumb-lines, and cutting wood and planing pieces which would become beams, ridge posts, rafters, components of *dougong*, and so on. These men, skilled carpenters one and all, did not learn their trade working on traditional

(Right) A column, already shaped and cut with mortises, is being shifted into position before it is raised.

(Left) Part of the roof structure.

buildings. Chang Qinghai began by making furniture in his village Chenggouzhen in Handan, more than 300 miles from Beijing. Without itinerant workers from the hinterland, the massive construction projects transforming the face of the city would hardly be viable. The workers are recruited by subcontractors (more often than not someone from their own village) and engaged on piecework rates — anything from 15 to 40 yuan (around U.S.$1.80 to $4.80) a day — in addition to a dormitory bed and three meals a day. These are people who have known each other all their lives, and the closeness of their relationships, in which fellow feeling, team spirit and occasionally personal animosity all play a part, affects the quality of their work as inescapably as the wage they are paid and the rations they are given.

Every opportunity is taken to work and save enough to remit to the family back home. 'If we give them Sunday off,' Li Yongge tells Happy, 'they'll simply moonlight for another contractor.' It's a hard life, says Miao Baoping, another carpenter from Handan: 'I discouraged my son from taking up this work.' Old Chang would agree, although he is more resigned to it, not having enjoyed a regular wage for over ten years. He left school at seventeen, but 'in our village there's no local industry and few kinds of employment,' he explains, 'we depend on farming, and the income from that is so small that you can't live on it. We had to learn some manual skills.' In his case, it was having a third child that forced a change of career, for this breach of the country's birth control regulations carried fines which he couldn't afford to pay on his basic earnings. Ironically, he hardly sees his family, working as he does now in the city while his wife and children remain in their village. He says, though, that he has become accustomed to going home only for the summer and fall harvests and for the new year holidays.

The seemingly unlimited supply of workers from the provinces certainly puts labor-saving devices in the shade: muscle power is easily more economical, and more practical too,

(Below) A particularly elaborate architectural feature is the carved ornamental moldings under the beams.

(Right) Much of the woodwork is done by hand.

on site, where there is little level ground to accommodate a crane or large mechanical power tools. As the Palace Museum's own head carpenter and foreman points out with a chuckle, 'The one thing China has plenty of is manual labor!' Most of the building materials are brought to the site on humble wheelbarrows. And when brute force is patently not enough to handle the enormous hunks of stone or massive columns of wood, the workers resort to an appliance which has changed little over the centuries — the block and tackle. Simple and effective, this device lifts the heavy loads by means of chains and pulleys suspended from a scaffold.

Erecting the scaffold seems the work of a moment, with four agile boys in their late teens and early twenties dexterously assembling wooden poles and pre-cut wire ties and scampering up and down the frame as it grows. Much to Happy's dismay, they wear no hard hats and use safety harnesses only when working above the second story. When she asks Li Yongge what happens if one of them fell off, his answer is laconically matter-of-fact: 'Well, then we send him to hospital.'

Instead of the bamboo scaffolding ubiquitous in southern China, a structure of fir poles is built, wood being more suitable in the drier northern climate. Four thirty-foot-tall 'golden columns' each shaped with a tenon at one end and two mortises at the other are lying on the terrace of the Pavilion of Prolonged Spring. They will form the central bay of the ground floor. A scaffold is soon raised in their midst, and once these four columns are upright, a second ring of scaffolding is built around them. In a repetition of this, the scaffolding spreads outward until, when all the columns have been hoisted into place, it is dismantled and re-erected around their perimeter.

The first four columns are to be raised on October 6, 2000, a dark, overcast day. A depressing opaque mist is rolling down from Prospect Hill to the north and blotting out everything in the distance. Happy nevertheless manages to generate a sense of excitement on site, where some twenty men are milling around

The Palace of Established Happiness

(Left) The Pavilion of Prolonged Spring would rise on a grid of sturdy wooden columns slotted into stone bases.

(Right) Sawing a piece of wood for the roof in the lumber yard. This will serve as a 'flying' rafter.

and making preparations for the key moment. She has bought candy for the workmen, and there is talk of cracking open a bottle of champagne. With no division of labor by skill, the same carpenters will move and lift all the heavy timbers as well as carve the most delicate patterns on them. One man loops a rope round a column at about a third of its length from one end. A second hooks a chain to it, tugging on the chain to make sure that it is properly threaded through the two pulley wheels attached to the scaffold above. Within seconds, two other men with crowbars are levering the column along as the top end is winched higher by the chain. When the column is almost vertical, hooks hanging from the chain of another block and tackle are used to grip and lift it slightly off the ground. By this time, two carpenters have wrapped their arms round the other end of the column, steering and sliding its tenon across the stones to shouts of 'Back a bit' and 'Just a little to the left'. At last a cheer goes up as the tenon sinks into the cavity of the stone base in a perfect dovetail. And so to the next column.

Afterward, the columns are tied to each other and to the scaffold: the tension of the taut, twisted rope will hold them all in place for the night. They will not move, says Li Yongge, even in a strong wind. The next morning dawns dazzlingly clear, the air crystalline, the cloudless sky a pale lapis lazuli. Now the beams — each piece already shaped and cut with tenons and mortises — will be taken up and laid across the columns. Once again the pulleys come to the fore, and slowly but surely the first beam, destined for the heads of the two central columns on the eastern side, is hoisted up to the scaffold platform. The projections at one of its ends are slotted in to the column head, but only halfway. The joints at both ends will have to come together simultaneously, and although there is a degree of give with timber the structure is, after all, rigid, and the pieces are enormous, so fitting the joint at the other end takes rather more effort. Old Chang, standing firmly on the scaffold platform and visibly straining, needs to push the column slightly outward if the tenons and mortises are to lock. When they do, and he detects with the help of a plumb-line a minute tilt in one column, a sliver of wood is shaved off the tenon to bring the column back to the perpendicular.

Thirty-six weeks into the restoration, Happy marks the advent of Chinese new year with a dinner for the construction team. She has often fretted over safety on site, blown the whistle on the way the debris and rubbish are strewn about, and complained about lax security. A few months earlier, as the nights were drawing in, arc lamps had to be installed on site to prolong the working day. This was easier said than done because the source of electricity was some distance away. 'On site the next day,' she remembers, 'I found wires trailing dangerously all over the place!' If the electricians were aware of what might have caused the fire in the Garden in 1923, they showed no sign of it. And when asked to coil up the wires, they tried to fob Happy off with 'excuses that sounded so stupid I felt ashamed for them.' All the same, her confidence in those working on the project has grown. She can see that the likes of carpenters Old Chang and Miao are good craftsmen, capable of producing high-quality joinery when motivated: 'I sense that Miao is taking increasing pride in his work. He jots down notes and calculations in a little book, and he wants to see this project through — he's told me that several times.' Old Chang is less forthright about his commitment but finds it satisfying, nevertheless, to be at the Palace Museum: 'The main difference between previous jobs and this Garden project is that a higher quality is called for here; but although the work is more demanding at least there are still some older craftsmen around to help me improve my skills.'

Directly after the dinner, Miao and Old Chang leave for their village in Handan, a seven-hour train and bus ride away. 'We bought chickens and pork and fish for the new year,' Miao recalled afterward, 'and we played mahjong.' They had five weeks off. Old Chang said it was a long time to be doing nothing, so he took in some local work, making windows for a new house nearby. Miao, too, was busy with furniture and fitting out an extension to his house for his son, who was to be married soon. He had been saving for the wedding banquet for five years.

Back in Beijing, Miao and Old Chang would work on windows — and doors and partition screens too — of a more intricate design. Emperor Qianlong had looked out of the Lodge of Viridian Jade through casements latticed in the form of 'cracked ice', a pattern 'both simple and elegant', according to Ji Cheng, the author of *The Craft of Gardens*, a landscaping manual written in the Ming dynasty. Garden pavilions, Ji Cheng decreed, 'should have many window-openings so that one can secretly enjoy looking through them into different worlds, as if in a magic flask'. Besides the 'cracked ice', there were other standard traceries, some based on the shape of the water-caltrop blossom, several of them geometrical. The latter ranged from frets of horizontal bars and short vertical struts to zigzags, repeating hexagons and intersecting circles. In Qianlong's day, lattice-work was combined with glass panes but more often than not with paper pasted on the frame inside.

> **Garden pavilions 'should have many window-openings so that one can secretly enjoy looking through them into different worlds, as if in a magic flask.'**

Two other lattice patterns in the Garden are the *bubujin*, a trellised design, and the 'lantern', a grid pattern with an open rectangle in the center. Both involve immensely time-consuming and complicated handwork. For

The skeletal frame of the Pavilion of Prolonged Spring in twilight.

Old Chang, Miao and others, it meant cutting hundreds of pieces of molding and carving them before assembly in the traditional way by mortise and tenon. Windows were clearly more than just functional, for the latticework on them was usually so delicately wrought, providing a visual lightness and flow in agreeable contrast to the solid columns and overhanging roofs, that they became ornamental features as well.

Calligraphy in the Garden

Calligraphy, considered the first among the arts in China, was everywhere evident in the Garden, most distinctly on the *bian* or inscribed wooden plaques placed over the portal of every pavilion. The inscriptions are believed to have been written by Qianlong himself. We know that the imperial hand was at work in other gardens as well, notably in the one built for his retirement, for each set of ideograms is accompanied by an impression of his seal. Qianlong both collected calligraphy and practiced it himself, taking pains to emulate the early masters but also to develop his own style. Specimens from his brush may be seen not only in the Forbidden City and his summer palaces but throughout the empire: not a single expedition to the holy mountains or the southern provinces was complete without him leaving his mark upon some stele or tablet.

There were thirty characters on ten *bian* in the Garden. To reconstruct them, Palace Museum historian Xu Qixian was commissioned to burrow through the archives for specimens of calligraphy over fifteen years of the emperor's early reign. The emperor's writing, according to Xu, was a blend of two styles, *kaishu* ('regular script') and *xingshu* ('running script'). All thirty ideograms in this distinctive style were found on scrolls and inscriptions written within Xu's time frame: here, then, were the templates for the plaques in the Garden, ready to be digitally photographed and enlarged to the appropriate scale.

But a comparison with the inscribed plaques in the Palace of Established Happiness threw all this into doubt. The calligraphy there is in an altogether less cursive and more angular style, one that is closer to *kaishu* than *xingshu*. So the question remained: how was Qianlong's formal but equally authentic autograph to be reproduced? Only, Xu had to admit, by charging a modern calligrapher to do as Qianlong did — to imitate, in other words, the models of the past.

The Manchu names were a different matter. When the semi-nomadic Jürchen tribesmen

Calligraphy in the Garden

(Right) The Qianlong emperor's calligraphy.

(Left) Plaque with the name of the Palace of Established Happiness (Jianfu gong) in Chinese and Manchu.

swept down from the Inner Asian steppe to conquer China in 1644, they made their language official along with Chinese, and bilingual plaques eventually went up over many doorways in the Forbidden City. After 1912 there were attempts by the Republican government to rid China of the Manchu script and other vestiges of the overthrown dynasty, but in the Forbidden City such cleansing was confined to the front audience halls, probably because the deposed emperor Puyi and his family were still living in the inner court. This accounts for the anomalous existence of bilingual *bian* today. What's more, Xu says, no uniformity in the Manchu inscriptions is apparent: both literal and phonetic translations of the Chinese are to be seen, the work very likely of anonymous officials in the Imperial Household rather than Qianlong. The emperor might have perpetuated his own culture in the matters of dress, customs and rituals, but maintaining his spoken and written Manchu at the same level of facility as his Chinese was more problematical. Concluding that Qianlong would have left the writing of Manchu to others, Xu looked around for a scholar of the Qing language, and soon a retired teacher living in Beijing was found and invited to submit a phonetic rendering of the thirty characters required for the Garden.

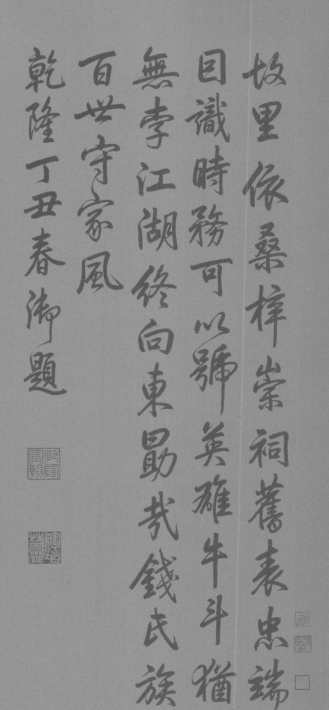

8 | Baked Earth

8 | Baked Earth

Clay has been used as a basic building material since the dawn of time. Rectangular blocks of it, dried in the sun and bound together by a simple mortar, provided a crude but effective barrier against the elements. Substituting sun-dried bricks with baked ones involved only a small technical advance, and in China, as elsewhere, the discovery was made very early that when ordinary clay was heated to a certain temperature, a chemical change took place and it became irreversibly hard. Fired clay or terracotta (from Italian, literally 'baked earth') also possessed the water-resistance and durability required for such structural components as walls, roofs and floors. Both sun-dried and baked bricks were used, along with tamped earth and stone, to strengthen stretches of what is called the Great Wall.

(Pages 138-139) Terracotta roof guardians marching down curving eaves, against a brilliant blue sky.

(Right) Glazed tile pieces bound in rope for protection.

Primitive bricks would have been made with clay found in the earth or dug up from river beds. Later it became possible to mine deposits from deeper sources and thereby to work with a greater variety of the material. The composition of clays from different sources varies, but it usually includes quartz and assorted quantities of mineral and organic substances. A brick or tile factory is also likely to blend different clays to ensure consistency, or combine the raw clay with gangue, a waste material derived from the separation and concentration of ores, which commonly includes traces of such minerals as quartz and calcite. Whatever its composition, the clay needs to be ground and mixed with water before it becomes plastic and malleable.

Fired clay is highly versatile. When used in facing a wall or a plinth, its exposed surface can be decorative. For example, fired-clay bricks may be laid in a pattern with their joints forming horizontal, vertical or diagonal lines. Or the bricks themselves are molded and carved. A further refinement is achieved when a thin slab of fired clay — a tile — is glazed. In the kiln, the plastic tile not only hardens upon heating but also, miraculously, turns from almost black to a shade of beige light enough to take any color. Color-glazed finishes are, of course, radiantly conspicuous on the yellow, green and blue roofs of the Forbidden City.

During the early Ming dynasty, when Emperor Yongle built his palace in the center of his chosen capital, Beijing, kilns to produce tiles were concentrated a short distance southwest of the imperial city. Canal and river boats brought the raw materials from the surrounding areas. But the impact of fumes emitted during firing proved so disagreeable that the kilns were later closed down and only remembered in the name of a street, Liulichang ('Glazed tile factory'), a district of antiquarian book stores and antique dealers today.

By the Qing dynasty kilns that supplied tiles to the Palace were polluting the air at two factories — Beiyao ('North Kiln') and Xiyao ('West Kiln') — in Mentougou, west of the city. Both factories found a trickle of demand and stayed in production long after the Palace's denizens had fled in the early twentieth century. In the 1950s Xiyao passed to the control of the Beijing municipal government, while Beiyao remained under the management of the Palace Museum. That the management of Beiyao left something to be desired eventually became apparent. Quality was always erratic, and when a trail of unpaid bills led to the discovery that Beiyao's factory head was corrupt, the managers were compelled to call it a day. A number of the craftsmen drifted to Shandong province, where they found work in a tile factory set up in Zibo.

Where did artisan traditions fit, if at all, in the machine age?

The process for manufacturing terracotta tiles has altered little since imperial times. Building technology, on the other hand, has seen an astonishing shift over the last century. Where did artisan traditions fit, if at all, in the machine age? In China, remarkably, the rise of concrete and steel did not immediately sound the death knell for such traditions. Beijing, for example, remained largely intact as the city planned

and built under the Ming and Qing dynasties, and craftsmen continued to find an outlet for their trades. At the same time as the Chrysler Building, Empire State Building and other skyscrapers were dramatically altering the skyline

of New York, Beijing was still a city with an ancient way of life. Visitors in the 1930s noted slow-moving two-wheeled carts, itinerant carpenters with their boxes of saws, and coolies with shoulder poles trotting along narrow *hutong* lanes around which low, gray-tiled courtyard houses clustered.

One of the first physical changes to the city after the Communist liberation of 1949 was the dismantling of the old city walls and the clearance of entire housing areas to expand Tiananmen Square. In a nod to Moscow, the opportunity was taken to line the square with the gigantic heavy-handed architecture of socialist realism, for this was the heyday of the Sino–Soviet friendship. And since political messages could be conveyed through the destruction of architecture as well as its construction, annihilating the decadent relics of the so-called feudal past was encouraged. The destruction accelerated further during the Cultural Revolution (1966–76), when Red Guards embarked on a rampage, smashing temples, historic buildings and cultural artifacts to prove their revolutionary fervor. Since then, even greater physical changes have been wrought, although the impulse has been economic rather than revolutionary. *Hutongs* and old neighborhoods are casualties of the bulldozer as Beijing transforms itself into a modern metropolis. Trophy public building designed by chic European and American architects and clad in steel, glass and titanium are the city center's new landmarks. For all the avant-garde architecture, though, large tracts of Beijing have become characterless landscapes of tower blocks and traffic-choked boulevards, prompting conservationists and citizens alike to complain that the old is demolished only to make way for the ugly.

(Left) A workman at the Zibo factory with his vat of color glaze.

(Right) Putting horn and feet on a 'celestial horse', one of the roof guardians that will decorate the ridge of a curving eave.

It is no wonder that master craftsmen stopped passing on their skills to a younger generation. However, here and there in Beijing one can see an attempt to return not so much to vernacular architecture as to a generic Qing-dynasty style, with upturned roofs and painted beams, particularly as a form of decoration for the facades of shops and restaurants. In the minds of many, it is a style that signifies wealth and grandeur. This 'Qing Revival', if one could call it that, has produced few successful examples; it has, nevertheless, kept decoration painters and tile factories in work.

The Shandong Zibo Glazed Tile Factory, which took in some of the craftsmen from the defunct works at Mentougou, is a flourishing concern and a regular supplier to the Palace Museum. In late 2000 Li Yongge was close to giving Zibo the tile order for the restoration. But Happy reminded him that the restoration was a joint effort: for her own satisfaction, she wanted to look into other suppliers — to show that research had been done, even if only for the record. Li's selection of the Zibo factory seemed to her puzzling and arbitrary:

(Below) Despite mechanization, part of the tile-making process is still done by hand. Here, a tile that has come out of a mold is given a finishing touch.

'Why Zibo and not some other factory?' she wondered. Here was another occasion where, improvising her own role in the project and feeling her way round the existing structure of authority as she went along, she nevertheless wanted to ensure that no decision was taken without her participation. 'I didn't feel that I had the authority to push the Palace Museum,' she admitted, 'I could only ask Mr Li if he would do this or that. Ultimately the decision was up to him.' But she needed to be certain that 'we can both defend our choices and convince the other side should there be a difference in opinion.' Fortunately, she added, 'this approach has worked out every time.'

Li Yongge conceded that the choice of the supplier was not a trivial one. This tile order was going to be the biggest that he would ever put his signature to, and only an established manufacturer which was known to him could be relied upon to deliver. Clearly nothing would be lost by falling in with Happy's request, and they spent some time that winter inspecting three factories. One of them was dismissed immediately: a small outfit, it clearly did not have the capacity. That left Zibo and a factory at Anhe in Haidian, a suburb of Beijing. On first impression, Zibo hardly inspired confidence: 'It felt as if a couple of farmers had got together and started running this factory,' Happy said. On the other hand, the woman factory director at the Anhe Tile Factory, Ji Ruiqin, seemed refreshingly eager.

> It was obvious…that the tiles were not up to scratch…'What was the point of showing us something of inferior quality?'

Li asked them to produce a *dishui*, a 'drip tile', as a test. A *dishui* functions as a dripstone and is designed to throw rainwater clear of the wall below. Consisting of a concave tile with a glazed triangular lip at right angles to it, a *dishui* may be found along the edges of the eaves. On imperial buildings the triangular lip was usually molded with a dragon motif. The factories would be judged on their carving of the mold. Happy later acknowledged that, at the time, she was not aware that there were 'many more relevant criteria when assessing the quality of tiles beyond a good mold.'

As it turned out, Zibo's carving was palpably superior, so in early 2001, as roofing boards were being prepared for the flying rafters of the Pavilion of Prolonged Spring, Li signed the contract. To make doubly sure, he planned to send Xiao Shi down to Zibo. Xiao Shi was one of the Palace Museum's own men who had previously worked at Beiyao. He knew about tiles: he would make himself available for consultation, and could keep an eye on things. Li thought he would also go down himself directly after the first firing.

But more urgent tasks intervened, and the visit to Zibo, which would have included Happy, was postponed. In the first week of May, at Happy's urging, Li telephoned the factory and asked it to send some trial pieces up to Beijing instead. After all, as Happy said, 'I would expect in my capitalistic way for a supplier to come to the client, for them to be on *my* doorstep.' On May 14 two factory representatives and the trial pieces duly arrived in Li's office. It was immediately obvious from the samples that the tiles were not up to scratch, as even Happy could tell: 'The tile I checked was a *dishui* in a blue glaze. Somehow it just didn't look right. The dragon molding was fine, but the shape of the tile was not regular, the color was not evenly spread, and the back of the tile, which was not glazed, was pretty rough.' The Zibo representatives did not seem in the least nonplussed by her comments. Their speech tinged with a Shandong accent which even Li found barely comprehensible, they suggested that those flaws were due to the tile having been placed in the kiln sideways — as if this was an acceptable excuse. Happy simply could not understand it: 'Why didn't they bring a sample of their best effort? What was the point of showing us something of inferior quality? What was in their mind? Did they think that we would be too stupid to know the difference? If they thought that, then they were the stupid ones, not us.'

For Happy there was a blindingly obvious matter of principle at stake — the principle of quality control. She saw no reason not to apply commercial standards and judgements to

A veritable bestiary is found on the roofs. The dragon (top right), placed at the end of a ridge, represents a powerful creature that can make rain.

this project. The principle was not, however, blindingly obvious to an organization like the Palace Museum. In fact the Museum still had trouble casting itself in the role of a demanding client vis-à-vis its suppliers. Such clear-cut business relationships were something new, as was competition. Not so long ago, 'everyone ate out of the common pot' in a state ownership system and there were no financial penalties for low productivity, inferior quality and huge wastage. According to Li, the Zibo factory would have no difficulty selling the tiles rejected by the Palace Museum — to those construction companies putting up the gimcrack 'Qing Revival' restaurants in the city, for example.

Such expectations might have helped Li to take a tough stance. He told the men from Zibo that if that *dishui* was the best the factory could do, then the 10,000 tiles it had fired would have to be scrapped.

Other questions remained. Xiao Shi was supposed to provide quality control. What happened to him, Happy asked, implacably.

'He never went down there,' Li divulged, 'because his father got sick.'

Happy replied in a calm tone, 'Fine, I'm just not going to get upset about such things any more. But you know, all along, maintaining quality was what I had in mind. Xiao Shi should be to the tile order what I am to this whole project: he needs to be in Zibo, constantly breathing down those people's necks. Now, since Zibo is likely to have to make the tiles again, why not send, if not Xiao Shi, then someone else?'

In fact Li went to Zibo himself shortly after this conversation. As he had suspected, the tiles that had gone through the first firing were indeed no better than the trial pieces shown to him in Beijing. It was clear to Li that the only way out of the impasse was to give the Zibo managers an ultimatum: did they want to attempt another batch, or should the Palace Museum rip up the contract there and then? Not surprisingly, the factory chiefs came back and said that they would make the order again. After all, Li later explained in an aside to Happy, 'They would lose face if the word got around that the Palace Museum had canceled a contract with them.'

He also said, 'We may have turned down the batch, but the factory can sell the tiles to other customers and make its money back. There are customers out there who don't have the same high standards that we insist on for our Garden.'

'High standards' was open to interpretation, Happy thought to herself. So far they had seemed arbitrary. 'You could have the world's best standards carved in stone, but does that prevent them from messing things up? No! We had checked out three of the better tile factories.

(Left) Sections of the glazed finial delivered to the site await installation.

(Right) Drawing of the finial for the Pavilion of Prolonged Spring.

Optimistically and naively, I thought there was one ideal factory out there but our research showed that tile craftsmanship is just substandard now, period. That's the reality. It's nobody's fault. And if these tiles are the best available — then these tiles go on the roof of the Pavilion of Prolonged Spring. If they're no good and people criticize, well, we'll just have to tell them that that's the best China is capable of now.'

It is June. Activity on site has almost ground to a halt, as most workers are preparing to leave for their villages to help bring the harvest in — *shoumai*, they call it, 'gathering the wheat'. On the 9th Li Yongge and Happy set off for Zibo, an eight-hour drive from Beijing.

Zibo is in Shandong, the coastal province famous as the birthplace of Confucius. Lying to the east of Jinan, the provincial capital, Zibo is at the northern fringe of the hill mass which dominates the center of the province. It is positioned on the Jinan–Qingdao railway and its proximity to sources of minerals as well as the sort of clay and earth suitable for the production of ceramics and pottery has made it a leading manufacturing center of glass, tiles and porcelain.

The Shandong Zibo Glazed Tile Factory was brought into being by Deng Xiaoping's dramatic economic reforms in the closing years of the 1970s. Previously, the rural sector was organized into communes subdivided into production brigades and production teams. These were large collectives: a production team, for example, might consist of all the inhabitants of a village.

Exemplifying self-reliance, a principle dear to Chairman Mao, production teams, brigades and communes were all-purpose units that held joint ownership of land, livestock and farm machinery and distributed the benefits flowing from those assets equally to its members. Each level provided a degree of local government and a range of social and cultural services. The larger units might even run collective enterprises like handicraft workshops and factories producing industrial goods to support agriculture on the one hand, and what was called 'the people's material life' on the other. At the height of the collectivization movement, there were some 24,000 communes in China.

With the return to economic pragmatism heralded by Deng Xiaoping's reforms, there was a rush to dismantle communes. Material incentive was re-introduced by a new arrangement, the so-called 'responsibility' or 'contracting' system. At its simplest, this provided for a production team to enter into a long-term contract with an individual household which would 'lease' a plot of land and undertake to sell a specified quota of the farm's output to the government at a fixed price. Anything the household produced over and above the quota was allowed to be kept or sold for profit. Households engaged in sideline occupations, whether it be tractor repair, dumpling-making or tile-manufacturing, similarly benefited from the new system. In fact, when those sideline occupations proved to be more lucrative than farming, many a peasant turned with alacrity to running former collective enterprises full-time. The Zibo tile factory was just such a collective enterprise: set up under a production brigade, it is now a business run by the Wu family under contract.

(Right) Part of the finial ready for firing.

There is no denying that privatization has brought enormous economic gain not only to the country as a whole but also to individuals who were entrepreneurial enough to seize opportunities as they emerged. 'Some people,' Li Yongge says, 'undoubtedly made lots of money. But perhaps too many enterprises making the same things were set up too quickly, and inevitably a number were unable to compete and went bust.' Although Zibo has survived, it has not shaken off habits inherited from its previous incarnation: keeping a bloated staff and paying virtually no attention to efficiency, productivity and management, to name just two.

Part of the tile-making process is mechanized, but much is still done by hand.

On this June day, not much appears to be going on in the cool and airy but poorly-lit workshop. Happy discovers that little noticeable progress has been made since the contentious samples were checked in May. It is of course harvest time, and most of the male workers have left for their villages. Xiao Shi and a colleague, Yang, billeted at the factory for over two weeks now, had asked some workers to stay behind. Most of them are girls. They are grouped round three assembly lines.

Part of the tile-making process is mechanized, but much is still done by hand. At one assembly line, wet black earth blended with gangue is shoveled into a machine with a large hollow tube at the end. Compacted in the machine, the clay comes out of the tube in a continuous solid roll. A girl sitting beside the tube chops lengths off. These sections pass along the line to

another girl who cuts them into equal lengths by shaving the ends with a wire slicer. Further along, the clay sections are dropped two by two into hemispherical troughs and subjected to a mechanical press. They emerge in the shape of concave ridge tiles. A third girl, placing each tile in a mold, flicks a blade around the edges, slicing and smoothing, until all the tiles are exactly the same size. Happy characterizes the process as 'stone-age'; it is certainly slow and laborious. The tiles are now ready for the first firing, a process that will take seven or eight days. Afterward, the glaze is poured on to the baked tiles which are then fired a second time.

A second group of girls is engaged on drip tiles, pressing lumps of earth into a wooden mold with the sunken carving from which a relief image of a dragon will emerge. The pressing is done first by hand, then with a wooden mallet, its head wrapped in layers of cloth. With a texture resembling rubber, the still plastic tile is then gently pushed out. Its impression of the dragon is surprisingly sharp and detailed, but one can see how difficult it is to maintain consistency at this step of the process. If the worker applies too much pressure, slight indentations may be imprinted on the clay by fingertips or the palm of a hand.

Hands are deftly at work on some 'roof guardians' in another corner of the workshop. Roof guardians are the glazed tile figures of mythical beasts set on the ridges of sloping eaves. Six-inch high *tianma*, 'celestial horses', and *haima*, seahorses, are just at this moment having their horns and feet shaped by some nimble fingers. The animals have come out of molds, but the horns and feet are added later by hand. A second girl prepares the ridge tile on which the figures will be fixed by scoring its surface with a fork. She dabs on a layer of paste, a second later rolling out a strip of mud, joining its ends together into a ring, and sticking the ring on the tile. Each tile takes two rings; these are, it turns out, 'seats' for the animal figures. Once the rumps of these are glued to the rings, the girl —patting, pressing, smoothing — works the circular projections into the joints, anchoring the animals more firmly to their base. And then, with another smear of paste, the feet and horns are put in place.

'What we have seen,' says Happy at the end of the inspection, 'is not bad.' She uses the phrase '*hai keyi*', a laconic and grudging comment much heard in Beijing speech. 'The problem here is not technique but management and quality control.' She later recalls an incident,

(Left) Preparing to place the end tile, in the shape of an open-mouthed dragon, on a top ridge.

when Mr Li and I watched a young woman engaged in extracting tiles from a mold. Mr Li noticed that the raw clay tile would take on the slight curvature of her palm, which was of course undesirable. He therefore made a suggestion and demonstrated how she could easily transfer the tile onto something flat, like a board, instead of her hand. She followed his instruction for literally as long as his gaze was on her. The second he turned his head, she was at the old method again as if Mr Li had never spoken. Throughout this episode, she never once raised her eyes to look at us.

I was dumbfounded by her 'so what?' attitude. Either she was so totally inane that she did not realize who Mr Li was, or, worse, she really could not care less. From that moment on, I began to have serious doubts about this factory. The fact that Mr Li did not seem too perturbed by this incident was also worrisome. But I was still new at all this, and therefore did not pursue the issue, wanting to give everyone the benefit of the doubt, at least for the moment.

(Right) These tile pieces will eventually decorate roof ridges and weigh down on the structures under them.

Back in Beijing, Happy and Li waited for Zibo to deliver, but as the summer wore on, her worst fears were realized. The site workers returned from the harvest, and still none of the tiles promised for mid-July appeared. When chased, the Zibo factory asked for an extension, then it asked for another. By early September any hopes that the roof of the Pavilion of Prolonged Spring could be completed before winter set in were rapidly vanishing. Mindful that, besides their waterproofing and decorative function, the tiles were needed to bear down on the structure and, by their sheer weight, 'set' the building, Li had to take steps to buttress the Pavilion with additional scaffolding. Zibo's failure to deliver finally forced his hand, and he had to go back to Anhe, to the factory that now turned out to be the winning tortoise to Zibo's complacent hare in the race: 'It is to be hoped,' Happy said, 'that Anhe will make up for their shortcomings in the carving by better management of the manufacturing process. A bonus is that they're only an hour and a half from Beijing, and we can be there often, making a nuisance of ourselves and showing them that we do have expectations. They know that we care — unlike some of their other customers. That should make a difference.' She confessed to a great sense of relief when she realized that her earlier insistence on researching suppliers in addition to Zibo had been justified.

Lime is to the fixing of tiles what clay is to the making of them. Varying proportions of lime are used to make a plaster, several layers of which will then be spread on a roof board before the tiles are laid. First there is the base layer: a blend of yellow mud and lime, this is arguably the most primitive form of waterproof roofing. Equally simple is the tool wielded to increase the density of the mixture; when the mud and lime are three-quarters dry, a round flat press held on a curved handle is applied to compact them. And while the plastering is in progress, particular attention is paid to the curvature in the pitch of the roof, steep as it slants downward from the ridge and flattening out above the eaves. It is true that the corner eaves are not as exaggeratedly upturned as those on the buildings of southern China, but they do curve back in an elegant sweep which the tile-worker must correctly align and render as each layer of plaster is patted down. Special care is also taken with the ridges, for at the meeting of two roof slopes the plaster is more likely to split open and let in rainwater. To provide additional protection, the ridges are covered in lead sheets.

In the old days, one or two further coats of plaster combined with a sprinkling of straw or wheat stalks were customarily laid on top of the base layer, particularly on ordinary houses. On palace buildings the straw or wheat stalks might be dispensed with; the roofs would instead be covered with two or three layers of

The Palace of Established Happiness

152

Roofs are treated with many layers of protective covering, made up of varying proportions of mud, lime, hemp fibers and plaster.

plaster stiffened with hemp fibers to prevent the plaster from cracking. The next layer on the roof — *qinghui*, a dark gray plaster — is also reinforced with hemp fibers. A smooth surface is finally obtained after much patting and squeezing with a flat, metal trowel. 'Another slow and laborious process,' Happy observes, 'involving hard, physical manual work. But then the process can't be improved upon, because it is already the most efficient.' The plaster hardens when dry. Afterward, a coat of size is applied, and when that is dry, the roof is ready for tiling.

Some sixty types of tile differing in shape, size and color are deployed on the roofs of the Garden's pavilions.

Some sixty types of tile differing in shape, size and color are deployed on the roofs of the Garden's pavilions. The most common ones are concave tiles and semi-cylindrical tiles, laid vertically from the top ridge down to the eaves in alternate rows in an undulating pattern peculiarly adapted to shed rainwater. The overlapping concave tiles lie with their curved side down, while the interlocking semi-cylindrical tiles straddle the joints between the rows. As they are being laid, a tiler fixes them with plaster, pushing it into any gaps and then leveling it down with his palette-like tool. His fellow tilers are working on the opposite slope, for the tiles are so heavy that, unless the weight is balanced, one side of the roof may sag and push the whole structure out of equilibrium. By the time the tiler has finished, each row of concave tiles has become a shallow trough, dropping away from the ridge to the eaves and

acting as a run-off for water when it rains. The very last semi-cylindrical tile in each row is secured by a nail with its own glazed-tile nail head. This one nail seems a flimsy device for resisting the weight of all the tile pieces above it, not to mention the force of gravity, but its effectiveness is demonstrated by the fact that the tiles do not all slide off the roof, even in a high wind.

At the end of a row, the last semi-cylindrical tile is closed with a molded disc, while the last concave tile is made with a triangular lip — the drip tile with its dragon design which the Anhe factory found so difficult to perfect. Effective, again, in the shedding of rainwater, these end tiles may also be decorative. For instance, the end tiles, together with two or three behind, could be in a different color from all the tiles above them. By this means, the roof acquires a sort of trim along the eaves — *jianbian* ('cut border'), as the feature is known. Examples of *jianbian* combinations abound in the Garden and include peacock-blue tiles with a yellow 'cut border' on the Studio of Esteemed Excellence, and yellow tiles with a green 'cut border' on the Chamber of Crystalline Purity. Equally ornamental are the glazed ceramic figures placed at the ends of the top ridge and along the ridges of the eaves. On the predominant building in the Garden, the Pavilion of Prolonged Spring, a climax to the entire structure is provided by its massive finial of glazed terracotta. In all, more than 126,000 pieces of tile were laid on the roofs of the pavilions and galleries of the Garden of the Palace of Established Happiness.

To the range of colors is added a variety of roof systems, each chosen in accordance with a building's rank. The Hall of Supreme Harmony

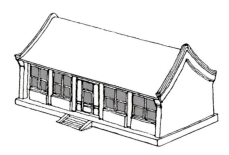

in the outer court of the Forbidden City is endowed with a double-eaved hipped roof to proclaim its position at the very top of the hierarchy. Such portentousness is out of place in a garden; instead we find at the Garden of the Palace of Established Happiness roofs similar to the ones atop the houses of common folk. Roofs with modest connotations include the *xieshan*, a hipped version having a small gable at both ends; the *xuanshan*, a roof with two sloping sides which overhang the gable ends; and the *yingshan*, which also has two sloping sides but these are flush with the gables at the ends. All three roof types may have a curved silhouette (*juanpeng* or 'rolled canopy') rather than a horizontal ridge. There is a single-eaved *xieshan juanpeng* roof on the Lodge of Viridian Jade, for example, and a *xuanshan juanpeng* roof on the Chamber of the Mystical Lotus. A fourth roof type distinguishes the Pavilion of Prolonged Spring and the Belvedere of Abundant Greenery. This is the *cuanjian* or pointed pyramid roof, crowned where its four sloping sides meet with an ornate four-color glazed ceramic finial.

The subject of roof lines came to the fore in the summer of 2001. It was then, at the commencement of phase two — involving four buildings along the western wall of the Garden — that a question mark over the Studio of Esteemed Excellence pressed for a solution.

In his painting *Peace for the New Year* (see page 59), Ding Guanpeng depicted the studio with a ridged roof; the studio's match in Qianlong's Garden, the Lodge of Retirement, on the other hand, is surmounted by a curved roof.

After some debate, the Palace Museum's panel of experts decided to give credence to Ding Guanpeng. After all, went the experts' argument, why should the court painter have invented a ridged roof if a curved one was in place? This opinion given, Shi Zhimin proceeded with the architectural drawings. But when faced with a dilemma, the more academic mind longs for a corroborating piece of evidence to resolve it. Quite accidentally, the possibility of further evidence presented itself in August, when a researcher by the name of Zhu Jie, whom Happy met through Shi Zhimin, happened to mention that an aerial photograph of the Forbidden City taken around 1900 existed in a museum in France.

Vague though it was, this was a lead intriguing enough for address books to be opened and networks to be tapped. An e-mail was sent off to John Sanday inquiring about his contacts in Paris; in the Palace Museum itself, a researcher suggested soliciting the help of Chiu Che Bing. Chiu, a Chinese architect based in Paris, is also a research fellow of the Centre de Recherche sur l'Extrême-Orient at the University of Paris-Sorbonne.

Traditional roof styles: (far left) *xuanshan*; (below) *xieshan*; (far right) *yingshan*.

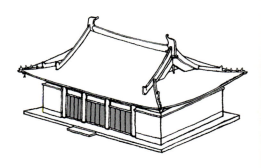

Both Sanday and Chiu were able to acquire a copy of the photograph in question. Not only was the aerial view published in the album *La Chine à Terre et en Ballon*, a 'Reproduction de 272 Photographies exécutées par les officiers du Genie du Corps Expéditionnaire 1900–1901', but, better still, the original glass plate was still kept in the Musée de l'Armée de Terre. Clearly, the allied troops who relieved the siege of the legations and occupied Beijing in the aftermath of the Boxer rebellion had time for some sightseeing. With the help of Jean-Marie Linsolas, curator of the Section des archives photographiques, Chiu soon had a print. This memento of a shot of the Forbidden City from the air was pored over with excitement at the Palace Museum when Chiu delivered it in person during the fall of 2001. It was promptly photographed so that a negative could be made. In an enlarged close-up, the relevant roof line was just perceptible from the dark and grainy background. Here at last was the evidence to convince the experts, and one by one, they put their signatures to a reversal of their earlier decision. Although Ding Guanpeng had painted the Studio of Esteemed Excellence with a ridged roof, he was evidently mistaken and the reconstructed building was to have a curved roof after all.

Before the reconstruction began, the sweeping away of the rubble strewn across the site of the Pavilion of Prolonged Spring brought a revelation. Under the debris were a good number of intact floor tiles. Those tiles, no doubt burnished to a luxurious sheen in Qianlong's time, are the so-called 'golden bricks' laid across the floor of some of the Imperial Palace's grandest pavilions. Belying their name, though, they are actually dark gray. There is a folk saying about this sort of tile, Director Pei points out, that goes like this: *sheng ru qing; ming ru jin* ('It resonates like a *qing* [jade chime]; it is as bright as gold'). Looked at another way, he goes on, the 'gold' might also be an allusion to its price, for it has always been an expensive artifact to produce.

Jin Meiquan concurs with a wide grin. Head of a tile factory in Wuxian, a township half an hour's drive from the garden city of Suzhou in Jiangsu province, he has been making golden bricks for more than a decade. The tiles *are*

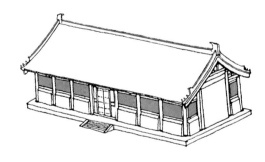

costly, Jin agrees, but then output is limited; this is due as much as anything to the long production process, as it takes about a year for the molded tiles to dry in a natural atmosphere before they are fired. They are also special, as the factory name proclaims, for it still calls itself 'Yuyao' — the 'Imperial Kiln'. No-one can say for certain whether it really is the same tile producer patronized by Emperor Yongle when he built the Forbidden City in the early fifteenth century, but the imperial association is obviously worth clinging to, and there is no denying that golden bricks were indeed sent to the new Ming capital from the vicinity of Suzhou over 500 years ago.

On an overcast day in June 2000 Director Pei, Li Yongge, Zhang Shengtong and Happy Harun arrive in Wuxian to spend a day at Jin's factory and clinch their order of a thousand golden bricks. They note that the surrounding country is green and lush: this is Jiangnan, the famous 'land of fish and rice' where rivers, lakes and canals crisscross an alluvial plain of fertile soil and agricultural plenty. Along one waterway running by the side of Yuyao, a punt stacked with tiles is coming in to unload. Midges rise in swarms from the bank and fill the air. A little further on, a man is lifting nightsoil from a cesspit into buckets. 'Excellent fertilizer,' says Zhang. Just ahead is a green hillock covered in scrub. Two cone-shaped brick chimneys and a massive terracotta water vat protrude from its summit; a firing is in progress, as the smoke surging from one of the chimneys makes clear.

It resonates like a *qing* [jade chime]; it is as bright as gold.

'My two partners and I bought the factory from the local prefectural authority,' Jin explains as he welcomes his visitors with bananas, lychees and tea, 'previously this was a collective village enterprise set up by the production team, one of eight that formed the brigade.' He subcontracts some of the work to local households. Even so, local people shun the more physically demanding functions in tile-making, and labor needs to be recruited from farther afield, especially Anhui, a less prosperous province to the west.

Anhui workers are found around the nearby pit where the clay for the tiles is drawn. 'We remove the topsoil and go beneath the surface by about a meter, where there's a layer of clay down to about two meters deep that is particularly viscous. Further below sand occurs and that's no good. The viscous mud makes for a sturdy tile.' Li confirms that this is so: 'Tiles from this factory were installed behind the Palace of Earthly Tranquility. Visitor traffic in that part of the Forbidden City is particularly heavy, but the tiles have stood up to the constant wear and tear really well.'

There is a direct relationship between a tile's quality and the clay from which it is made, Jin claims. The clay has to settle, so after it is moved to the factory yard, it must be left for two to three years before it is spread out to dry in the sun and crushed. Water is then sprinkled until the mixture is thoroughly wet. Jin is precise on the time taken for this part of the treatment: 'After soaking the clay, you turn it over two or three times, the first time after a lapse of twelve hours, the second after waiting for two hours. On the second turning, the mud is trampled on by bare feet: this releases its adhesiveness.'

Then the batch is shaped into a large circular pile before being cut into slices of no more than three-quarters of an inch thick. There is more treading to compact each slice. Finally the clay, which is by now quite dense, is pressed into a wooden mold and smoothed down. To show what happens next, Jin leads his visitors across the road and into a warehouse. Inside, straw stuffed into the window cavities effectively screens out most of the daylight, although it is actually put there to block drafts so that the serried rows of black tiles, now taken out of

Decorative tiling, the Pavilion of Prolonged Spring.

their molds and standing on end, can dry out slowly, and in the shade. The tiles are turned periodically. Jin's next stop is the homestead of a subcontractor, Mr Yao, whose wife, daughter and neighbor are squatting on the porch cracking melon seeds. At the back of the house, in a concrete warehouse with a high ceiling, a child's bicycle shares space with fifty tiles. 'I believe these are ours,' Li Yongge tells his colleagues. For all that the factory is now a privatized enterprise, it is still very much a village affair.

Those tiles have lodged with Mr Yao for nearly a year. Soon they will be ready for the kiln. 'We use rice husks as fuel,' Jin says, 'about 40,000 kilos for each firing, or enough to fill two of these warehouses.' Rice husks generate consistent heat, a critical factor in successful firing. The kiln consists of high brick chambers built into the hillock seen on arrival. It has space for hundreds of tiles, all manually stacked on shelves before they are fired. It is a long, slow firing, for the tiles remain in the kiln for sixty days. During the first week the heat is kept very low to allow the tiles to dry out further. Gradually, the furnace would be stoked until a more intense heat is produced. Toward the end of the firing, water is poured down the chimney to turn the tiles into their distinctive hue of dark gray.

The Palace of Established Happiness

Roof Guardians

Bizarre gaping dragons at the ends of ridges and a fantastic bestiary marching down the curving eaves — these glazed terracotta objects are as integral to the roofs of the buildings in the Forbidden City as overlapping tiles. If they served a practical purpose once (perhaps as counterweights), their function is now merely symbolic and ornamental. The open-mouthed dragon with a double-edged sword planted in its back, placed so that it appears to be swallowing the end of the top ridge, is called a *chiwen* ('owl's lips'). Its name refers to a legendary fish whose tail, which resembled that of an owl, was powerful enough to whip up the waves in the sea and create rain. For this rainmaking faculty,

A procession of animals, some of them mythical, traditionally protected a building against fire.

it was adopted as a mascot and protector against fire.

The animals (*zoushou*), too, are guardians of sorts. Here, again, a hierarchical code is in play: except for the highest-ranking Hall of Supreme Harmony, whose sloping eaves are uniquely endowed with the entire bestiary of ten, official buildings would have nine animals, whereas garden pavilions generally made do with seven, five or three. Odd numbers are associated with the masculine and positive principle in nature, *yang*, the cosmic force that pairs with the feminine and negative *yin*. Predictably, the sloping ridges on the Pavilion of Prolonged Spring each boasts seven animals, while the Chamber of Crystalline Purity displays only three.

An immortal riding an equally strange creature heads the procession of animals. Some say his mount is a chicken, others that it is a phoenix. His full retinue consists of one each of: dragon, phoenix, lion, celestial horse, seahorse, *yayu* (a fish with a dragon's head, adept at quenching fires), *suanni* (a legendary beast of prey), *xiezhi*, *douniu* and *xingshen* (all composite animals with magical powers to discriminate between good and evil, ward off calamities or bring good luck). A fabulous horned creature brings up the rear.

Symbols of another order decorate the huge finial that surmounts the Pavilion of Prolonged Spring. This many-layered affair, molded and fired in pieces at the Anhe factory and then assembled on site, has the eight Buddhist and Taoist emblems in two decorative bands. The Buddhist emblems are the wheel of law, the conch-shell, the parasol, the canopy, the lotus flower, the jar, the fish and the mystic knot. Separated from these by a frieze of lotus petals are the devices representing the eight immortals of the Taoist pantheon: a fan, a sword, a *yugu* (a musical instrument, either a bamboo pipe or a drum with two drumsticks), a pair of jade clappers, a gourd, a flute, a flower-basket and a seedpod of the lotus.

9 | Palaces of Gold and Jade

9 | Palaces of Gold and Jade

For Beijing, 2001 was a momentous year. On July 13 the city was chosen to host the 2008 Olympics, a decision greeted with euphoria by its denizens. Four months later China achieved membership of the World Trade Organization after fifteen years of lobbying and negotiation. The two events were widely seen as symbolic of China's admission into the community of economically and politically powerful nations.

(Pages 160-161) Glittering painted decoration on eaves and brackets sets.

(Right) Ceiling of the Belvedere of Abundant Greenery.

In the Palace Museum, the euphoria might have been more muted but the excitement was no less real. To prepare for the Olympics, the government had pledged billions of dollars to smarten up Beijing, including U.S.$75 million for the repair and conservation of historical relics. A hefty proportion of that largesse was to be spent on a thorough overhaul of the Forbidden City.

As the central government officials had it, the Forbidden City would be restored to its former glory, and the inspiration for this renewal would be drawn from the heyday of the emperors Kangxi and Qianlong, generally seen as imperial China's final golden age. Their catchphrase for describing the grandeur and opulence of that age, rapidly taken up by the media and by the Palace Museum staff, was *jinbi huihuang*: gold, jade and resplendence.

Words conjuring up palaces of gold and jade do not seem far off the mark when one comes upon some newly-painted pavilion in the Forbidden City, glittering under a cerulean sky. Typically rising on a terrace of white marble, the pavilion's columns and walls will be bright vermilion, a striking contrast to the mustard yellow of its roof tiles. On the complex designs adorning its beams, lintels, brackets and rafters, pigments from deepest emerald green and blue to gold and scarlet will have been applied by hand, square inch by square inch. One of the most distinctive characteristics of the buildings in the Forbidden City is this seemingly infinite variety of colors painted on all wooden surfaces.

Happy Harun added the term *youshi caihua* to her vocabulary as 2000 wore on. It referred to a two-part process, she was told: *youshi* — preparing the paint ground, followed by *caihua* — decorating with the polychrome designs found on most Ming and Qing architecture. Now that the structure of the Pavilion of Prolonged Spring was up, it was time to think about painting it, and the matter of *youshi caihua* was duly raised at a meeting in the fall.

Weekly meetings, instigated by Happy, had been held since the earliest stage of the project, bringing together round a table the key people responsible for getting the Garden built on time and within budget. Happy, Li Yongge and Zhang Shengtong — effectively the construction management team — formed the core group, and other participants were asked to attend as necessary.

Looking forward to the completion of phase one the following spring, Li notified those present at the meeting that the moment had come to determine the details of the Garden's *youshi caihua*. At that point two master-craftsmen with close to a century of experience between them were introduced to the project. One was Zhang Decai, designer and pattern-maker working under Li in the construction division. The other was his senior colleague Wang Zhongjie, the Palace Museum's resident expert on painted decoration. Based at the department of traditional architecture, Wang had been engaged in historical and technical research on behalf of the Garden project since the previous winter. In December he was asked to make a presentation.

Seventy-year-old Wang speaks loudly and with conviction. His didactic manner comes as no surprise when one remembers that, having devoted his entire working life to *youshi caihua*, he has accumulated an unrivaled knowledge of the craft and is widely regarded as the authority in the field. Everyone expects him to lay down the law on painting: even color matches are submitted to his eye, no other standard being considered necessary. The question now put to him by China Heritage Fund was: what patterns, motifs and pigments should be applied in the Garden?

The presentation was attended not only by the management team and Director Pei but also by several 'old experts' in traditional Chinese architecture. As in the controversy over stone, the experts' views needed to be solicited before decisions could be made.

Wang Zhongjie unveiled his scheme by first recapitulating the structural history of the Palace of Established Happiness and its Garden. Archival records show, he said, that after 1742 the Palace and Garden were expanded, rebuilt or refurbished several times, notably in the

(Left) A configuration of rafters and brackets under a corner eave, the Pavilion of Prolonged Spring. The character for fortune (*fu*) decorates the round rafter ends.

seventeenth, nineteenth, twenty-third and twenty-ninth years of Qianlong's reign. They further reveal that a comprehensive overhaul of the roofs, paintwork and stone bases was carried out at a cost of 48,000 taels of silver in 1802, the seventh year of Emperor Jiaqing's reign. Less extensive repairs were undertaken in the late Qing period.

It was understood from the start that exact reproductions of the original decoration would probably be impossible given the absence of plans and drawings. Wang and his team had

couple of assistants from his department. Where there were gaps in knowledge about possible decoration designs, he put the corresponding pavilions in Qianlong's Garden into the equation, for all that these were built some thirty years later. Two other precious pieces of material evidence were available to him: Sirén's photograph of the Pavilion of Prolonged Spring (see page 60), and the group shot in front of the Chamber of Crystalline Purity (see page 166). Such clues formed the vocabulary from which the designs for the Garden pavilions would be reconstituted.

(Right) Priming the wooden surfaces before the paint goes on.

instead to reinvent the designs from whatever documentation and material evidence they could find. Fortunately there were enough clues for them to discern some connections and to posit a time line.

A significant clue was the cluster of buildings comprising the Palace of Established Happiness, contemporary with the Garden and untouched by the fire of 1923. Wang had already surveyed the painted decoration on those pavilions with a

The survey had begun by dating the extant decoration of the Palace of Established Happiness, all of which was, Wang confirmed, in the official Suzhou style. He thought that the dates would logically fall into three periods — the years of initial construction, the 1802 improvements and a 'late Qing' stage encompassing the nineteenth to the early twentieth century. To his surprise, he did find a spot where the composition of the *caihua* might have remained unchanged from when it

Puyi (sitting on a rock), dowager empress Longyu (fourth from right) and palace women in front of the Chamber of Crystalline Purity.

was first painted. Below the inner eaves of the Hall of Controlling Time within the Palace of Established Happiness complex, the decoration has two distinct characteristics. First, one feature of the decoration, the perpendicular bands in blue and green known as *gutou*, are plain; secondly, the painted dragons, a predominant imperial motif of *youshi caihua*, appear to have fish-like scales. In later depictions the dragons lost such scales and acquired something approaching linear markings, while the *gutou* bands became visibly more ornate.

By the same token, Wang was able to make a case for dating the decorations below the outer eaves of the Hall of Controlling Time, as well as those on the Belvedere of Favorable Breezes and the Palace of Established Happiness, to around 1802, the year of renovations under Jiaqing. Part of the evidence for this lies in the elaborate *gutou* which, with its representation of rings entwined with ribbons, was not seen on Suzhou-style *caihua* until the end of the Qianlong era. All this exactly chimes with what is known about the development of *caihua* styles. It seemed reasonable to assume, Wang added, that the decoration on the Pavilion of Prolonged Spring, as registered in Sirén's photograph of 1922, was done at the same time.

Wang then presented the last piece of his jigsaw: the photograph of Puyi, his aunt the dowager empress Longyu, and several palace women against the backdrop of the Chamber of Crystalline Purity. 'We don't know the date of this photograph,' he observed, 'but it couldn't have been taken after 1913, when the dowager empress Longyu died. Puyi, sitting there on a rock, looks about four, or only a year or so older than when he ascended the throne in 1908.' Those two dates framed and gave direction to Wang's conjectures, as did Shi Zhimin's efforts on the computer, which resulted in a digitized and enlarged image of the photograph: 'We can see the painted decoration behind them quite clearly. The motifs are simpler than those characteristic of the middle Qing. Besides, the *caihua* looks crisp and in very good condition. I would guess that it had not been painted many years before the photograph was taken. That makes it the work of the late Qing period.'

Bringing all these factors together, Wang concluded that the painters should attempt a return to the style prevalent at the close of Qianlong's reign and the beginning of Jiaqing's. And if corroboration was needed, the decorations on matching pavilions in Qianlong's Garden were on hand for reference. There was, however, one incongruity for which no satisfactory explanation was forthcoming. The Lodge of Fragrant Bamboo in Qianlong's Garden was dignified by decoration of the highest rank — the design called 'dragon *hexi*' — which was highly unusual in an informal setting. Does this signify some religious connotation to the small building? If so, the same protocol would have to be observed on its model in the Garden of the Palace of Established Happiness, the Lodge of Viridian Jade.

Approval for Wang's scheme was unanimous. One of the experts, Luo Zhewen, praised the thoroughness of his research: 'The argument for adopting the *caihua* style of the mid-Qing period is most persuasive. More importantly, this is a design scheme that can be implemented.'

Despite the consensus, there was one small ripple. A representative from the State Administration of Cultural Heritage raised an issue that had not cropped up before with the project in quite the same way: traditional methods were revived in the push for authenticity, but up to then no-one had made a point of insisting on traditional materials. Could the construction team, asked that expert, look into the possibility of using mineral-based pigments?

This query was to receive short shrift from the architect. 'That's totally unrealistic — they're much more expensive than chemical pigments,' Shi Zhimin said later, 'and sourcing will be a headache too.' Here again, Happy was presented with one of the many odd contradictions generated by the nature of the project. In *replacing* rather than conserving the past, should one still regress to the circumstances of the mid-eighteenth century, or is it legitimate to take advantage of technical and industrial developments since then?

In replacing rather than conserving the past...is it legitimate to take advantage of technical and industrial developments...?

Zhang Decai is little troubled by such dilemmas. It is enough for him that the paint is applied in the traditional way: 'We are employing techniques that are a direct inheritance from those practiced in Qianlong's time. I learnt my skills from my teacher, who in turn learnt the same skills from *his* teacher, and so on.' As for the pigments, the deciding factor must be the availability of supplies. In a reflective moment Zhang compares *youshi caihua* to a woman's make-up: while the timber structure of a building, he says, may be thought of as a skeleton, and the roof tiles and brick walls the flesh and skin, *youshi caihua* is equivalent to foundation, powder and rouge, which mask a face and camouflage any flaws. And as in cosmetics, a rich palette of colors is demanded.

One way of classifying pigments is to designate them as either mineral, extracted from the earth and crushed into powder; or chemical, which involves a fusion or conversion of one

sort or another. 'There was a time,' Zhang explains, 'when we used only mineral pigments — all domestically manufactured since China conducted little foreign trade.' But tradition has long given way to practical considerations. As Zhang remarks, 'Now that local supplies are not available, what can we do but buy chemical pigments from abroad? Mind you, I think it's possible that the Imperial Palace already began importing chemical green pigment as far back as Emperor Yongzheng's time in the early eighteenth century.'

He is referring to the pigment known as Schweinfurth green which, as its name indicates, is manufactured in Germany. Sometimes described as Paris green, this is a mixture consisting of several double salts of copper arsenate and copper acetate. Besides its beautiful tint, the pigment is highly toxic and notable as an insecticide. In fact, Zhang claims, all pigments used in *youshi caihua* are more or less poisonous.

Another predominant pigment is yellow, which comes from the mineral realgar, a rare soft orange ore of arsenic. Equally indispensable is a brilliant red pigment, an oxide of lead called *hongdan* in Chinese. Then there is ultramarine, so named in Europe because its chief ingredient was originally sourced from Asia, the landmass beyond the seas. This vivid blue to purplish-blue hue was obtained by pulverizing lapis lazuli but is now synthetically produced from sodium, aluminum silicates and sodium sulphide.

Outlines are drawn with paints containing white lead or carbon black. Titanium white was traditionally not widely applied, but became more extensively used because of its prized qualities of high covering power and durability. Cinnabar continues to be a component of one of the other pigments used.

A spectator might find all these colors, patterns and motifs overwhelming. However, as Zhang points out, they are usually observed at a distance. Indeed, there is a deliberate distortion of perspective in the painting of certain figures, for example the ritual vessel motifs on the Hall of Concentrating Brilliance, because they are not expected to be viewed frontally but from below. What rescues the painted decoration from appearing meretricious may be the gilding,

(Right) *Youshi caihua* patterns and motifs include (top row from left) the *kuilong* and the five-clawed dragon; (middle row) peaches, ring and knots, cranes, bats and peony; (bottom row) dragons playing with flaming pearl and flowers in a gilded lattice.

(Left) A rich palette of colors all applied by hand.

9 | Palaces of Gold and Jade

probably *caihua*'s most distinctive feature. The patina of gold somehow transforms the decoration, giving it an opulent, luminous and layered effect — layered because the gilt is laid on top of an embossed design.

The technique of rendering an embossed pattern, whether of geometric lines or a more complex motif like a floral scroll or an ascending dragon, is simple but back-breaking. Anyone who has piped icing to decorate a cake could probably do it, especially as it does not have to be so delicate as to bear scrutiny. In fact, the work can be fairly crude when seen close up. The Chinese term for the procedure is *lifen*, literally 'trickling powder'. This involves squeezing a sticky white putty of plaster, glue size and tung oil out of a forcing bag through a small pointed nozzle along a line of dots. These dots, marking out a motif or pattern, will have been transferred onto a prepared wooden surface with the aid of a stencil and pounce. The putty is left to harden and becomes the raised design on which a yellow size for the gold leaf is then smeared. Old craftsmen would say that, for the gold leaf to stick fast, it is best to apply two coats of the size.

Two shades of gold leaf enhance the richness and provide further visual depth. One is a light-hued alloy containing seventy-four per cent of gold, and the other a purer and more yellow kind, with a ninety-eight per cent proportion of the metal. According to the construction division's estimate, it was going to take more than 182,700 sheets of gold leaf, each measuring between three to four inches square, to gild the decorations on the buildings in the Garden. That comes to just under 16,000 square feet of gold leaf or six pounds of gold.

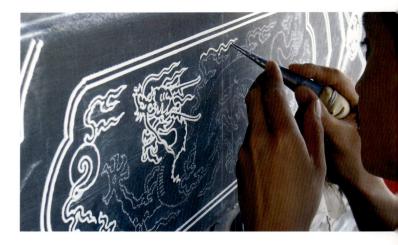

Zhang Decai is to be found every weekday in a dark, cabin-like office within the compound of the construction division. His office is a narrow room floored in cement, containing not only a desk but also a low bed against the far wall. A large wooden cabinet protrudes into the room. When opened, it is seen to be overflowing with pattern books in kraft paper. The light filtering in from windows on either side of the door is so faint that Zhang has long become accustomed to switching on an overhead fluorescent tube as soon as he walks in. Yet, astonishing for a man in his late sixties, he has no need of spectacles as he begins sketching freehand on the rolled-out sheets of paper on his desk. His hands are notable: long-fingered and dexterous, they trace the outlines of dragons or clouds or lotuses with quick, deft strokes. These drawings are Zhang's way of communicating his age-old craft, for the sheets will become stencils once every drawn line has been pricked with tiny holes. At the construction site, the perforated templates are placed over

(Left) 'Trickling powder' to create an embossed effect.

beans and lintels and dusted with flour. When the pouncing is completed, a design emerges from the network of powdery white dots, ready for a painter to fill in with his brush and paints, and eventually to create the ravishing effect summed up in the phrase 'gold, jade and resplendence'.

'My father was engaged in *youshi caihua*: he was a decoration-painter,' Zhang says, 'my brother, too, and both my sons. I thought of doing something else, perhaps joining the army, but my parents still had somewhat feudal notions of sons following in their fathers' footsteps.' Zhang duly did so in 1953, when he was seventeen:

> Traditionally, one was never apprenticed to members of one's own family. But the master-painter I wanted to learn from, He Wenkui, wouldn't accept me as his apprentice. A modest man, he said he was not qualified. I always regarded him as my teacher, though.
>
> Most of the time I hung around my father and Mr He in the traditional architecture department of the Palace Museum. Their work involved tracing *caihua* designs *in situ* and transferring them onto paper. The designs were then reduced in scale, to be enlarged with complete accuracy to the size of the original when required.

(Below) Sheets of gold leaf applied with a pair of bamboo tweezers.

Work stopped during the Cultural Revolution in the mid-1960s. But I persevered with Mr He. Almost every day, I would go to his house, taking the tram to the east of the Drum Tower nearby. Sometimes I went after dinner, and would spend the evening chatting and playing chess with him. If I had skipped dinner, I would make noodles for us both.

His nephew came to live with him some time in the 1960s. Mr He had no children of his own. I went to his house as usual. One day my teacher turned to his nephew and said, 'Pour a glass of water for your *shige*, your senior fellow apprentice.' That was when I knew he had finally acknowledged me as his apprentice.

Mr He and my father were responsible for producing the templates, while I learnt every aspect of the craft by filling in the colors or laying on the putty for the gilding. Occasionally they would let me trace their designs to make stencils. By 1964 I had been under Mr He's tutelage for ten years. He said to me one day, 'Here, why don't you draw some yourself?' At first I was bashful and demurred. But he clearly saw some potential in me and insisted, most gently, as he never raised his voice to anyone. When he saw my stencils, he smiled and said, 'They're all right, aren't they?'

After my mentor retired, a group of young people came to the Palace Museum. They were *chadui* students, and someone had to show them the ropes.

Zhang does not dwell on the *chadui* movement or the Cultural Revolution of which it was a facet. To *chadui* meant to go and work in a production team of a rural commune. In the early 1970s millions of students in middle and higher education, politicized by Chairman Mao, dropped out of school to participate in glorious productive labor. Many were sent to factories; still more were posted to the countryside to live as peasants — all this to inculcate self-reliance and egalitarianism. 'But,' says Zhang, 'I did want to give some training, to pass on what techniques I had acquired over the years. Eventually I took on some students myself. We must make the most of our cultural legacy and carry it forward.'

It is plain to see that he takes pride in his work. The likes of Zhang Decai are addressed as *xiansheng* — a term of respect applied to teachers and gentlemen — because *youshi caihua* is generally considered a higher craft than masonry or carpentry. Zhang counts himself fortunate to have worked on the Garden: 'All the stenciling on the Pavilion of Prolonged Spring is my handiwork. As long as the decoration is here, a part of me will always be left on this building.' He has, he says, given his best shot at imitating the original signature of Qianlong's craftsmen, and although 'there's room for innovation or creativity in a new building, in a reconstruction one must follow the historical model and turn out decoration as close to its former appearance as possible. I don't attempt to reinterpret or to express myself. Rather, I try to mirror and convey the spirit of the original master-painter.'

Much apparent indecisiveness and mind-changing attended the preparations for painting. Fixing a timetable proved especially difficult. Priming and painting are ideally done well before or after the rainy season, with a long spell of fine weather afterward to allow for drying. Spring and fall are therefore the best times but, slated to begin in March 2001, painting did not commence until late February 2003. Of course unforeseen problems crop up in any project; what had not immediately

struck the management team, for example, was one thrown up by the very imperatives of construction: while building activity was still so hectic, the site was not at its cleanest, and all those floating particles of dust and grime could damage wet paintwork. Once the problem was recognized, though, a solution was not long in presenting itself. Why not undertake the painting for phases one and two at the same time, Li Yongge suggested? Postponement of the last stage of the construction process would not delay the project as a whole, and the number of painters could be doubled if necessary to ensure that the work was still finished on time. Li's recommendation proved particularly prudent, for the fall of 2002 turned

Part of the painting crew: young women from Hebei.

the following spring, materials must be sourced without delay. Wang said that most of the materials were manageable: lime and flour were standard items which were either already in stock or easily purchased; as long as three weeks could be allowed for delivery, tung oil was most readily procured from Sichuan; for pigs' blood there were several abattoirs in Beijing. It was only the availability of flax that gave him some concern.

In 2003 Chinese New Year fell on 1 February. Work on site had stopped nearly a month before. Soon after mid-February, when the workers were due to return, the Pavilion of Prolonged Spring would be shrouded in scaffolding once more. This time the workforce would include a thirty-strong painting crew from Yixian in Hebei province. Some of the crew were to spend the next two weeks preparing the Pavilion's wooden surfaces for priming.

out to be a short one, with winter starting unusually early that year and limiting all work on site.

On a freezing cold and misty day in November 2002, Happy went with Wang Zhongjie, Zhang Decai and Li Yongge to look at the Pavilion of Met Expectation in Qianlong's Garden, as much as anything to remind herself what clumsily executed *caihua* looked like. She was told that the painted decoration, first completed in 1776, was last renewed — far from proficiently, it seemed — in 1959. The visit brought the imminent painting work at the Garden of the Palace of Established Happiness into sharp focus: if it was to start

'As long as the decoration is here, a part of me will always be left on this building.'

To increase the new timber's absorption of the primer, shallow notches are scratched all over it with a small hatchet. With timber there is always the inevitability of cracks or shakes developing as it dries and settles, not to mention the likelihood of shrinkage or expansion in response to changes of weather. The customary method of securing the timber is to wedge short bamboo nails in the shakes and seal them with a filler. But before the filler is applied, the timber is brushed with a size.

By the time a column or beam is painted, its glossy surface gives no hint that the wood has been covered with as many as six or seven layers of a primer which, before it dries, resembles nothing so much as thick mud. Preparation of this primer or paint ground — *dizhang* in Chinese — is dirty and arduous. Xu Chuntao supervises the first part of this procedure in a couple of sheds at the back of the construction division. He is a man of few words, quietly purposeful as he watches his two young assistants at their tasks. But then he has seen it all before, more times than he can count, for he joined the staff of the Palace Museum when he was a lad of seventeen.

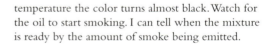

Like Zhang Decai and Wang Zhongjie, he has seen some fifty years of service; indeed, all three had begun their training in the Palace Museum together.

The paint ground, Xu explains, is made up of a number of basic ingredients, all of which have to be first processed. It is a windy day, and the wood-burning stove beside which he stands is roaring away, the flames giving off such heat that the two boys stoking and stirring the cauldron on top are bright red in the face. Xu continues:

This is literally a cooking process. We stir-fry pellets of manganese dioxide and powdered red lead until all the moisture content evaporates. A barrel of tung oil is then poured into the cauldron. You stir with a ladle while the mixture is heated. With rising temperature the color turns almost black. Watch for the oil to start smoking. I can tell when the mixture is ready by the amount of smoke being emitted.

This oily concoction is then combined with wheat flour, limewash and pigs' blood to form a viscid paste. Pigs' blood mixed with limewash is a bonding agent and an indispensable component of the paint ground. By combining these ingredients with coarse-grained or fine brick dust in various proportions, several grades of mortar are made. The mortar is spread on the timber, layer after layer, the first one or two coats applied merely to fill and cover the shakes and even out the surface, the uppermost coats to form a polished base for the paint. Between each coat, the surface is rubbed with a piece of pottery shard or, as it becomes progressively smoother, with sandpaper.

(Left) Pouring coagulated pig's blood into the mix for the paint ground.

This oily concoction is then combined with wheat flour, limewash and pigs' blood to form a viscid paste.

Then there is 'glossy oil'. As its name implies, this is a varnish laid on top of the paint ground, although it is just as useful in combination with the blood and the paste for priming small structural pieces such as brackets and windows. Its salient constituent is the light yellow perilla seed oil, derived from a mint plant long cultivated in China. Perilla seed oil is heated with tung oil and combined with small quantities of clay and lead monoxide to yield a dense liquid that not only dries quickly but also forms a hard and even film, imparting a lustrous finish to the varnished surface.

(Right) Flax is combed and then pressed into the primer.

Before the varnish, however, one other operation is carried out. Well away from the vats of pigs' blood, oils, paste and limewash, another team of artisans is sorting out bundles of stringy flax, untangling, combing through and shaking it loose. Despite Wang Zhongjie's worries, a sufficient quantity of flax was secured for the project in time. After more combing by hand, the threads of the fiber are draped on or wrapped round structural pieces such as doors and columns and pressed into a sticky primer which has been daubed on beforehand. This mesh of threads makes a veritable grass cloth, strengthening the *dizhang* and helping it to cohere more firmly. It is literally beaten into its backing with a wooden mallet until, compacted and dry, it appears as streaks of gold against the dark brown ground, an effect that is surprisingly beautiful. On the beams and in awkward corners of the woodwork, small squares of woven fabric serve the same purpose.

Craftsmen describe the thickness of the paint ground in terms of the number of layers applied, labeling each set as, for example, *yima wuhui* (one layer of flax, five layers of mortar) for large structural pieces like columns and external beams, or *san dao hui* (three layers of mortar) for windows, moldings and brackets.

By June 2003 the paint ground on the Pavilion of Prolonged Spring was ready to be

emblazoned with all the glorious colors of Suzhou-style *caihua*.

A slogan written in pink chalk on a blackboard outside the offices of the construction division warmly greets the inauguration of the *Liang hui*, the 'Two Meetings', in Beijing. The annual National People's Congress and the Chinese People's Political Consultative Conference, platforms for debates on national policies and central government performance, opened on March 5, 2004. Around the city center, the daily traffic gridlock at rush hour is exacerbated by a diversion: the southern half of Tiananmen Square has been put out of bounds to all cars except those used by the delegates. A full year has elapsed since President Hu Jintao and Premier Wen Jiabao assumed leadership of the country. On this their first anniversary in power, they will present the government's work reports before unveiling its political and economic priorities for the coming twelve

The Palace of Established Happiness

(Left and right) In the less formal versions of Suzhou-style *caihua*, illustrations vary from landscapes and architecture to scenes from nature and folk tales. The bird on the right is framed in the outline of a pomegranate, which is a Buddhist emblem of favorable influences and, because of its numerous seeds, a symbol of prosperity as well.

months. Where the economy is concerned, says the Premier, a critical year lies ahead, for while growth has been impressive, it is also becoming increasingly uneven. This time round, investment will be diverted from such overheated areas as construction and property to development of the poor rural areas.

The priorities for the Palace Museum are clear. By the 2008 Olympics, when Beijing will be in the spotlight, this most visible of tourist sites must present an immaculate and exemplary face to the world. As a first step, more attention will be paid to maintenance. Already, measures are afoot to foster some good habits. Teams of cleaners in bright uniforms are suddenly rather evident in the public as well as closed-off areas. The construction division has tidied up the courtyard in front of its offices.

Before the Olympics, however, another important date looms. In 2005 the Palace Museum will have been established for eighty years. Plans have to be made for such a momentous occasion. Among the various possibilities there is the imminent completion of the Garden of the Palace of Established Happiness: its opening on the eightieth anniversary will not only be a happy coincidence but also a timely excuse for a joint celebration.

For China Heritage Fund, a new direction has already unfolded: simply finishing the Garden is not enough any more, and a possible answer to the question 'what will you do with it?' is starting to form. Having reached the last stage of the construction, Happy Harun can also look back on the five years with some perspective. Probably because she had been involved from

the beginning, dealing daily with apparently mundane matters like bad weather, the lack of hard hats or the woeful quality of the roof tiles, Happy had given little thought to the Garden's final appearance. But there was a moment when the reality of the restoration revealed itself to her with absolute clarity: 'It was an unusually beautiful day; the sky was a brilliant blue. I walked into the site, as I do every day, and looked up to the top of the Pavilion of Prolonged Spring. And there, in between the protective covering, I caught a glimpse of the paint and the gilt, and all that just sparkled. I never thought I could be that impressed again — and here it was.'

(Above and following pages) Polychrome decoration under the eaves of the Pavilion of Prolonged Spring.

Painted Decoration

The Chinese expression 'carved beams and painted rafters' (*diaoliang huadong*) has long been a metaphor for a magnificent mansion. Built in timber, architecture of the remote past did not survive, but we know that buildings were treated with paint from the very beginning of China's recorded history. Archeological and literary sources tell us also that mineral derivatives such as cinnabar, a coloring substance, and plant products like tung oil, acting as a coating vehicle, have been in use for more than two thousand years. Lacquer was employed as far back as prehistoric times.

Paint serves two purposes. First, it helps to protect the exposed structure underneath, whether that is of stone, metal or wood, from the ravages of weather and rot. Besides its preservative qualities, paint is also ornamental, and in China the impulse to use it to adorn gave play to a creativity out of which the craft of *youshi caihua* was developed. This produced the vivid and dramatic polychrome painted decoration that is so distinctive a mark of the Chinese architecture that has endured.

Designs for *caihua*, the illustrative or pictorial part of the craft, evolved historically. A whole repertoire of motifs was introduced from the late Eastern Han period (25–220) onward by Buddhism, which had a profound influence on the development of several types of art and crafts. These motifs, including for example floating clouds, lotus petals, leaf scrolls and the Buddhist swastika (*wanzi*), first appeared on religious artifacts and architecture. It was only a matter of time before they were applied to the ornamentation of secular buildings as well. They entered the stock of designs used by painters of *caihua* and were, in the tradition of craftsmen everywhere, passed from master to apprentice together with practical expertise.

Anyone could see at a glance that many hours of skilled labor and a great deal of expense were involved in creating the painted decoration's gorgeous appearance. Not surprisingly, therefore, *caihua* became a palpable symbol of wealth and status along with such architectural features as the height of a building or the color of its roof tiles. While not entirely losing their association with the Buddhist faith, *caihua* designs were gradually absorbed into a general concern with status and rank. No commoner was permitted to apply painted decoration to his house — sumptuary laws saw to that — while ceremonial halls used by the emperor would have an abundance of gilt and dragons. Eventually *caihua* developed a hierarchy of its own, with certain patterns designated as more exalted than others.

By the Ming and particularly the Qing dynasty, the ranking of *caihua* designs had arrived at a complexity and rigor not seen before. Take any decorated beam in the Forbidden City. It would have been painted in a style consistent with the importance and function of the building. This

Painted Decoration: Section of a Hexi Design

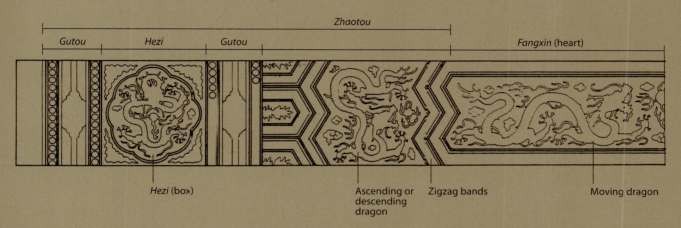

was achieved by varying certain details of the basic composition, which divides a beam or lintel panel — the span between two columns — into three sections: the *fangxin* ('heart') in the middle and a *zhaotou* on either side, each section measuring roughly a third of the entire width of the panel. Within the span of the *zhaotou* there would be two perpendicular bands or loops in blue and green known as *gutou*. For aesthetic balance, the bands might be repeated at intervals and even enclose a cartouche (*hezi* or box) if the beam were particularly long.

Just as richly ornamented are the coffered ceilings of the important halls, around a central cupola usually dominated by a coiled dragon playing with a flaming pearl, or by a paired dragon and phoenix. The four sides around the cupola would be a checkerboard of sunken squares in vivid green, each embellished with a gilded dragon or a white crane inside a roundel.

(In the Pavilion of the Rain of Flowers the ceiling's squares are decorated with Sanskrit characters.) Adding to the sumptuousness, colored clouds or bats accompany the central motif in each corner, while the designs on the crosspieces of the squares, called 'swallow tails', commonly consist of lotus patterns and symbolic clouds.

Buddhist symbols, particularly swastikas, are to be seen also on the square rafter ends. Round rafter ends tend to be painted with stylized characters for longevity (*shou*) or fortune (*fu*). If a floral design is used, favorites are the lotus, persimmon flower and cape jasmine. *Dougong* brackets are more often than not painted in plain blue and green accented with black, white and gilt contour lines. A design involving repeated curved striations of dark blue, pale blue, white and gold, which is applied on the underside of the corner beam end immediately under the

eaves, is described as 'cicada's belly'. The braces at the junction of beam and column are often richly gilded with a leaf scroll pattern.

In the Qing dynasty, the loftiest form of *caihua* in terms of status is called *hexi* ('combined seal'). Its application was sacrosanct, being confined to altars, temples and the ceremonial halls used by emperors. One would not have looked for *hexi* in a garden, even an imperial one, so that its surprising appearance on the exterior of the Lodge of Viridian Jade must be put down to the building having served some religious purpose, possibly as a repository for Buddha figures or sutras.

A subtle hallmark of the *hexi* style is the series of angled or zigzag bands, in the shape of a V or W turned on its side, placed between the *fangxin* and the *gutou*. A more conspicuous feature is the abundance of gilded dragons. The dragon is, of course, an auspicious creature in Chinese mythology, so much so that it was adopted as the emblem of the empire and of majesty. It was thought to live in several elements and was ascribed with supernatural powers. One myth tells of the dragon rising from its palace at the bottom of the sea to fly up to heaven at the arrival of spring. On the way it sports with the clouds and dispenses life-sustaining rains. In architectural decoration it is shown in a number of postures — either moving, sitting, ascending (in which case it is posed against a blue background, signifying the sky) or descending (into its green watery home). An equally nimble creature which is also prevalent in the painted decoration on imperial buildings is the *kuilong*, a hybrid of the dragon and an earthbound one-clawed monster of legend. As depicted on architecture, the *kuilong* is a minimalist version of the dragon, shorn of scales and an altogether simpler figure for the painter to portray. The dragon is sometimes matched with a phoenix, which is widely thought of as the female counterpart to the male dragon.

The illustrations . . . vary from flowers, fruit, birds and landscapes to human figures in narrative scenes depicting some folk tale or legend.

A step down in the *caihua* pecking order is the swirling pattern known as *xuanzi*, named for the floral scrolls painted on either side of the *fangxin*. Seen on the lesser imperial halls, temples, aristocratic mansions and government offices, the *xuanzi* style has several permutations which correspond to the amount of gilt employed. There are other, less widely-seen styles, such as *jixiangcao*, with its central motif of auspicious grass, or *haiman*, which is based on a design featuring bamboo. But in the more relaxed setting of a garden, most pavilions would carry the painted decoration that originated in Suzhou. The humblest of genres in terms of rank, Suzhou-style *caihua* gained tremendous popularity during the Qing dynasty. Its

comparative informality, not to mention its greater range of subject matter, gave craftsmen some scope for expression and experimentation. Only in the Suzhou style is there any concession to imagination; even so, certain conventions rule, especially when it was embraced by the imperial court and was deemed 'official'. The official version also became subject to ranking, the order generally correlating with the extent of gilding.

A Suzhou-style composition is divided into three sections, similar to the *hexi* and *xuanzi*, but differing from the other two in the treatment of the central section, *fangxin*. This is less easily seen in the Garden of the Palace of Established Happiness, where dragons are still the standard feature, than in the few halls within the Forbidden City decorated with the design known as *baofu* ('bundle wrapped in cloth'). In a *baofu* composition, instead of the central motif being enclosed in an oblong, the framing device is a semi-circle painted with a scalloped and frilled trim and extending over two or three stacked beams or lintels. It is said that this unique design, suggestive of beams and lintels draped in richly embroidered hangings, evolved from attempts to copy actual tapestries. The illustrations inside the 'bundle' vary from flowers, fruit, birds and landscapes to human figures in narrative scenes depicting some folk tale or legend. Beside them, the *zhaotou* may be covered in more illustrations with analogous themes, each fancifully framed in an outline shaped like a fan, a gourd, a rhombus, an open scroll, a Buddha's hand or finger citron, or a *qing* ('stone chime' percussion instrument made of jade). The themes, chosen for their auspicious associations, include brocade patterns (*jindi*), bats, goldfish, branches of prunus, fruits such as pomegranates and peaches, creepers and leaf scrolls, floating clouds, the eight Buddhist emblems, and the omnipresent flowers like lotus, peony and dahlia.

Between this riot of motifs and the end of the panel, a *qiazi* design is often painted. Shaped like a pair of pincers, *qiazi* can be 'hard' or 'soft', the former delineated with straight lines, usually on a blue or red background, and the latter with curved lines, frequently against a green background. Enjoying more freedom when painting Suzhou-style *caihua*, however, the craftsman did not always follow these conventions. Instead of the usual bands in blue and green, the *gutou* could be an elaborate geometric pattern between two strings of pearls. Another singular Suzhou-style *caihua* design may be seen on the beam ends above the columns of the Hall of Concentrating Brilliance. This is the so-called *bogu* — an archaic composition of ritual vessels, scrolls and books.

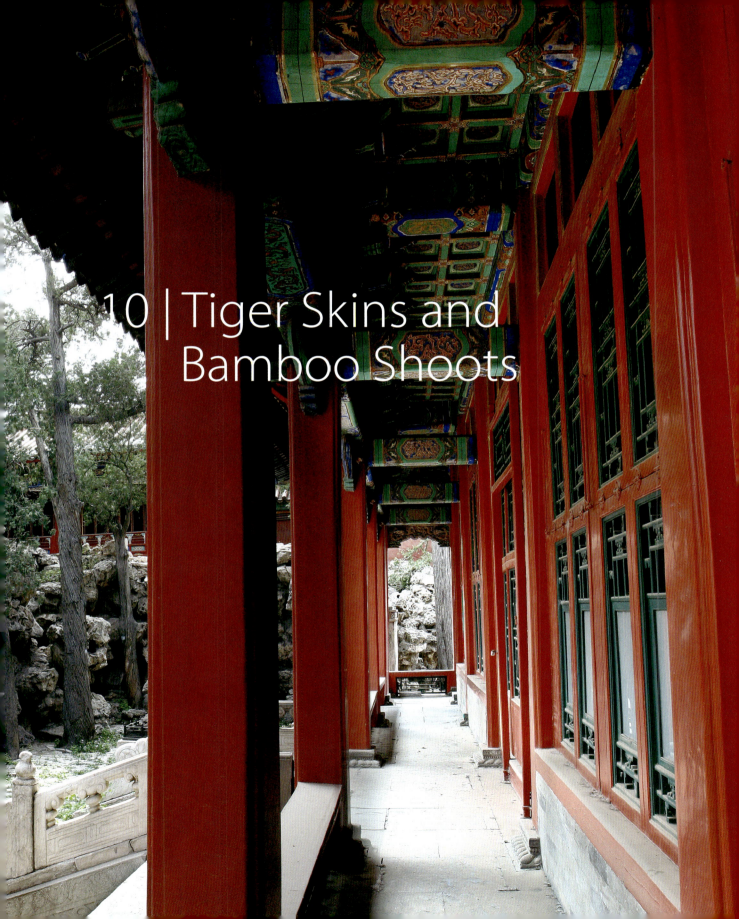

10 | Tiger Skins and Bamboo Shoots

10 | Tiger Skins and Bamboo Shoots

Besides painted pavilions and zigzagging galleries, a variety of other features help to deepen the effects and charms of a Chinese garden. There are trees and plants, of course, but vistas are generally more architectural than flowery, with most of the features built rather than cultivated. A garden could include decorative walls, fancy arches and doorways, pebble and flower-pattern paving, screens with relief carving, bridges, and inscriptions engraved in stone or written on wooden plaques. And almost invariably, a garden would contain sculptural rocks on plinths or a large rockery.

(Pages 182-183) In Qianlong's Garden, which was modelled after the Garden of the Palace of Established Happiness: on top of the *jiashan* is the Belvedere of Green Snail and, at the right, the Pavilion of Met Expectation.

(Right) The *jiashan* in the Garden of the Palace of Established Happiness on a winter's day.

At the southern perimeter and in the northern quarter of the Garden of the Palace of Established Happiness sit two built-up masses of rocks, which are referred to as *jiashan* or 'artificial mountains'. Mountains are implied in the Chinese term for landscape, *shanshui* (literally mountains-and-water), so that it is almost impossible to think of a garden worth its name without those two elements. Water is not present in this Garden, though, a deficiency that Puyi might have tried to remedy when he had a pond dug some time before 1923 in the courtyard in front of the Studio of Esteemed Excellence, as some rusty pipes revealed when the rubble was cleared away. Perhaps he was thinking of a 'winecup-floating stream'. There is one, for example, in Qianlong's Garden; cut into the tiled floor of an open-sided pavilion, this is a meandering watercourse used for a versifying game in his ancestor's day. Puyi's system of pipes included spouts as well, although there is no evidence that it was actually connected to a water source, so the fountain probably never played. Nor are mountains actually present in the Garden, but their essence — as wild, vast and rather perilous natural formations, with pinnacles, plateaus, cliffs and caverns — is represented, if in miniature, by artful groups of distorted rocks.

Qianlong certainly had a great affection for

rocks. Reginald Johnston was told that in the Palace of Tranquil Longevity there was a hall furnished only with a pile of rocks 'arranged to represent a wild and rugged mountain'. Qianlong would sit among the rocks to meditate and 'imagine himself to be a lonely hermit qualifying for the high destiny that awaits those who live on herbs and water and commune with the spirits of hills and rivers'. Of course the emperor had real hills to ramble over if he so wished, for vast imperial estates lay not too distant from the Forbidden City. 'But there was something in him', Johnston thought, 'that craved for a wonderland which, with the aid of a few heaped stones, would be wholly the creation of his own mind — a wonderland within the four walls of his own house . . .'

This was probably an exaggeration. Johnston's rocks were most likely a reference to three large jade sculptures which have remained in the Hall of Joyful Longevity within the Palace of Tranquil Longevity from Qianlong's time to the present day. Of the three, the Hill of

Jade, rising to a height of over seven feet and carved to depict the story of Yu the Great, is the most outstanding. Yu the Great, legendary founder of the Xia dynasty in 2200 BC, is credited with executing massive drainage works and controlling the floods that devastated the land. Weighing some five and a half tons, the enormous block of jade which commemorates Yu's feat was found in Xinjiang province and carved by the fine craftsmen of Yangzhou before its presentation to Qianlong.

'Rocks without *qi* are dead rocks, just as bones without the same vivifying spirit are dry, bare bones.'

Thus rocks could be appreciated in two ways: as *jiashan* or as sculptural art. As sculpture, they are given pride of place on a plinth out in the open, on a stand inside a hall or, if they are smaller, on a desk in a study. They could also form part of a miniature landscape composition. 'Mountains without rocks are commonplace;' a saying goes, 'water without rocks lacks clarity; a garden without rocks is inelegant; a room without rocks is unrefined.' Coral-like rocks from Lingbi in Anhui province are generally considered the best for display purposes; they are also distinctive for the clear ringing sound they produce when struck. In all instances, rocks are thought to encapsulate the vitality of nature, to embody the living quality of *qi*. As an artist once wrote: 'Rocks without *qi* are dead rocks, just as bones without the same vivifying spirit are dry, bare bones'. The equation of rocks and bones echoes a belief from very early times, when mountains were thought to be the bones of the earth, and rivers its arteries. Such myths might well have fueled the intense interest in stone, dubbed 'petromania' by art historians, that began in the Tang dynasty and reached a zenith in the Song. Scholars and artists, not to mention an emperor or two, elevated the appreciation of rocks as *objets d'art* or *objets trouvé* into a kind of connoisseurship.

Rock connoisseurs are often also collectors, and metamorphic rock — that is, rock that has been substantially altered from its original structure and composition by natural pressure and heat over several millennia — is exactly the sort of natural oddity which appeals to them, especially if they have a taste for the bizarre. Not for nothing are collected rocks called *qishi* — stones at once strange and rare. Strangeness may be discerned in the texture and color of a piece of rock, but what is most prized is an extraordinary form, as when a specimen is shaped like a living creature — a flying bird perhaps, or, in the case of two collector's pieces, deer antlers and 'a monk with a sack'. Rock-fanciers also find satisfaction in contemplating an object's venerable age. Either way, the queerer the rocks are, the more they are valued, says Li Jianguo, the man put in charge of restoring the Garden's rockeries in the third year of the project.

(Right) The Lodge of Viridian Jade and its small rockery

(Left) Model of the Belvedere of Abundant Greenery, with its pyramidal roof, atop the rockery.

Formerly a stonemason in the Palace Museum construction division, Li was set the task of building up two artificial mountains, one along the southern boundary, and one in front of the Lodge of Viridian Jade. In the former, the roots of a tree, which had grown just below the patch where the Belvedere of Abundant Greenery used to stand, had pushed up some of the rocks

and cracked them. As for the latter, it had in all likelihood collapsed after the fire, for the rocks that remained proved too brittle and fragmented to be re-used. Some sixty tons of new rocks to bolt on or bond to the old would have to be found. Everyone agreed with Li Jianguo when he proposed sourcing them from the area around Tai Lake in Jiangsu province, traditional home of the most celebrated rocks since petromania in China began. Time was when the most pleasing samples were dredged up from the bottom of this lake.

In the old days, it is said, there were even rock farmers who not only hauled rocks up from lake and river beds but also 'planted' large pieces of limestone by the water's edge, to let the flow and current work their magic until the stones, eroded into interesting configurations, took on the qualities of sculpture. The stones would then be 'harvested' and set in a garden for the farmer's descendants to enjoy. Nor would rock farmers feel any qualms about manually shaping them, by boring holes or chiseling off bits here and there, to make them even more interesting.

Today, Tai Lake rocks are not scooped out of the water but excavated from the hills round about. Quarry contractors and merchants who make a good livelihood selling rocks to landscape architects and garden-makers may be found clustered around the town of Yixing, a city lying to the west of Tai Lake, so it was to Yixing that Li Jianguo, Zhang Jinian (project supervisor and a member of the Palace Museum construction division) and Happy Harun went rock-hunting in November 2003. This was already Li's third attempt at procuring rocks, two earlier trips having yielded less than enough for the courtyard of the Lodge of Viridian Jade. Reflecting on the sourcing problems later, Happy remembered being perplexed by the haphazard way in which Li had approached his assignment. This time, to forestall a repetition of his unsuccessful expeditions, she recruited the help of Hu Xiaoxian, manager of one of Ronnie Chan's business operations in Shanghai and Yixing. Hu promptly sent members of his staff to scour the area around Yixing for suppliers offering the best specimens of garden rock.

Situated at the juncture of three provinces — Jiangsu, Zhejiang and Anhui — Yixing is known as China's 'ancient capital of pottery', its chief distinction being the purple-brown unglazed earthenware that has been produced in the vicinity for more than 2,000 years. But its fame also rests on the large number of karst caves nearby. Hollowed out by subterranean rivers coursing through limestone rock, the caves are filled with stalactites and stalagmites. So this is particularly fine rock country, and the types found around Yixing, according to *The Craft of Gardens*, are 'hard, with eyeholes and strange grooves . . . One kind is black, coarse-grained, with some yellow in it; another kind is white and smooth-grained'. In other words, they are possessed of decorative rock's most desirable qualities, which are summed up in four rhyming words: *shou, tou, lou* and *zhou*.

...decorative rock's most desirable qualities...summed up in four rhyming words: *shou, tou, lou* and *zhou*.

Two kinds of rock were required for the Lodge of Viridian Jade. One kind needed to be *shou*, which means 'thin' — that is, vertical pieces of rock in the shape of a pillar, and as tall or taller than a man. The Chinese name for such rock, *shisun*, invokes the bamboo shoot, a slender, tapered and edible sprouting of that most versatile of plants. But Li Jianguo was also in search of another kind of rock from the Tai Lake area, and for this, different criteria apply. Ideally, the specimens ought to be 'penetrable' (*tou*), which is a reference to hollows and cavities, of which no decorative rock should be without. They must also leak or ooze (*lou*), which they generally do, being full of holes. Put another way, explains Happy the geologist, the rocks should be 'porous (full of holes) and permeable (when the holes are connected)'.

Finally, to be utterly pleasing, the rocks should also be wrinkled and furrowed (*zhou*).

The rock-hunting party's destination is the Yixing Guoda Natural Rock and Stone Carving Factory at Jurong, a supplier turned up by Hu Xiaoxian's researches. Three hours out of Yixing, the car turns off into a wide paved road lined with every imaginable product of the quarry, from massive lumps of stone to marble that has been wrought in the configurations of lions, pillars, pedestals and dolphins, the last clearly destined for fountains in European style. But this is not Jurong yet. As the car travels on, the terrain becomes more rural. It stops at a spot where the land falls away to a little valley of checkerboard fields planted with rice. Jurong is not in the mountains, but a mountain may be seen in the distance through the opaque light of a drizzly afternoon. Li Jianguo is hardly bothered by the rain, so excited does he become when, on arrival at the factory, he happens upon four tapering *shisun* lying beside the road. These are yellow in tone, owing to the mineral elements embedded in them, Happy points out. Equally thrilling for Li are the pieces of green stone he sees strewn here and there in the yard. These will do for the decorative walls in the Garden, he observes to his colleagues. At this point the factory chief, a Mr Tang, makes himself known. He points to the *shisun* and says, 'These aren't even local but come from a hilly area in Zhejiang province. The truck driver started well before daybreak to bring them here this morning.' Soon a mutually acceptable price is reached: 'Rmb 3,000 is most reasonable,' Li mutters under his breath to Zhang Jinian. 'There's not nearly enough of the other kind here to fulfil our order, though.'

'Plenty more up in the mountain,' Tang assures those present, 'it's only this rain that prevents us from bringing the rocks down. There's too much slippery mud for the convoy to transport them safely. You can go up and look, but transportation must wait until the weather is dry.'

A chain and pulleys are used to hoist this heavy rock into place.

It is now late afternoon and getting dark; clearly the sensible course would be for Li to stay behind in Jurong while Happy and Zhang Jinian return to Beijing. The next day Tang escorts Li Jianguo up the mountain. Li takes up the story:

> At the crack of dawn we started climbing to the quarry. The quality of the rock was certainly satisfactory. I made my selection and took some photographs for my own record. But back down at the factory, Tang suddenly became uncooperative. As I had chosen the best pieces, he said, the price had to be raised by Rmb 120 to Rmb 480 per ton. Of course I stalled by saying that I needed to discuss this with the head of my department in the Palace Museum.
>
> After a telephone consultation with Li Yongge, I was authorized to negotiate a price below Rmb 450. Much haggling later, Tang and I came to terms.

It was then off to the haulage companies to arrange transportation.

By two o'clock the next day, the truck and trailer were loaded and ready to depart. I thought I could also now go home, only to find on reaching the railhead at Nanjing that tickets for the next day were sold out. The earliest hard-sleeper berth on the Nanjing–Beijing service that I could secure was for the 16th, two days later. Then, just after I'd left the station, my cell phone rang. Our truck had been involved in a road accident near Shuyang, some five hours out of Nanjing!

Advised by the haulage company to go to the scene of the accident as soon as I could, I took a long-distance bus to Shuyang. I reached the town just when daylight was fading, so there was nothing I could do but find a hostel and wait to inspect the truck the following day. The damage was fortunately not as grievous as I'd feared. It seemed that the accident had actually happened to another vehicle. Nevertheless, our truck was forced to brake suddenly, propelling the rock forward into the back of the cab. Bits of the smaller pieces of rock were broken off on impact, and I found cracks in two of the larger pieces.

What followed were arduous negotiations with the driver, the haulage company and their insurance agent. We finally settled on Rmb 3,000 in compensation for our damaged rock. After some work by a mechanic, the truck was able to proceed on its way while I, stumped once more when I tried to buy a train ticket to Beijing, had to kick my heels in Nanjing for another two days. The rain never stopped the whole time I was there. I had barely Rmb 100 after paying for the ticket, so it was reduced rations as well — eight hardboiled eggs over two days — in order to leave myself with enough money for the hostel and the fourteen-hour journey back to Beijing. I had expected to stay around Yixing for three to four days; I ended up staying for twelve

Besides suggesting the abode of immortals, an artificial mountain is also a device for creating surprise and suspense. The idea is that it should act as a screen, concealing a view to one entering a garden or a courtyard until, passing around the mountain or through it via a tunnel, the next vista is revealed in all its breathtaking glory. Then there is altitude, which the larger of the two artificial mountains in the Garden of the Palace of Established Happiness provides, so that an altogether different view is gained from the top. Qianlong very likely lingered over more than the view, if the stone chessboard table and four drum stools on the artificial mountain are anything to go by. The table and stools survived the fire, as did several inscriptions carved on the rock surfaces here and there. Accentuating the views or notable features of the rockery — whether real or imaginary — the inscriptions include 'Reaching the clouds', 'Beautiful cliffs', 'Soughing of the wind in the pines', 'Massed mountain ranges', 'Peak of accumulated jade' and 'Screen of brocade clouds'. Some of them are in the dowager empress Longyu's hand, or so it is claimed.

Broken pieces of masonry found in the Garden, fragments of what were once quaintly-shaped entrances set into internal walls at the sides of the Pavilion of Prolonged Spring, carried inscriptions in the same vein. One opening was a moon gate; the other had the silhouette of a vase. These entrances and walls — described as 'tiger skin' because they are made up of a patchwork of colored stones which Li Jianguo had to assemble anew — served to conceal and reveal at the same time. And the inscriptions, much abraded but still legible on the arch above the openings, suggest as much: *huaifen* or 'harboring fragrance', and *hanxiang* or 'aspect contained', were promises of sensory and visual effects lying beyond in the next courtyard. They were meant to arouse a sense of anticipation which a partial view through the openings would only heighten.

Chips of different colored stone, and bricks, pebbles and tile shards too, were used in paving the open trails that alternate with covered galleries (*lang*) to link the pavilions and provide a promenade. The paving along the path in the courtyard east of the Pavilion of Prolonged Spring had not been repaired or tampered with, and was, Happy was told, the only original pebble mosaics left in the Forbidden City. 'When laying walks in a garden,' Ji Cheng instructed in *The Craft of Gardens*, 'you should use small stones of irregular shape, fitting them together like the seeds in a pomegranate; this is both hardwearing and elegant.' Li Jianguo would agree as he scraped away the mud and debris from a pebble mosaic with a lion as its theme. Ji Cheng's manual is dismissive, however, of certain types of work: 'Pebbles are suitable for laying on paths that are not frequently used. It is best if you can intersperse large stones with small, but

(Left) Moon gate set into a 'tiger skin' wall.

(Right) Is it a mosaic lion or a dog? The figure was later identified as a tiger.

I am afraid most workmen are incapable of this. It is also effective to use bricks or tiles, and inlay them to form various brocade-like patterns. But if you lay them in the form of cranes or deer or lions playing with a ball, and the lion ends up looking like a dog, it is just ridiculous.' But the lion Li uncovered, even if it does rather resemble a dog, is charming.

When restoration began, the only plant life that remained in the Garden besides weeds were several trees. All of them cluster around the artificial mountain on the south or have their roots buried deep in the rock. Most of them are old trees, or so the small metal plaques nailed on the trunks have designated them. A horticultural survey of the Forbidden City conducted some years ago came to the conclusion that there were 3,800 trees within its walls. Of these, some 600 were more than eighty years old, 300 were over a hundred years old, and a hundred were aged between 300 and 500 years.

Four evergreen conifers on the east of the artificial mountain, hardy survivors of the 1923 fire, are more than a hundred years old. According to the plaque on one of them, their scientific name is *platycladus orientalis*; in Chinese they are called *cebai* ('lateral cypress'), possibly on account of their characteristically flattened, fanlike branchlets. In front and on the west are three deciduous trees with large leaves and pink flowers in summer, the *qiushu* (*catalpa bungei C. A. Mey*), a common species in northern China. The prettiest tree is undoubtedly a *sophora japonica*, standing close to the southern boundary of the Garden. With its feathery foliage and sticky pod, it is better known either as the Chinese scholar tree or the pagoda tree; it has been cultivated in China since ancient times. Both the *cebai* and the *sophora japonica* have been designated emblems of the city of Beijing since 1987.

We may safely assume that other species grew in the Garden, such as white-bark pine, willow and Yulan magnolia, all of which are found in the Forbidden City. There might even have been a Chinese jujube (*ziziphus jujuba*) — a particularly fine 'Tortuosa' specimen, all gnarled and crooked branches and oddly-shaped fruit, flourishes in the Imperial Garden and in the courtyard of the construction division. From several poems he composed at the Palace of Established Happiness, we know that Qianlong took aesthetic pleasure in the Garden's botanical features. One poem referred to a juniper standing outside the Lodge of Viridian Jade; another celebrated the 'three friends' of the cold season — by which he was referring to the pine, bamboo and flowering plum growing together outside its window. These trees were considered 'friends' because, flowering before winter's end, they presented a cheerful prospect when all around would still be gray and bleak. We also know that two more plum trees could be seen from the Pavilion of Tranquil Ease.

'I would gladly wander in Paradise... But it is far away and there is no road.'

Regard for the lofty pine was traditional in China. Often depicted in landscape painting clinging tenaciously to a cliff, it is a symbol of endurance and longevity. Bamboo, strong and flexible, swaying with the wind but never breaking, has always been identified with virtue and perseverance. It remains one of the most popular motifs in Chinese painting; admired for its beauty and manifold practical uses, no other plant has been so bound up in China's culture. As for the flowering plum or *prunus mume*, it is one of the first trees to bloom in early spring, typically at the Chinese new year along with the peach. The blossom of the *mei*, as it is called in Chinese, appearing on branches bare of leaves and before snow and frost have entirely melted, is a promise of new life. It is abundantly lauded in poetry and painted in works of art. So picturesque are the blooms that sprigs of the *prunus* would frequently be plucked and arranged in a vase for display, as they were once in the Pavilion of Tranquil Ease, inspiring Qianlong to several lines of verse in praise of their fragrance and efflorescence.

We know from Qianlong's poems that other species of *prunus* were planted in the Garden, including the peach, apricot and pear. The peach was, in a sense, ever present, for the fruit is an emblem of longevity and profusely portrayed in the decorative painting on pavilion beams. As the fruit is usually shown in a pair, it also makes an oblique allusion to felicity in marriage. Its flowers appear even before that of the plum, and are white or a delicate pink. Every Chinese knows the story of Peach Blossom Spring (*Taohua yuan ji*), which tells of

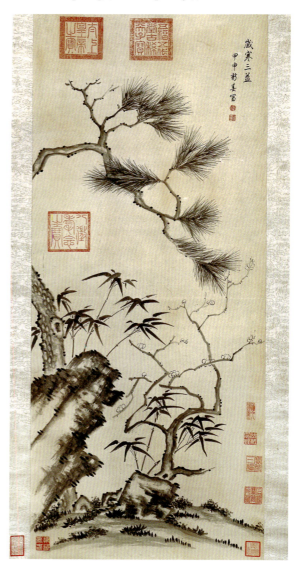

Pine, bamboo and rock: popular elements in a Chinese garden.

a fisherman's accidental discovery of an earthly paradise. One day, following the course of an uncharted stream, a fisherman stumbles upon an orchard of peach trees. He passes through this as if in a dream, for the air is filled with drifts of fragrant petals which tint the banks with their delicate splendor. The stream ends at a spring. Nearby is a hill with a narrow cave through which light glimmers. Following the light, the awe-struck fisherman suddenly emerges into a secret place of peace and beauty, where people know nothing of the mundane and troublesome world outside, and where time stands still. For several days the fisherman stays with these happy, contented people. When he leaves Peach Blossom Spring to return to his own village, he is careful to mark his route. Later, try as he may to re-trace his way back to that paradise, he is never to find it again, for the spring has mysteriously vanished. 'I would gladly wander in Paradise,' wrote Tao Qian (372–427), the author of *Taohua yuan ji*, in a poem, 'But it is far away and there is no road.'

Qianlong's poems mentioned the peach in the same breath as the apricot, another tree grown as much for its flowers as its fruit. Just as pleasing to his eye was the pear tree. Savoring the perfume of flowers carried on the breeze, he contrasted the white blossom of the pear tree with the rich red of the crabapple, a vision enhanced by a lustrous jadeite moon hanging in the night sky. In lyrical mood, the emperor could rise to an intense appreciation of nature; not surprisingly, the poem went on to imply that all this made up a scene lovely enough to entice the immortals.

A change of season brought other sights and colors to the Garden. Qianlong is known to have invited his mother to the Garden to dine and view the flowers at springtime. She would have found much to enjoy. There would have been varieties of the tree peony, a favorite among gardeners throughout China. Like Qianlong, whose 'Peonies at the Pavilion of Prolonged Spring' is an unusually rapt paean to the beauty of spring, she would have luxuriated in the gorgeousness of this quintessential Chinese bloom. Another plant Qianlong referred to in a poem is the *zidingxiang* (*syringa oblata*), a sweetly-fragrant purple lilac that makes a magnificent show in April. By May or so, the pomegranate is in bloom. An ornamental shrub with bright red flowers, it would have been cultivated in pots. As we are told by yet another poem, the pomegranate was shown to honored guests invited to the Studio of Esteemed Excellence when it was in flower. And before the onset of fall, there would be a brief blooming of the cottonrose hibiscus.

The Interior Decoration of the Studio of Esteemed Excellence

Two and a half centuries after they were built and more than eighty years since they were destroyed by fire, the pavilions of Qianlong's first garden have been reconstructed as closely to their original forms as possible. But what about their interiors? How much do we know of their decor besides the furniture and bric-à-brac listed in the Imperial Household's inventories?

In one pavilion — or at least a section of it — we can be certain that the interior design was distinctive and playful, notably in its use of *trompe l'oeil* to bring the garden indoors, thereby creating a garden within a garden. As it contained a theater, we may also conclude that it was a place of entertainment. This pavilion is the Studio of Esteemed Excellence, the one duplicated in Qianlong's Garden as the Lodge of Retirement. The latter's ceiling and wall murals, though they have deteriorated over time, are still extant (and, at the time of writing, being restored with the help of the World Monuments Fund). Nie Chongzheng, art historian and senior research associate at the Palace Museum, believes that they are reproductions of those in the Studio of Esteemed Excellence. It is thus possible to recover a likeness of the original from its copy. What follows is a precis and translation of Nie's essay on the subject, 'Ceiling and Wall Murals in the Lodge of Retirement'.

> There is a small theater in the Lodge of Retirement, whose western half is taken up by a stage built in the form of a belvedere surmounted by a pyramid roof. This creates the impression of there being one building inside another. Partition screens in latticed bamboo flank three sides of the stage. The partition parallel to the south wall of the Lodge has a moon gate set into it.

But what draws the eye more than anything else in this chamber is the *tieluo* which covers the entire ceiling and two of the walls. Literally 'pasted on-taken down', *tieluo* refers to large murals that are more akin to wallpaper than paintings. A single *tieluo* might cover a whole wall or half a wall. With a composition painted on paper or silk, it would be mounted with a silk or damask border and placed in position with the help of glue. Equally easily, it could be taken down and changed.

The mural on the north wall of the Lodge of Retirement is of a latticed partition in speckled bamboo pierced in the middle by a moon gate. Beyond the lattice and the gate is a garden in which pavilion, belvedere, flowers, flying magpies, wall and distant mountains are so painted as to deceive the eye momentarily into apprehending the composition as an actual vista. Two red-crowned cranes may also be seen, one of them shown preening its feathers just outside the moon gate. The cranes are finely observed and realistically portrayed, as is the bamboo. On the west wall, the scene through the bamboo lattice is of pine trees and cypresses against a backdrop of mountains and rocks.

Most ingenious of all is the mural on the ceiling, which depicts a riot of climbing wisteria hanging from a trellis, with patches of a blue sky peeping through the bright green foliage and violet pea-like blooms. To the spectator, the mural offers a range of perspectives: from a point in front of the stage, the viewer sees the clusters of wisteria drooping directly overhead; a few steps back, and the flowers seem to be at a slant; still further away, they appear even more deeply angled, almost as if they are lying flat against the trellis.

All these murals were affixed after they were painted, yet they differ from other *tieluo* in presenting a single, unbroken landscape in adroit juxtaposition with the surrounding decor and fittings so that a painted bamboo partition, for example, is contiguous with and all but

Red-crowned cranes in a detail of Castiglione's *trompe l'oeil* mural.

The Interior Decoration of the Studio of Esteemed Excellence

indistinguishable from the real one.

The technique of creating a painted illusion of reality was then already familiar to European artists engaged in the interior decoration of religious architecture. Using perspective devices, they painted angels and saints against blue skies and white clouds on cathedral vaults to represent a vision of heaven and to deepen the spiritual atmosphere. Andrea Pozzo (1642–1709), a Jesuit painter and architect, was greatly renowned in his day for his illusionist ceiling decoration such as that on the dome of San Ignazio in Rome. His work and the textbook on perspective he published, *Perspectiva Pictorum et Architectorum*, were much admired by the Italian artists who came after him. One of them, Giuseppe Castiglione, went as missionary to China in 1715 and stayed on as a painter at the imperial court, enjoying Qianlong's favor for his singular blending of Chinese brushwork with European realism.

The Western influence is quite evident in the style of the murals in the Lodge of Retirement, and this is borne out by the records. On the twenty-fifth of the fifth month in the seventh year of the Qianlong era (1742), the Imperial Household Department's workshop noted that the painters Lu Jian and Yao Wenhan were ordered to assist Lang Shining [Castiglione's Chinese name] with the painting of a wisteria trellis in the Palace of Universal Happiness. A month later, it was minuted that 'Lang Shining is to paint a wisteria trellis in the four western chambers of the Studio of Esteemed Excellence at the Palace of Established Happiness, in the manner of the pasted silk hanging at the Banmu Garden.' [Banmu Garden was at the Garden of Perfect Brightness.]

The interior decoration of the Palace of Universal Happiness has long disappeared, and the Studio of Esteemed Excellence burnt down in 1923. We know that the exterior design of the Lodge of Retirement was based entirely on the Studio of Esteemed Excellence; the document mentioned above strongly suggests that its interior decoration echoed that of the earlier pavilion as well. The Lodge was, however, built in 1772, six years after Castiglione's death. Who then painted its wisteria trellis? There were other European artists at Qianlong's court, of course. Among them, only Wang Zhicheng [Father Jean-Denis Attiret, 1702–68] could be considered the equal of Castiglione, but he too had died, in 1768. As for the Bohemian Ai Qimeng [Father Ignatius Sichelbart, 1708–80], it is doubtful that he was accomplished enough to have so successfully tackled the mural. We find another chronological difficulty when we set the red-crowned cranes in the mural against others attributed to Castiglione, for a stylistic comparison offers compelling testimony that the paintings are by the same hand.

One clue to unraveling the puzzle is provided by another document in the Imperial Household's workshop archives. On the twentieth of the second month in the thirty-ninth year of the Qianlong reign (1774), it says, the eunuch Hu Shijie passed on the following decree: 'The four walls, pillars, balustrades and partitions in the three bays [chambers] of the Lodge of Retirement are all to be painted by Wang Youxue in emulation of Derixin.' 'Derixin', the inscription on a plaque hanging in the western half of the Studio of Esteemed Excellence, frequently stood for the chamber itself. Wang Youxue, a painter at Qianlong's court, was a disciple of Castiglione, as was his brother Wang Ruxue. No-one was more suited to the task of decorating the Lodge of Retirement. However, since his skills fell far short of his master's, he could not possibly have painted the red-crowned cranes, even if he was responsible for the rest of the mural. My guess is that parts of the mural, including the section featuring the cranes, were painted by Castiglione earlier as *tieluo* for the Studio of Esteemed Excellence. Perhaps he painted more pieces of *tieluo* than could be used at the time. If so, it would have been unexceptionable for Wang Youxue to augment a new mural by using *tieluo* panels that were already in existence.

It goes without saying that, as a living example of the transplantation of European painting style and technique to a Chinese palace, the entire mural deserves to be cherished and studied further.

11 | A Museum of Chinese Architecture

11 | A Museum of Chinese Architecture

As in any complex project, with several parts advancing at the same time, it was easy to lose sight of issues raised by such fundamental questions as 'Is there a point to this?' and 'What will the restored Garden be used for?' Such questions had been in Happy's mind from the beginning, but events had overtaken her and 'there was just too much going on at the time. I had to devote all my attention to getting the construction started.' She had also, early on, stressed China Heritage Fund's particular interest in 'supporting self-sustainable projects', regarding such factors as 'conservation training, project management and, where relevant, the development of appropriate technology' as key to any cultural heritage work.

(Pages 196-197) Inside the Pavilion of Tranquil Ease. (Right) Natural light supplemented by ceiling track lights in the Pavilion of Prolonged Spring.

Halfway through the Garden restoration, these questions crystallized into a number of options. One of them, at its earliest, inchoate stage, was sparked by something John Sanday had said about presenting a work of conservation: 'What we want to try and do is always to save examples of a structure so that it can be read historically. I've been very impressed in my visits to the U.S. by the strong emphasis Americans place on the presentation of a site or a museum. They go to immense lengths to give people an experience.' Happy was to add later that she applied this idea of presentation to the Garden and 'carried it further.'

Several critical developments occurred in the spring of 2002. At the end of April Director Pei officially retired. The prospect of a change of guard is often unsettling; Pei had been directly responsible for architectural matters in the Palace Museum, and having devoted enormous energy to building trust and respect among those involved in the Garden restoration project, Happy awaited the announcement of his successor with apprehension. To her delight, Pei's replacement turned out to be someone already familiar to China Heritage Fund — Jin Hongkui from the State Administration of Cultural Heritage. Later that fall, and after more than a decade, China's central government finally appointed a full director to the Palace Museum, a ministerial-level official named Zheng Xinmiao.

During a farewell lunch hosted by Ronnie Chan for Director Pei, at which his successor was also present, the possibility of restoring the Hall of Rectitude, destroyed by the fire of 1923 like the Garden to its north, hung tantalizingly over the conversation. In fact Ronnie Chan was supportive from the first: 'I'd always wondered

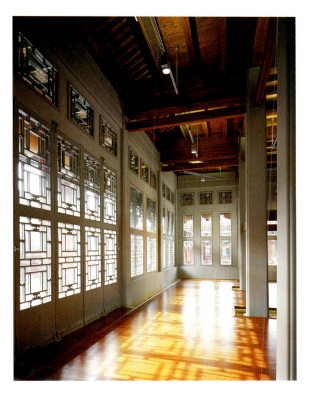

what was going to happen to that empty piece of ground. As the Garden restoration progressed, what we were doing became quite obvious to all, and we had also developed a good working relationship with the Palace Museum. From my own perspective, I wanted to be certain that what goes next to the completed Garden is done to the same high quality. So when they asked me if I would like to collaborate on the Hall of Rectitude, I said "my pleasure," of course.'

The prospect of a continuing role for China Heritage Fund in the Palace Museum brought the subject of the future of the Garden into sharp relief. Come handover time, the Fund was not going to pack up and leave. This was when the idea of presenting the Garden and what it exemplified took root. During one of his visits

199

to Beijing, John Sanday asked: 'Wouldn't it be entirely fitting to set up a museum of Chinese architecture in the Garden?'

With the assurance of Ronnie Chan's support, Happy began considering the possibility of adapting the Pavilion of Prolonged Spring to such a purpose. But she found that Jin Hongkui and his colleagues at the Palace Museum were already looking at a different option. For years the Museum establishment had felt that it lacked a venue imposing enough to receive visiting dignitaries — a minister of state or an ambassador, for instance. For various other reasons, not least location and security, a pavilion in the Garden would be particularly suitable for such a use. There was the Garden's proximity to the Gate of Divine Prowess, one of the main gates into and out of the Forbidden City, as well as its separateness from the tourist areas, which would lessen the difficulty of making security arrangements should these be necessary. In a new building where no interior decoration had as yet been undertaken, there would also be comparative freedom to design a tailor-made reception center.

In the course of discussions it became clear that the aspirations of the Palace Museum and China Heritage Fund were not in conflict with each other. There was no reason why the schemes should not be combined. After all, there would be two large buildings in the Garden — the Pavilion of Prolonged Spring could serve as a place of reception, and the internal space of the Pavilion of Tranquil Ease would certainly lend itself to adaptation as an exhibition gallery. Happy noted afterward that, given its size and the fact that it is a single-storied building, the latter would actually be more appropriate as a museum space than the Pavilion of Prolonged Spring.

The idea of a museum of Chinese architecture is at once obvious and compelling. As Happy put it, the Pavilion of Tranquil Ease is 'an exhibition in itself: what inspired me was the rawness and natural beauty of its lines.' Indeed, the entire Garden site and its buildings could be the star of the show, complementing whatever is designed to fill the exhibition, whether that is an illustrated historical narrative or a collection of models, tools and artifacts. For a start everyone agreed that there should be models of a series of *dougong*, the very symbol of the carpenter's art. Here, then, would be a means of 'presenting' the restoration and inculcating in visitors a positive awareness of the project's significance. The display would not just offer things to look at but also an environment to experience.

To convert a copy of an eighteenth-century building into a modern space for display is actually an immensely complicated undertaking. New architecture embodies shafts and ducts for the services and mechanical and electrical systems to run through. With the Pavilion of Tranquil Ease there is no such structural flexibility. In fact, since the structure does not allow anything

Before (right) and after (left): interior fixtures of the Pavilion of Prolonged Spring include a new staircase in contemporary design, one which harmonizes totally with its surroundings.

to be easily hidden, integrating contemporary elements and then making them invisible becomes nothing less than an engineering nightmare. But both Ronnie Chan and Happy came to see that, given the will and architects with experience of designing museums in an international context, it could be done. In a letter to the Palace Museum directors toward the end of 2004, Ronnie Chan made another point about the proposed collaboration and its consequence for China and Chinese culture:

> Today the West is focused only on China's manufacturing accomplishments, robust exports and relatively low value-added products flooding the global market. These are indeed realities. But China's economic resurgence is bound to enrich the world's spiritual civilization as well.
>
> The synthesis of an intrinsically Chinese cultural relic in the Forbidden City with state-of-the-art technology from around the world would be nothing less than astounding and increase China's prestige on the international stage. Such expectations may strike some people as exaggerated, but from the standpoint of one long-time observer of the politics, economics and cultures of both East and West, they do not seem far-fetched. I believe that with our joint and wholehearted efforts, these intentions can be realized.

'The synthesis of an intrinsically Chinese cultural relic ... with state-of-the-art technology ...would be nothing less than astounding...'

For Happy there is another aspect to the presentation of a museum experience. Museums have always played a didactic role, she says. A museum of Chinese architecture may be both a reflection of the artisan and his craft and a transmitter of that heritage. It will call attention to the value of traditional activities that are rapidly disappearing from the modern world. Was it being too quixotic to think that, through reconstructing the Garden of the Palace of Established Happiness, these traditional crafts were being revived? Happy had been conscious of a growing sense of pride among her best craftsmen and of their increasing willingness to meet her expectations as the buildings took shape. But she was equally aware of the strong pressures exerted on them to change to a more lucrative livelihood. The likes of Old Chang and Miao had seemed totally committed to the project until lured away by other jobs and the prospect of higher pay, as they were before the project's completion. After passing his test, Zhang Jiye, the young mason, abandoned stone-carving to become a driver. All this contributed to contradictory feelings about the survival of the Chinese way of building. It was indisputable, nevertheless, that the destroyed Garden had been restored entirely by traditional methods at the end of the twentieth and the beginning of the twenty-first century.

These ambivalences ran against the certainty felt by people like Li Yongge, who was unequivocal

(Left) Roofline and rafters of the Pavilion of Tranquil Ease. (Right) Contemprorary and traditional effects are blended in the decor of the Studio of Esteemed Excellence, the Pavilion of Prolonged Spring and the Pavilion of Tranquil Ease. The lanterns were modelled on Qing originals in the Palace Museum collection.

that rebuilding was the natural thing to do. As much as anything, that piece of devastated ground in the Forbidden City, like a gaping wound, represented bad *fengshui*. The Imperial Palace is resonant with manifestations of the belief that 'cosmic breath' or 'magic energy' flowed through the landscape, and the symmetry, equilibrium and symbols of harmony that were infused in its design were there for a reason: they attracted fortune and repelled catastrophes. He is not superstitious, Li says, but he respects the ancestral belief that the *fengshui* of the Forbidden City had a direct bearing on the stability and well-being of the country. Wholeness was clearly vital to this geomantic scheme.

With the end in sight in the fall of 2004, the director of the Palace Museum, Zheng Xinmiao, was just as adamant on the desirability of completeness. He shared the old experts' view that refilling the void in the northwest corner of the Forbidden City was something devoutly to be wished; like them, he stands in a cultural tradition that regards conscious archaism not as a pretentious or counterfeit act but a worthy and reverential attempt to re-engage with the glorious past. Imitation and reproduction of the works of ancient masters has long been practiced in China. Similarly, copying the craftsmanship of Qing-dynasty builders is a way of preserving it. The Garden of the Palace of Established Happiness was rebuilt in a way that mirrored the original techniques faithfully. It is, says Zheng Xinmiao, an authentic restoration.

One of the most interesting writers to have confronted the issue of restoration and historical correctness is Howard Mansfield. The title of Mansfield's book, *The Same Ax, Twice*, refers to the story of 'a farmer who says he has had the same ax his whole life — he only changed the handle three times and the head two times.' The question leading from this is: does the farmer have the same ax? 'To remake a thing correctly is to discover its essence,' Mansfield concludes; in other words, yes, the farmer does possess the same ax — and with a truer sense of that ax than, say, another farmer who has never repaired

11 | A Museum of Chinese Architecture

203

his own ax. 'A tool has a double life. It exists in the physical sense, all metal and wood, and it lives in the heart and the mind . . . The farmer who restored his ax has . . . the history of ax building in his hands . . . A repaired ax is a living tradition.'

'The authenticity is really in the process.'

Happy tends to steer any debate about historical authenticity toward more practical considerations such as techniques and materials, almost all of which were replicated in the Garden reconstruction. She said while contemplating the shiny paint on the Pavilion of Prolonged Spring: 'Give this building a few years and it will grow old. It's really not about something new and something old.' After all, 'the other buildings in the Forbidden City were new five, six hundred years ago' and have evolved over time, with some demolished and rebuilt and others destroyed by earlier fires and replaced. 'When something fell down you put up a replacement — and so it continues, in the original surroundings and faithful to the traditional methods. The authenticity is really in the process.'

In the China of today this attempt to recover a lost eighteenth-century imperial garden contrasts dramatically with what many see as a breathless rush to discard the past and embrace the future. But the restoration says as much about China's present ambitions and confidence as the titanium-clad national theater on the edge of Beijing's Tiananmen Square, the construction of which marched exactly in step with that of the Garden of the Palace of Established Happiness. Ronnie Chan expresses the same analogy when he ponders upon the timeliness of his own participation: 'It is always easier to destroy than to build. This is as true for a palace as for a garden. Equally it is true for a nation. Culture flourishes in times of prosperity and withers in times of turmoil or war. Isn't it appropriate that as China finally re-enters the family of great nations, and as China rises economically and politically on the world scene, that somebody should come along and restore this Garden?'

At the top of the stairwell, Pavilion of Prolonged Spring.

A Contemporary Space Inside the Garden

Alexander Beels, *China Heritage Fund*

To meet the challenge of creating a contemporary space inside the Garden, Happy put together a team of top-flight international architects, designers and engineers from firms in Guangzhou, Hong Kong and New York. The common factors uniting these people were expertise in state-of-the-art materials and techniques, and experience of working in China.

The eventual team coalesced around Happy's choice of lead architect for the project, Calvin Tsao. Born in Hong Kong and educated in the U.S., Tsao had worked under I. M. Pei on projects such as the Fragrant Hills Hotel in Beijing in the mid-1980s before establishing his own firm, Tsao & McKown, in New York. Happy was drawn to Calvin Tsao because she saw that he could bring a special sensitivity, both social and aesthetic, to the project. In Tsao she saw both excellent instincts for understanding a client's aspirations and true needs and an appreciation for structures and their background. Here was someone who might look at the Garden the same way as she did, and would not let his own agenda overrun the project. With the architect on board, the rest of the team came together naturally, encompassing Tsao's long-time collaborator, Pei Partnership; the mechanical engineers, Parsons Brinckerhoff China; and Levett & Bailey, which had been generously providing professional support to China Heritage Fund since 2000.

For Calvin Tsao, the challenge was to design a space that would not clash with the Qing exteriors of the buildings; in his words, he had to make the new architecture 'disappear':

> The first approach we took was to try to make the contemporary interventions invisible, but we found this impossible. Not carrying out the sort of interior decoration that the building would otherwise have had was already an intervention ... So we ended up trying to harmonize the contemporary devices with the traditional. We didn't try to look for commonalities in actual style elements. Instead, we use contemporary materials, but in a way that does not detract from the historical. We work with undercurrents of the overall style, things like proportion, size, order, even the mathematical progressions which help to hold a style together.

Sometimes, Tsao's efforts to keep the contemporary interventions from interfering with the historical structures were hard for the Palace Museum officials to understand. He had, for instance, chosen a very subdued color scheme and minimal decorative detail because he didn't want something so attractive that it would compete with the historical material or upstage it. 'But the officials didn't understand why we are putting out such effort for something they think is "drab." They probably were thinking, "Why are we bringing in international designers to make something so plain?" I think they were looking for something more glamorous.'

The technical challenges facing the engineers were just as great. 'When I was introduced to this project last December, it really scared me!' recalls Shiu-Wo Lam, lead engineer for Parsons Brinckerhoff. 'We have decades of experience — but with concrete buildings, not wooden structures. So I had to learn all about traditional structures, reading lots of books and visiting many other sites.'

Lighting plan for the Pavilion of Prolonged Spring.

A Contemporary Space Inside the Garden

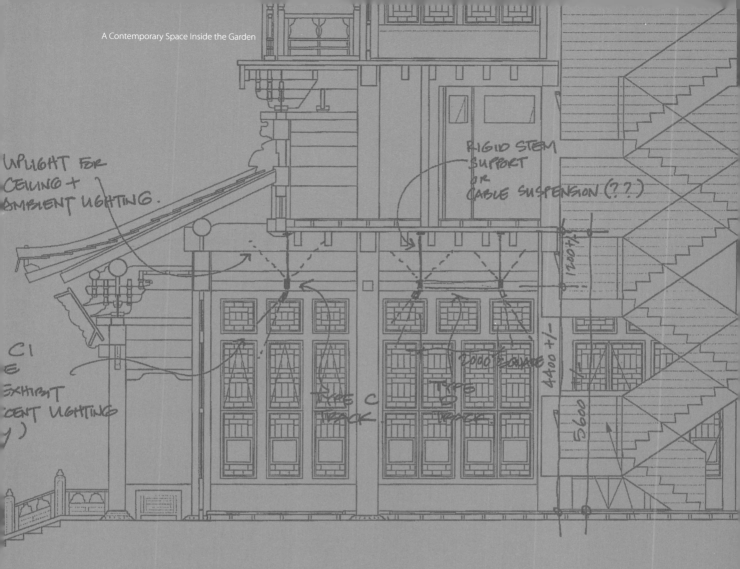

The site presented Lam with a number of unique problems. Conventional facilities, such as hidden spaces for mechanical equipment, were not available. Installation of standard sprinkler systems would have violated museum policy. The wooden buildings would provide no sound proofing. To solve these problems, eventually careful testing of all possible lines of sight was required to find unobtrusive locations for the air-conditioning units. State-of-the-art air sampling systems were needed to provide adequate fire protection. But some resources turned up fortuitously. The acoustic consultant Lam found happened to have trained in England: 'I can handle it,' the consultant told Lam. 'The buildings I learned on in the U.K. were all wooden structures!'

In the end, says Lam, what made this project special was the team. 'We have a great team, from the architect and the Palace Museum to the contractor, and we all appreciate the significance of the project.' Drawing on their broad international experience, and united by their respect for the special space they are creating, Happy's team has been able to realize the Garden as a piece of living heritage in the modern world.

Afterword

Michael Petzet, *President, International Council on Monuments and Sites*

On 27 May 2007, a group of delegates concerned with World Heritage and conservation, including myself, were shown round the recently reconstructed Garden of the Palace of Established Happiness. We left that evening with the impression that what we had seen was an almost perfect reconstruction of an imperial garden from the Qing dynasty, probably similar in all its essentials to the one built by the Qianlong Emperor in the middle of the 18th century.

As this book explains, the Garden includes nine structures in a rectangular space, each sumptuously painted with polychrome decorations that are highlighted in gold leaf. The interiors of these traditional buildings with their vividly ornamented facades are fitted in a contemporary style and equipped with modern lighting and air-conditioning, combining historical architecture with present-day design. It is a generally accepted conservation doctrine that reconstructions of historical buildings which no longer exist can only be accepted in exceptional cases and under special circumstances. A few such buildings may be reconstructed *in situ*, however, if certain conditions are met; if, for example, there is strong support from experts, and if it involves no damage to the existing site. The Florence Charter (1981) gives us the necessary guidelines for historic gardens: *No reconstruction work on a historic garden shall be undertaken without thorough prior research to ensure that such work is scientifically executed and which will involve everything from excavation to the assembling of records relating to the garden in question and to similar gardens. Before any practical work starts, a project must be prepared on the basis of said research and must be submitted to a group of experts for joint examination and approval.* In the case of the Garden of Established Happiness, there was overwhelming consensus for reconstruction from both the museum officials and architectural historians. Perhaps the integrity of the Forbidden City was foremost on their minds, for the integrity and intactness of the Imperial Palace had long been undermined by the loss of the Garden.

In old China, where timber was the most extensively used building material, what we now consider as heritage sites and historical monuments were repeatedly damaged or destroyed and repeatedly restored and rebuilt over the centuries. Nevertheless, for each reconstruction the questions of authenticity are inevitably posed. During the preparation and implementation of the concept for the Garden China Heritage Fund showed that, far from being insensitive to such questions, it has welcomed debate on them, as well as on the principles and practices of conservation. During our visit three points of particular interest were discussed: First, all those concerned in the project had the abundant archives of the Palace Museum to draw from, so that their efforts were based on a wide range of documentary evidence. China Heritage Fund was also helped by the existence of an invaluable physical reference — that of the Qianlong Garden in the opposite corner of the Forbidden City, a near copy of the original. Secondly, they were scrupulous in protecting the site, preserving the existing historical fabric, and adopting as far as possible the traditional crafts and traditional

The completed Pavilion of Prolonged Spring.

Afterword

materials deployed in the 18th century. Finally, China Heritage Fund clearly recognizes that interpretation for visitors rounds out the entire conservation process, as shown by its plan to create an exhibition of traditional Chinese architecture at the site.

I am delighted to contribute an Afterword to this narrative of the Garden's history and its restoration. Each pavilion, hall, studio and belvedere tells myriad stories — past and present — and this book helps the reader to discover some of them.

Glossary

This glossary provides Chinese characters for references in the text that are translated or rendered in pinyin, such as place names, proper names and architectural terms. Well-known names of people, cities, provinces and reigns have not been included, nor have the names of authors and the titles of books and journals listed under Acknowledgements and Sources.

Admonitions of the Instructress to the Court Ladies (*Nushizhen tu*) 女史箴图
ang (cantilever 'arm') 昂
Anhe 安河
Anhe Tile Factory (Anhe Liuliwachang) 安河琉璃瓦厂
Attiret, Father Jean-Denis (Wang Zhicheng) 王致诚

baishijian ('hundred assorted pieces') 百式件/百什件
Banmu Garden (Banmu yuan) 半亩园
baofu (design in decorative painting: 'bundle wrapped in cloth') 包袱
bay (*jian*) 间
Beiyao (North Kiln) 北窑
Belvedere of Abundant Greenery (Jicui ting) 积翠亭
Belvedere of Favorable Breezes (Huifeng ting) 惠风亭
Belvedere of Green Snail (Biluo ting) 碧螺亭
Belvedere of Purest Jade (Yucui xuan) 玉粹轩
bi (jade disc) 璧
bian (inscribed plaques) 匾
bingyin (1746) 丙寅
bogu (design in decorative painting: archaic composition of ritual vessels, scrolls and books) 博古
bubujin window (lattice pattern) 步步锦
Buddhist swastika (*wanzi*) 万字

cai (standard measurement for timber) 材
Castiglione, Giuseppe (Lang Shining) 郎世宁
cebai (cypress) 侧柏
'Ceiling and Wall Murals in the Lodge of Retirement' ('Ji Gugong Juanqin zhai tiandinghua, quanjinghua') 记故宫倦勤斋天顶画. 全景画
chadui (to live and work in a production team) 插队
Chamber of Crystalline Purity (Yuhubing) 玉壶冰
Chamber of the Mystical Lotus (Miaolianhua shi) 妙莲花室
Chang Qinghai 常青海
Chenggouzhen 称勾镇

China Cultural Property Promotion Association 中华文物交流协会
China Heritage Fund 中国文物保护基金会
'China royal white' stone (*hanbaiyu*) 汉白玉
Chiu Che Bing 邱治平
chiwen (ridge tile: 'owl's lips') 鸱吻
Cixi 慈禧
concave tiles (*ban wa*) 板瓦
'cracked ice' window (lattice pattern) 冰裂纹
Craft of Gardens, The 园冶
cuanjian (roof type) 攒尖

Daoguang 道光
department of traditional architecture (gujian) 古建部
Derixin, *see* 'Virtue Renewed Daily'
dian (hall) 殿
diaoliang huadong ('carved beams and painted rafters') 雕梁画栋
Ding Guanpeng 丁观鹏
dishui (drip tile) 滴水
dizhang (paint ground) 地仗
Dong Bangda 董邦达
Dong Qichang 董其昌
dou (bearing block of a bracket set) 斗
dougong (bracket set) 斗拱
doukou (mortise of the bearing block of a bracket set) 斗口
douniu (tile figure: animal with magical powers) 斗牛

Fan Youliang 范友良
Fan Yubin 范毓宝
Fangshan 房山
fangxin ('heart' section in painted beam) 枋心
Feng Yuxiang 冯玉祥
Fifth Western Abodes 西五所
Firmiana simplex (Chinese Parasol tree) 梧桐树
First Historical Archives of China 中国第一历史档案馆
Forbidden City 紫禁城
Fourth Western Abodes 西四所
fu (fortune) 福

Garden of Everlasting Spring (Changchun yuan) 长春园
Garden of Gorgeous Spring (Qichun yuan) 绮春园
Garden of Perfect Brightness (Yuanming yuan) 圆明园
Garden of the Palace of Established Happiness (Jianfu gong huayuan) 建福宫花园
Gate of Divine Prowess (Shenwu men) 神武门
Gate of Heavenly Peace (Tianan men) 天安门
Gate of Preserving Integrity (Cunxing men) 存性门
Gate of Supreme Harmony (Taihe men) 太和门

ge (pavilion) 阁
'golden bricks' (*jinzhuan*) 金砖
'golden columns' (*jinzhu*) 金柱
Golden River (Jinshui he) 金水河
gong (crossed 'arms' of a bracket set) 拱
'greenish-white stone' (*qingbaishi*) 青白石
Gu Congyi 顾从义
Gu Kaizhi 顾恺之
guan (lodge) 馆
Guangxu 光绪
guangyou (glossy oil) 光油
Gugong 故宫
gutou (design in decorative painting) 箍头

haima (tile figure: sea horse) 海马
haiman (form of decorative painting: design featuring bamboo) 海墁
Hall of Concentrating Brilliance (Ninghui tang) 凝晖堂
Hall of Controlling Time (Fuchen dian) 抚晨殿
Hall of Imperial Peace (Qin'an dian) 钦安殿
Hall of Joyous Longevity (Leshou tang) 乐寿堂
Hall of Martial Valor (Wuying dian) 武英殿
Hall of Mental Cultivation (Yangxin dian) 养心殿
Hall of Precious Prosperity (Baohua dian) 宝华殿
Hall of Preserving Harmony (Baohe dian) 保和殿
Hall of Rectitude (Zhongzheng dian) 中正殿
Handan 邯郸
hanxiang ('aspect contained') 含象
He Wenkui 何文奎
Heshen 和申
hexi (form of decorative painting: 'combined seal') 和玺
hezi ('box': design on painted beam) 盒子
hongdan (red pigment) 红丹
Hongli 弘历
Hongxian 洪宪
Hu Shijie 胡世杰
huagong (bracket arm at right angles to the wall of a building) 华拱
huaifen ('harboring fragrance') 怀芬
Huang Jinfu 黄进福
Huizong 徽宗
hutong (lanes) 胡同
Hu Xiaoxian 胡孝贤

Imperial Garden (Yu huayuan) 御花园
Imperial Household Department (Neiwufu) 内务府
Institute for Research in Chinese Architecture 中国营造学社

Jade Spring Mountain (Yuquan shan) 玉泉山

Ji Cheng 计成
Ji Ruiqin 姬瑞琴
Jia (empress) 皇后贾氏
jianbian ('cut border') 剪边
Jianfu gong huayuan, *see* Garden of the Palace of Established Happiness
Jianfu gong, *see* Palace of Established Happiness
Jiaqing 嘉庆
jiashan (artificial mountain) 假山
Jin Hongkui 晋宏逵
Jin Meiquan 金梅泉
jinbi huihuang ('gold, jade and resplendence') 金碧辉煌
jindi (design in decorative painting: brocade pattern) 锦地
Jingdezhen 景德镇
jixiangcao (form of decorative painting: 'auspicious grass') 吉祥草
juanpeng (roof type: rolled canopy) 卷棚
Jurong 句容

kaishu ('regular script') 楷书
kang (heated brick platform) 炕
Kangxi 康熙
kuilong (legendary creature) 夔龙

lang (galleries) 廊
'lantern' window (lattice pattern) 灯笼锦
Li Gonglin 李公麟
Li Jianguo 李建国
Li Jie 李诫
Li Yongge 李永革
Liang hui (the 'two meetings') 两会
Liang Sicheng 梁思成
lifen ('trickling powder': embossing) 沥粉
Lingbi 灵璧
liu'an (wood) 柳桉
Liulichang ('Glazed tile factory') 琉璃厂
Lodge of Fragrant Bamboo (Zhuxiang guan) 竹香馆
Lodge of Retirement (Juanqin zhai) 倦勤斋
Lodge of Viridian Jade (Bilin guan) 碧琳馆
Longyu 隆裕
lou (of rock, 'leak or ooze') 漏
lou (tower) 楼
Lu Guanli 卢观藜
Lu Jian 卢鉴
Luo Zhewen 罗哲文

Ma Lailu 马来禄
mei (flowering plum) 梅
Mentougou 门头沟
Miao Baoping 苗保平

Minguo ribao 民国日报
'mugwort-leaf green' stone (*aiyeqing*) 艾叶青

Nanmu (wood) 楠木
Neiwufu, *see* Imperial Household Department
'New Thoughts, New Orientation, New Program, New Prospects' (*Xin siwei, xin dingwei, xinguihua, xinqianjing*) 新思维,新定位,新规划,新前景
Nie Chongzheng 聂崇正
Nine Songs (*Jiu ge*) 九歌
nuange (warm chamber) 暖阁

Office of Eunuch Affairs (Jingshi fang) 敬事房

Palace Museum (Gugong bowuyuan) 故宫博物馆
Palace of Earthly Tranquility (Kunning gong) 坤宁宫
Palace of Established Happiness (Jianfu gong) 建福宫
Palace of Great Blessings (Jingfu gong) 景福宫
Palace of Compassion and Tranquility (Cining gong) 慈宁宫
Palace of Multiple Splendors (Chonghua gong) 重华宫
Palace of Nurturing Joy (Yuqing gong) 毓庆宫
Palace of Tranquil Longevity (Ningshou gong) 宁寿宫
Palace of Universal Happiness (Xianfu gong) 咸福宫
Pavilion of Met Expectation (Fuwang ge) 符望阁
Pavilion of Prolonged Spring (Yanchun ge) 延春阁
Pavilion of the Rain of Flowers (Yuhua ge) 雨花阁
Pavilion of Tranquil Ease (Jingyi xuan) 静怡轩
Pavilion Over a Pond (Linxi ting) 临溪亭
Peace for the New Year, *see Tai cu shi he*
Pei Huanlu 裴焕禄
Prince Chun 醇亲王
Prospect Hill (Jing shan) 景山
Pujie 溥杰
Puyi 溥仪

qi 气
Qianlong 乾隆
Qianlong's Garden 乾隆花园
qiazi (design in decorative painting: pincers) 卡子
qin (Chinese zither) 琴
qing (jade or stone chime) 磬
qinghui (gray plaster) 青灰
qishi (strange stone) 奇石
qiushu (catalpa) 楸树

Rehe 热河
'Reunion of Four Beauties' (*Si mei ju*) 四美具
Ru ware 汝窑瓷
ruled-line painting (*jiehua*) 界画

Ruzhou 汝州

san dao hui (three layers of mortar) 三道灰
Sanctuary of Buddhist Essence (Fanhua lou) 梵华楼
Sanctuary of Buddhist Light (Fori lou) 佛日楼
Second Western Abodes 西二所
semi-cylindrical tiles (*tong wa*) 筒瓦
Shandong Zibo Glazed Tile Factory (Shandong Zibo Liuliwachang) 山东淄博琉璃瓦厂
shanshui (mountains-and-water) 山水
Shao Ying 绍英
sheng ji er shuai ('zenith to protracted decline') 盛极而衰
sheng ru qing; ming ru jin ('It resonates like a *qing*; it is as bright as gold.') 声如磬,明如金
Shi Zhimin 石志敏
shifu (master) 师傅
shige (senior fellow apprentice) 师哥
shisun ('bamboo shoot stone') 石笋
Shiwo (Stone Pit) 石窝
shou (longevity) 寿
shou (of rock, 'thin') 瘦
Shu River 蜀川图
Shuntian shibao 顺天时报
Shuyang 沭阳
shuyao ('girdle') 束腰
Si mei ju, *see* 'Reunion of Four Beauties'
Sichelbart, Father Ignatius (Ai Qimeng) 艾启蒙
'speckled stone' (*huabanshi*) 花斑石
State Administration of Cultural Heritage 国家文物局
Structural Regulations (*Gongcheng zuofa zeli*) 工程做法则例
Studio of Character Cultivation (Yangxing zhai) 养性斋
Studio of Esteemed Excellence (Jingsheng zhai) 敬胜斋
suanni (tile figure: legendary beast of prey) 狻猊

Tai cu shi he (*Peace for the New Year*) 太簇始和
Tai Lake 太湖
tang (hall) 堂
Tang Yinian 唐益年
tangyang (scale model) 烫样
Tao Qian 陶潜
Taohua yuan ji (*Peach Blossom Spring*) 桃花源记
Temple of Universal Peace (Puning si) 普宁寺
'thunder god column' (*leigong zhu*) 雷公柱
tianma (tile figure: celestial horse) 天马
tieluo (murals) 贴落
ting (kiosk, gazebo or belvedere) 亭
tongyou (tung oil) 桐油
tou (of rock, 'penetrable') 透
Tower of Auspicious Clouds (Jiyun lou) 吉云楼

Glossary

Tower of Illuminating Wisdom (Huiyao lou) 慧曜楼
Tower of Lustrous Clouds (Yunguang lou) 云光楼
Treatise on Architectural Methods (*Yingzao fashi*) 营造法式
Tsinghua University 清华大学

utility room (*jing shi*) 净室

'Virtue Renewed Daily' (Derixin) 德日新

Wang Limei 王立梅
Wang Ruxue 王儒学
Wang Youxue 王幼学
Wang Zhongjie 王仲杰
Wanli 万历
West Garden 西花园
Western palaces (Xiyang lou) 西洋楼
Wutai shan 五台山
Wuxian 吴县

xi (brush washer) 洗
Xiang Yuanbian 项元汴
xiansheng 先生
Xiao and Xiang Rivers 潇湘游图
xiao chaoting ('little court') 小朝廷
xieshan (roof type) 歇山
xiezhi (tile figure: animal with magical powers) 獬豸
xingshen (tile figure: animal with magical powers) 行什
xingshu ('running script') 行书
Xiyao (West Kiln) 西窑
Xu Chuntao 徐春涛
Xu Jinxi 讦进喜
Xu Qixian 徐启宪
Xu Shichang 徐世昌
Xu Xuekun 续学坤
xuan (pavilion) 轩
Xuan paper 宣纸
xuanshan (roof type) 悬山
Xuantong 宣统
xuanzi (form of decorative painting: 'swirling pattern') 旋子
xumizuo (stone terrace) 须弥座

Yang Yongzhan 杨永占
Yao Wenhan 姚文瀚
yayu (tile figure: fish with a dragon's head) 押鱼
Yi Peiji 易培基
yihai (1779) 乙亥
yima wuhui (one layer of flax, five layers of mortar) 一麻五灰
yingshan (roof type) 硬山
Yixian 易县

Yixing 宜兴
Yixing Guoda Natural Rock and Stone Carving Factory 宜兴市国达天然石材雕刻厂
Yongle 永乐
Yongzheng 雍正
youman (mortar used in paint ground) 油满
youshi caihua (priming and decorative painting) 油饰彩画
Yu (legendary ruler) 禹
Yuan Hongqi 范洪琪
Yuan Shikai 袁世凯
Yuanming yuan, *see* Garden of Perfect Brightness
yugu (Taoist emblem: pipe or drum) 鱼鼓
Yung Ho Kung Temple (Yonghe gong) 雍和宫
Yuyao (Imperial Kiln) 御窑

zhai (studio) 斋
Zhang Decai 张德才
Zhang Deqin 张德勤
Zhang Hua 张华
Zhang Jinian 张吉年
Zhang Jiye 张继业
Zhang Shengtong 张生同
Zhang Xun 张勋
Zhang Zhongpei 张忠培
zhaotou (side section in painted beam) 找头
Zheng Xinmiao 郑欣淼
zhou (of rock, 'wrinkled') 皱
Zhu Jie 朱杰
Zibo 淄博
zidingxiang (*syringa oblata*) 紫丁香
Zou Ailian 邹爱莲
Zou Yigui 邹一桂
zoushou (tile animal figures: roof guardians) 走兽

Ming and Qing Reigns
(*Only era names are shown*)

MING DYNASTY (1368 – 1644)
Hongwu   1368 – 1398
Jianwen   1399 – 1402
Yongle   1403 – 1424
Hongxi   1425
Xuande   1426 – 1435
Zhengtong 1436 – 1449
Jingtai 1450 – 1456
Tianshun 1457 – 1464
Chenghua 1465 – 1487
Hongzhi 1488 – 1505
Zhengde 1506 – 1521
Jiajing 1522 – 1566
Longqing 1567 – 1572
Wanli 1573 – 1620
Taichang 1620
Tianqi 1621 – 1627
Chongzhen 1628 – 1644

QING DYNASTY (1644 – 1911)
Shunzhi 1644 – 1661
Kangxi 1662 – 1722
Yongzheng 1723 – 1735
Qianlong 1736 – 1795
Jiaqing 1796 – 1820
Daoguang 1821 – 1850
Xianfeng 1851 – 1861
Tongzhi 1862 – 1874
Guangxu 1875 – 1908
Xuantong 1909 – 1911

The Garden of the Palace of Established Happiness: constructed, seventh year of the Qianlong reign; destroyed, 1923; restored, 2005.

Acknowledgements and Sources

China Heritage Fund commissioned me to write this book, providing me with the simplest of briefs: an account of the course of the reconstruction. Happy Harun agreed that I should have access to all the correspondence, reports and background papers. Besides giving constant support, she helped with gathering material, showed me hospitality in Beijing and allowed me to interview her at regular intervals during the five years of the project, for all of which I am immensely grateful. Zhang Liping dealt with my frequent requests for information with patience and good humor. This book could not have been written, though, if I had not observed the process from design to completion at first hand. The craftsmen and their supervisors on site and in the factories had little choice about answering my questions but were always unfailingly helpful. Through interviews with other participants, I learnt something about heritage conservation and management in general, and about the Palace Museum's policies and progress in particular. All those who were generous with their knowledge and time are named in the book, and I thank them collectively here. I would be remiss, however, if I did not single out Li Yongge and Zhang Shengtong, who cheerfully answered questions at every stage of the research and writing. Hu Chui, long-time photographer of the Forbidden City and head of its information center, deserves special mention for many of the illustrations and for his steadfast support and friendship.

In the preliminary stages of the restoration, members of the Palace Museum undertook research in the First Historical Archives of China under the direction of a panel of scholars and experts including Yu Zhuoyun, Luo Zhewen, Fu Xinian, Shan Guoqiang and Du Xianzhou. Every record and document relating to the Palace and Garden of Established Happiness, from the Qianlong emperor's poems to Imperial Household memorials on construction and repair expenditure and the inventories of furnishings and ornaments in several of the pavilions, was reproduced in a volume published for internal circulation. This compilation, *Zijincheng Jianfugong huayuan ziliao huibian* (*ziliao huibian* hereafter), is the main source for my descriptions of the historical garden. Separately, China Heritage Fund commissioned the First Historical Archives to trawl through the so-called 'Puyi archives' for further information on the 1923 fire. This task, directed by senior researcher Tang Yinian who was, as ever, gracious and forbearing, was accomplished with dedication and care. Finally, I should like to thank my editor, Ralph Kiggell.

Footnotes and detailed references would not be appropriate in a book of this kind, but I acknowledge below the main reference works consulted as well as the publications from which I have directly quoted; the translations are mine unless otherwise specified. Among general books on Chinese architecture and the Forbidden City, these have been particularly useful: Liang Sicheng, *A Pictorial History of Chinese Architecture: A Bilingual Edition*, (trans.) Wilma Fairbank (Baihua wenyi chubanshe, Tianjin, 2001); Yu Zhuoyun, *Palaces of the Forbidden City* (The Viking Press, New York, 1984 and Allen Lane, London, 1984); and Institute of the History of Natural Sciences, Chinese Academy of Sciences, *History and Development of Ancient Chinese Architecture* (Science Press, Beijing, 1986). For insights into the 'little court', I have drawn from Reginald F. Johnston, *Twilight in the Forbidden City* (Victor Gollancz, London, 1934) and *From Emperor to Citizen: The Autobiography of Aisin-Gioro Pu Yi*, (trans.) W. J. F. Jenner (Foreign Languages Press, Beijing, 1964). Further details of quotations from these and other sources appear in the notes below.

1 | The Fire

To reconstruct the fire I relied on a draft memorial by eunuch-lama Ma Lailu, eunuch Wang Jinfu's report to Neiwufu, and newspaper articles, in particular *North China Daily News*, June 27, 1923, which mentioned the assistance of M. Riva and described the 'very good and valuable work' of the Italian Legation guard fire brigade. In the Chinese media there were accounts in *Jing bao*, *Shuntian shibao*, *Beijing ribao*, *Xin bao*, *Xiao gong bao* and *Minguo ribao*.

Mrs Joseph Carson's accounts of life in China were recalled for me by her daughter Mrs Tatiana Browning, who also lent me her mother's letters from Beijing in the early 1920s. She provided a translation from Russian of Miss Irene Staheyeff's letter to her mother of June 28, 1923, a cutting of 'The Emperor's Thanks' from the *North China Daily News*, June 27, 1923 and copies of the memorial from Neiwufu expressing thanks for the Carsons' help in fighting the fire, and showed me the oxblood vase given to her parents by Puyi.

The fire is mentioned in Jenner (trans.), *From Emperor to Citizen* and Johnston, *Twilight in the Forbidden City*.

Hu Jianzhong's 'Gugong zhenbao liushi ji' in *Zijincheng*, volume 106 (Zijincheng chubanshe, Beijing, 2000), details the imperial treasures lost through looting and unpaid bank loans. Dr Stacey Pierson, Curator of the Percival David Foundation of Chinese Art, drew my attention to the Ru ware dish which survived the fire. Rosemary Scott, *Percival David Foundation of Chinese Art: A Guide to the Collection* (School of Oriental and African Studies, University of London, 1989) contains information about Sir Percival's connoisseurship and the history of his unique museum. I have also consulted Stacey Pierson, *Illustrated Catalogue of Ru, Guan, Jun, Guangdong and Yixing Wares in the Percival David Foundation of Chinese Art* (School of Oriental and African Studies, University of London, revised edition, 1999).

2 | Qianlong Builds a Garden

Emperor Qianlong is said to have composed 43,000 poems. Those associated with his Palace and Garden of Established Happiness, together with much else, are reproduced in *ziliao huibian*. If not greatly distinguished for their literary merit, his verses have nevertheless been immeasurably valuable in this attempt to reconstruct the historical garden in words. 'Colors fade from the pavilions' painted columns . . .', translated by Wee Kek Koon and the author, is one of several poems entitled 'Summer at the Palace of Established Happiness ('Xiari Jianfu gong'), attributed to Qianlong and reprinted in *ziliao huibian*. Qianlong's 'Song composed at the Pavilion of Tranquil Ease' ('Jingyi xuan zuo ge'), beginning with the line 'Voices from the town bemoan the unusual heat . . .', translated by Wee Kek Koon, is from the same source. His justification for garden-building ('An emperor or king . . .') is from Qing Gaozong, *Yu zhi Yuanming yuan tu shi* (Shiyin shuwu, Tianjin, 1887, reprinted by Wenhai chubanshe, undated).

'It is as well to lay in bricks and lime . . .' is one of the memorials on expenditure (*zou xiao dang*) reprinted in *ziliao huibian*. The translation is by Wee Kek Koon.

I quoted from the bilingual edition of Liang, *A Pictorial History*. The famous poem from which the name of the Chamber of Crystalline Purity (Yuhubing) derives is 'Farewell to Xin Jian at Hibiscus Pavilion' by Wang Wei (699–759). Several of Wang's poems were inspired by his study of Buddhism. 'Yuhubing' means 'ice in a jade flask' (or 'cup', as the following translation has it):

A cold rain mingled with the river at evening, when I entered Wu;/In the clear dawn I bid you farewell, lonely as Chu mountain./My kinsfolk in Luoyang, should they ask about me,/Tell them: 'My heart is a piece of ice in a jade cup!'

For the article on the Admonitions scroll, I am grateful to the Trustees of the British Museum for allowing me to reproduce the extract from pages 110–117 of Shane McCausland, *First Masterpiece of Chinese Painting: The Admonitions Scroll* (The British Museum Press, London, 2003). All the papers presented at the colloquy referred to in the text were published in Shane McCausland (ed.), *Gu Kaizhi and the Admonitions Scroll* (The British Museum Press, London, 2003). I drew the translation of Qianlong's colophon from the latter (Nixi Cura, 'A "Cultural Biography" of the Admonitions Scroll: The Qianlong Reign (1736–1795)').

As any calligrapher knows, *Xuan* paper is a high-quality paper, traditionally produced in Anhui province and particularly favored for Chinese ink painting and calligraphy.

Acknowledgements and Sources

3 | The Garden in Twilight
The gloss ('It had long been a cherished wish of mine . . .') to Qianlong's poem, *Changchun yuan tiju*, is quoted in 'Changchun yuan mingming zhi youlai' by Yang Naiji in *Zijincheng*, volume 111/2 (Zijincheng chubanshe, Beijing, 2001). Qianlong's warning about garden-building ('later generations should not dispense . . .') comes from *Yu zhi Yuanming yuan tu shi*. Jenner (trans.), *From Emperor to Citizen* is the source of Puyi's words. I also quoted from Johnston, *Twilight in the Forbidden City*.

Peace for the New Year is reproduced in Lin Lina, *The Elegance and Elements of Chinese Architecture: Catalogue to the Special Exhibition 'The Beauty of Traditional Chinese Architecture in Painting'* (National Palace Museum, Taipei, 2000). The photograph of the Pavilion of Prolonged Spring appears in Osvald Sirén, *The Imperial Palaces of Peking*, Volume Two (Libraire Nationale D'Art et D'Histoire, G. Van Oest, Paris and Brussels, 1926). You Xinmin, *Jiehua jifa* (Renmin meishu chubanshe, Beijing, 1998) gives an exposition of 'ruled-line painting'.

4 | What Caused the Fire?
This chapter relied on research in the 'Puyi archives' undertaken by Zou Ailian, Tang Yinian and Yang Yongzhan of the First Historical Archives of China. The documents relating to the fire were photocopied for me, and I translated the material quoted here; I have also benefited from written comments on those documents from Zou, Tang and Yang. The clippings from *Shuntian shibao* and *Minguo ribao*; the extract of Ma Lailu's draft report; the letters from the Imperial Household, the Office of the Palace Guard and Lu Guanli; and the Imperial Household's memorial on what was salvaged are all from this source. For details of articles from the imperial collection sold to antique dealers or pledged to banks, I referred to Hu Jianzhong's 'Gugong zhenbao liushi ji' (see notes to chapter 1).

Yuan Hongqi provided information on the artifacts, curios and *baishijian* in the Palace Museum. This was supplemented by Imperial Household inventories of furnishings, furniture and ornaments (*chenshe dang*) reproduced in *ziliao huibian*. I quoted from Jenner (trans.), *From Emperor to Citizen*, Johnston, *Twilight in the Forbidden City* and Irene Staheyeff's letter (see notes to chapter 1).

5 | China Heritage Fund
For this chapter I had access to the files of China Heritage Fund: correspondence between Ronnie Chan, Zhang Deqin, Wang Limei, Diane Woo and Happy Harun filled in much of the background to the years between the conception of China Heritage Fund and the launch of its first project. The papers also included the Palace Museum's preliminary proposals for the restoration. John Sanday produced a report on his mission on behalf of China Heritage Fund to Beijing, March 10–14, 1998. A project meeting with the experts of traditional architecture was arranged by the Palace Museum on October 9, 1999 and recorded on tape. Associated Press quoted John Sanday on May 24, 1999. Interviews were conducted with those quoted in the text. 'New Thoughts, New Orientation, New Program, New Prospects' ('Xin siwei, xin dingwei, xin guihua, xin qianjing'), the policy statement on architectural conservation, was posted on the Palace Museum's website at the time of writing.

6 | Saving the Stones
Ding Wenfu (ed.), *Yuyuan shang shi* (Joint Publishing, Hong Kong, 2000) contains information on decorated stone in the Forbidden City. I quoted from *Principles for the Conservation of Heritage Sites in China, English-language Translation, with Chinese Text, of the Document Issued by China ICOMOS* (The Getty Conservation Institute, Los Angeles, 2002). The book from which Happy Harun quoted is Alexander Stille, *The Future of the Past* (Farrar, Strauss and Giroux, New York, 2002).

7 | The Timber Frame
This chapter contains quotations from Liang, *Pictorial History* and Ji Cheng, *The Craft of Gardens*, (trans.) Alison Hardie (Yale University Press, New Haven and London, 1988). Other quotations are taken from transcripts of interviews. I consulted *Historic Chinese Architecture*, compiled by the Department of Architecture, Tsinghua University (reprint with corrections, Qinghua daxue chubanshe, Beijing, 1990).

8 | Baked Earth
The following books contain chapters on roofs and tiling: *History and Development of Ancient Chinese Architecture*, compiled by the Institute of the History of Natural Sciences, Chinese Academy of Sciences (see above); Yu Zhuoyun, *Palaces of the Forbidden City* (see above); Liu Dake, *Zhongguo gujianzhu wa shi yinfa* (Zhongguo jianzhu gongye chubanshe, Beijing, 1993).

9 | Palaces of Gold and Jade
He Junshou and Wang Zhongjie, *Zhongguo jianzhu caihua tuji* (Tianjin University Press, 1999) is a helpful reference, and so is Zhao Lide and Zhao Menwen, *Qingdai gujianzhu youqizuo gongyi* (Zhongguo jianzhu gongye chubanshe, Beijing, 1999). But this chapter owes most to the patient guidance of the master-craftsman Zhang Decai and the direct experience of watching the painters at work. The quotations from Zhang Decai were taken from two filmed interviews. A course of lectures (February 4–5, 2004) he gave at the Palace Museum made the subject of *youshi caihua* both comprehensible and fascinating.

10 | Tiger Skins and Bamboo Shoots
I owe the quotation about Qianlong imagining himself 'to be a lonely hermit' and 'But there was something in him ...' to Johnston, *Twilight in the Forbidden City*. The source of 'Rocks without *qi* are dead rocks' is *The Mustard Seed Garden*, translated and edited by Mai-mai Sze (Princeton University Press reprint, New Jersey, 1956). Li Jianguo wrote a report of his prolonged stay in the vicinity of Yixing.

Peter Valder, *The Garden Plants of China* (Timber Press, Portland, Oregon, 1999) is an invaluable and delightful work of reference for my reconstruction of the Garden's flora. Li Runde, 'Gugong dui wenwu gushu de baohu' in Gugong Bowuyuan, *Jincheng yingshan ji* (Zijincheng chubanshe, Beijing, 1992) throws further light on trees in the Forbidden City. For a description of rocks from the mountains around Yixing ('... hard, with eyeholes and strange grooves'), and the methods of paving ('When laying walks in a garden ...' and 'Pebbles are suitable ...'), I drew from Ji Cheng, *The Craft of Gardens* (trans.) Alison Hardie. Another standard reference work is Du Wan, *Yunlin shi pu* (Shandong huabao chubanshe, Jinan, reprint, 2004). There is no equal to Maggie Keswick, *The Chinese Garden* (Academy Editions, London, 1978) for a general guide to the subject of artificial mountains and much else besides.

Nie Chongzheng graciously allowed me to abridge and translate his 'Ceiling and Wall Murals in the Lodge of Retirement' ('Ji Gugong Juanqin zhai tiandinghua, quanjinghua'), which was reprinted in *ziliao huibian*.

11 | A Museum of Chinese Architecture
The story of the farmer's ax is taken from Howard Mansfield, *The Same Ax, Twice: Restoration and Renewal in a Throwaway Age* (University Press of New England, Hanover, New Hampshire, 2000).

Illustrations

Liu Zhigang, one of the photographers in the Palace Museum's information center, was assigned to document the Garden project visually through its five-year span. Born in Beijing, Liu has worked in the Palace Museum since 1978. Climbing up and down scaffolds and on several occasions shooting from the top of a fire-engine ladder, he produced a strong and memorable record of the restoration. Cheng Shouqi, a Beijing native, is a well-established professional photographer whose work has appeared in *Metropolis*, *Interior Design* and *Yin Yu Tang: The Architecture and Daily Life of a Chinese House* by Nancy Berliner. He played a dual role for China Heritage Fund in documenting the restoration both in photographs and on film. Hisun Wong took an interest in the project after visiting the site as an observer while pursuing a postgraduate course on architectural conservation at the University of Hong Kong; he is responsible for some of the most stunning architectural photographs in this book. Alex Beels, Happy Harun, May Holdsworth, Or Sing-pui, Ronald Tam and Yan Dan contributed a number of pictures of the site and of the reconstruction process. China Heritage Fund holds the copyright in all these images.

Most of the historical photographs and the images of paintings and relics are reproduced courtesy of the Palace Museum. Guo Yaling, also of the Museum's information center, was helpful beyond the call of duty in locating and scanning those images for this book. The drawings of the Forbidden City and of the Garden (pages 4-5, 12-13 and 35) are courtesy of Chiu Kwong-chiu — graduate of the Academy of Art at Besançon and the University of Paris I (Panthéon-La Sorbonne) and author of several books on Chinese architecture and painting. Illustrations from other sources are credited in the list below. China Heritage Fund wishes to thank the photographers and institutions for permission to reproduce them in this book.

Picture Credits

Tatiana Browning: page 23
First Historical Archives of China: pages 21 (right), 62-63, 65, 70-71
Hu Chui: pages 48, 49, 68, 69, 78-79
Reginald Johnston, *Twilight in the Forbidden City*: page 17
Liang Sicheng, *A Pictorial History of Chinese Architecture*: page 127, 154-155
Lin Zhongxing, calligraphy: page 27
National Palace Museum, Taipei: pages 37, 59
Nie Chongzheng: page 195
Palace Museum, Beijing: pages 18, 19, 20, 24-25, 30. 31, 33, 47, 50-51, 52, 53, 54, 57, 66, 67, 90, 116, 137, 166, 192
Qinding shujing tushuo (published 1905): pages 32, 88
Osvald Sirén, *The Imperial Palaces of Peking*: page 60
The Stewart Lockhart Collection, National Galleries of Scotland: page 56
Trustees of the British Museum: pages 38-39, 40-41, 42-43

The emblem used to divide sections in the book is a silhouette of the Pavilion of Prolonged Spring enclosing the five characters of the Garden's name – Jianfu gong huayuan. It was created by Zhang Decai, the master-craftsman who drew all the designs for the painted decoration in the Garden.

Index

Admonitions of the Instructress to the Court Ladies, 38-43
Alston, Lucy, 22
Alston, Sir Beilby, 22
An Qi, 40
Anhe Tile Factory, 144, 151, 153, 159
artificial mountain, 31, 36, 72, 74, 75, 185, 186
'Articles of Favorable Treatment of the Great Qing Emperor after his Abdication', 53, 68, 69
Attiret, Father Jean-Denis, 195

baishijian, 79
Banmu Garden, 155
Beiyao (North Kiln), 141, 144
Belvedere of Abundant Greenery, 36, 74, 154, 187
Belvedere of Favorable Breezes, 34, 75, 166
Benoist, Father Michel, 48
bian, 136
bracket set, *see dougong*
British Museum, 39, 41
Browning, Tatiana, 22
Bush, Barbara, 89

cai, 125, 127
caihua, 163, 165, 166, 167, 173, 178, *see also* painted decoration
calligraphy, 136-137
Carson, Tatiana and Joseph, 17-20, 22-23, 70
Castiglione, Giuseppe, 48, 195
Chamber of Crystalline Purity, 36, 103, 153, 165, 166
Chamber of the Mystical Lotus, 36, 154
Chan, Ronnie, 8, 85-89, 110, 187, 199, 201, 204
Chang Qinghai, 130, 133, 134, 201
Chengde, *see* Rehe
China Heritage Fund 8, 9, 70, 85-87, 90, 93-95, 101, 102, 104, 113, 122, 164, 177, 199
Chiu Che Bing, 154, 155
Cixi, Dowager Empress, 23
Computer Associates International, 89
Conable, Barber, 89
Courtauld, Caroline, 85, 86
Craft of Gardens, The, 134

Daoguang Emperor, 51
David, Sir Percival, 23
Derixin, 17, 71, 72, 73, 195
Ding Guanpeng, 58, 154, 155

dizhang, 174
Dong Bangda, 42
Dong Qichang, 40, 41, 42
dougong, 126-127, 129, 200

Fan Youliang, 107, 110
Fan Yubin, 34
Fangshan, 105, 107
Feng Yuxiang, 69
Fifth Western Abodes, 31, 33, 34
fire, the, 17-20
    cause of, 64, 65, 70-75; treasures lost in, 78-79
First Historical Archives of China, 70
First Masterpiece of Chinese Painting: The Admonitions Scroll, 41
Forbbiden City, The, 16, 17, 18, 29, 30, 31, 34, 36, 53, 67, 104, 125, 129, 141, 154, 155, 163, 185, 201, 204; approaches and exits, 18, 200; as museum, 83; building of, 27, 128; conservation of, 83, 85, 96-97; electricity in, 73-74; *fengshui* in, 202; gardens in, 36, 50; heating in, 116; trees in, 191; water in, 19, 72
Fourth Western Abodes, 31, 33, 34

Garden of Everlasting Spring, 47, 49
Garden of Gorgeous Spring, 47
Garden of Perfect Brightness, 23, 28, 29, 47-49, 79, 195
Garden of the Palace of Established Happiness, 8, 9, 49, 50, 60, 69, 79, 90, 128, 128, 153, 154, 164, 165, 167, 173, 177, 181, 185, 190, 191
    building of, 27-28, 31-34; destroyed by fire, 17-20; future use of, 198-201; restoration of, 86, 89, 202, 204; size and layout of, 34-37
Garden of the Palace of Compassion and Tranquility, 50
Garden of the Palace of Tranquil Longevity, *see* Qianlong's Garden
Gascoigne, Mr, 18, 20, 70
Gate of Divine Prowess, 18, 69, 72, 200
Gate of Heavenly Peace, 49
Gate of Preserving Integrity, 34, 103
Gate of Supreme Harmony, 72
Gavrilovic, Predrag, 108, 111
Golden River, 72
Greenberg, M.R. 'Hank', 85, 86
Gu Congyi, 40, 41
Gu Kaizhi, 38, 41, 42
Guangxu Emperor, 52, 54, 78

Hall of Concentrating Brilliance, 36, 116, 168, 181
Hall of Controlling Time, 34, 75, 166

Hall of Imperial Peace, 50
Hall of Joyous Longevity, 185
Hall of Martial Valor, 97
Hall of Mental Cultivation, 28, 53, 54
Hall of Precious Prosperity, 17, 71
Hall of Preserving Harmony, 105
Hall of Rectitude, 9, 17, 19, 71, 72, 74, 75, 199
Hall of Supreme Harmony, 153, 159
Harun, Happy, 8, 9, 95, 121, 129, 130, 131, 133, 156, 163, 164, 167, 173, 177, 190, 198; background of, 90-91; and contracts, 93, 94, 103, 120; and craftsmen, 134, 201; and the Garden as museum, 199-201; and language problems, 91; and pavilion interiors, 206-207; goes rock-hunting, 187-189; and stonework, 107-114; and tiles, 143-151; view of conservation of, 101, 204
Heshen, 47
Hongli, *see* Qianlong Emperor
Huang Jinfu, 72, 73, 74
Huizong Emperor, 40
Hu Shijie, 195
Hu Xiaoxian, 187, 188

Imperial Garden, 50, 191
Imperial Household Department, 18, 34, 38, 64, 68, 69, 70, 72, 74, 76, 194, 195
Imperial Palaces of Peking, The, 59

Jade Spring Mountain, 72
Ji Cheng, 134, 190
Ji Ruiqin, 144
Jia, Empress, 38
Jianfu gong, 17, 27, *see also* Palace of Established Happiness
Jianfu gong huayuan, 27, *see also* Garden of the Palace of Established Happiness

Jiaqing Emperor, 49, 51, 165, 166, 167
jiashan, *see* artificial mountain
Jin Hongkui, 9, 121, 199, 200
Jin Meiquan, 155, 156, 157
Johnson, Captain Clarence, 41
Johnston, Reginald, 20, 53, 54, 56, 64, 67, 68, 69, 74, 185

kang, 116
Kangxi Emperor, 29-30, 47, 49, 121, 163

Lam Shiu-wo, 206, 207
Lee, Dr Q.W., 87
Levett & Bailey, 206
Li Gonglin, 40, 41, 42

Li Jianguo, 186-189, 190, 191
Li Jie, 33, 125, 126
Li Yongge, 94, 110, 128, 129, 130, 131, 133, 143, 144, 146, 147, 149, 150, 151, 156, 157, 172, 173, 189, 201, 202
Liang Sicheng, 33, 92, 124
Liulichang, 141
Lodge of Fragrant Bamboo, 141
Lodge of Retirement, 194, 195
Lodge of Viridian Jade, 36, 37, 134, 154, 167, 187, 188, 191
Longyu, Dowager Empress, 52, 53, 166
Lu Guanli, 73, 74
Lu Jian, 105
Luo Zhewen, 92, 112, 167

McCausland, Shane, 41
Ma Lailu, 17, 71, 72, 74, 75
Mansfield, Howard, 202
Mentougou, 141, 143
Miao Baoping, 130, 134, 201
mortise-and-tenon joint, 124, 135

Neiwufu, *see* Imperial Household Department
Nie Chongzheng, 194
Nine Songs, 38, 41, 42

Office of Eunuch Affairs (Jingshi fang), 17, 71
Olympic Games, 97, 162, 177

painted decoration, 178-181
Palace Museum, 39, 91, 107, 109, 111, 121, 131, 134, 136, 141, 143, 144, 146, 154, 155, 163, 174, 177, 187, 194, 199, 206, 207; anniversary of, 177; inauguration of, 83; collection of, 83-84; directors of, 84, 92; and negotiations with China Heritage Fund, 89-90, 93, 94
Palace of Earthly Tranquility, 71, 156
Palace of Established Happiness, 17, 34, 69, 73, 75, 79, 90, 136, 164, 165, 166, 191, 195
Palace of Compassion and Tranquility, 50, 97
Palace of Multiple Splendors, 31
Palace of Nurturing Joy, 31, 54
Palace of Tranquil Longevity, 49, 90, 185
Palace of Universal Happiness, 195
Parsons Brinckerhoff China, 206
Pavilion of Met Expectation, 122, 173
Pavilion of Prolonged Spring, 36, 58, 60, 65, 73, 74, 78, 103, 107, 116, 121, 124, 126, 131, 144, 147, 153, 154, 155, 159, 163, 165, 166, 172, 173, 175, 177, 193, 200, 204
Pavilion of the Rain of Flowers, 17, 71, 72, 86, 179

Pavilion of Tranquil Ease, 28, 34, 37, 38, 42, 65, 78, 103, 116, 192, 200
Pavilion Over a Pond, 50
Peace for the New Year, 58, 154
Peach Blossom Spring, 192
Pei Huanlu, 9, 84, 85, 89, 105, 156, 164, 199
Pei Partnership, 206
Percival David Foundation of Chinese Art, 23
Prince Chun, 52, 69
Pujie, 55, 67
Puyi, 52, 64, 100, 137, 166, 185; abdication of, 52-54, 55; archives, 70; departure from the Forbidden City of, 69-70; and eunuchs, 65; and the fire, 18, 19, 20, 69; and losses from the fire, 76-78; and the restoration of 1917, 56; and thefts from the imperial collection, 67-69;

Qianlong Emperor, 28, 29, 30, 67, 69, 90, 100, 110, 116, 121, 122, 134, 163, 165, 166, 167, 190, 191, 194, 195; and the *Admonitions* scroll, 40-43; and calligraphy, 58, 136-137; as collector, 78, 79; and garden-building, 27-28, 31-34, 47; and Lord Macartney, 50, 51; poems of, 27, 28, 30, 31, 37, 192, 193; rock-appreciation of, 185, 186
Qianlong's Garden, 50, 101, 173, 185

Rehe, 30, 47, 50, 79, 121
'Reunion of Four Beauties', 38, 42
roof guardians, 158-159
roof systems, 153-155
ruled-line painting, 58

Sanctuary of Buddhist Essence, 101
Sanday, John, 92, 93, 101-105, 107-111, 113, 114, 121, 154, 199, 200
scaffolding, 131
Second Western Abodes, 31, 33
Shandong Zibo Glazed Tile Factory, 143, 147, *see also* Zibo
Shao Ying, 18, 72, 73, 74
Shi Zhimin, 89, 95, 122, 154, 167
Shiwo, *see* Stone Pit Factory
Shu River, 38, 41, 42
Si mei ju, *see* 'Reunion of Four Beauties'
Sichelbart, Father Ignatius, 195
Simpson Thacher & Bartlett, 89
Sirén, Osvald, 59
Staheyeff, Irene, 18, 19, 70, 75
Standard Chartered Bank, 87
Starr Foundation, The, 85, 86
Stone Pit Factory, 105
Structural Regulations, 33, 127

Studio of Character Cultivation, 60
Studio of Esteemed Excellence, 17, 36, 72, 74, 75, 78, 116, 153, 155, 185, 193, 194-195
Sun Jiazheng, 9
Sun Yat-sen, 52, 55

Tai cu shi he, *see* Peace for the New Year
Tai Lake, 187
tangyang, 33
Tao Qian, 193
Taohua yuan ji, *see* Peach Blossom Spring
tieluo, 194, 195
Tower of Auspicious Clouds, 36, 58, 103
Tower of Illuminating Wisdom, 34, 101, 103
Treatise on Architectual Methods, 33, 125, 127
Tsao, Calvin, 207
Twilight in the Forbidden City, 20

'Virtue Renewed Daily', *see* Derixin

Wang, Charles, 89
Wang Limei 9, 85, 86, 87
Wang Ruxue, 195
Wang Youxue, 195
Wang Zhongjie, 164-167, 173, 175
Wanli Emperor, 50
West Garden, 50
Western palaces at the Garden of Perfect Brightness, 48
Woo, Diane, 85, 87, 94
World Monuments Fund, 102, 108, 194

Xiang Yuanbian, 40
Xiao and Xiang Rivers, 38, 41, 42
Xiyao (West Kiln), 141
Xu Chuntao, 174
Xu Jinxi, 65
Xu Qixian, 136, 137
Xu Shichang, 56
Xu Xuekun, 107
Xuantong Emperor, *see* Puyi

Yao Wenhan, 195
Yi Peiji, 83
Yixing, 187, 188
Yixing Guoda Natural Rock and Stone Carving Factory, 188
Yongle Emperor, 27, 50, 105, 128, 141, 155
Yongzheng Emperor, 28-29, 31, 47, 127, 168
youshi caihua, 163, 166, 168, *see also* painted decoration

Yu the Great, 186
Yuan Shikai, 52, 53, 55, 56
Yuanming yuan, *see* Garden of Perfect Brightness
Yuyao (Imperial Kiln), 155, 156

Zhang Decai, 164, 167, 168, 170-172, 174
Zhang Deqin, 86, 87
Zhang Hua, 38
Zhang Jinian, 187, 188, 189
Zhang Jiye, 107, 110, 201
Zhang Shengtong, 95, 107, 121, 122, 156, 164
Zhang Wenbin, 9
Zhang Xun, 55, 56
Zhang Zhongpei, 84
Zheng Xinmiao 9, 10, 199, 202
Zhu Jie, 154
Zibo, 144, 146, 147, 148, 149, 151
Zou Yigui, 41

图书再版编目（CIP）数据

建福宫花园重建记事＝The Palace of Established Happiness:
Restoring a Garden in the Forbidden City: 英文／潘蔓著.
—北京：紫禁城出版社，2008.3
　ISBN 978-7-80047-331-9

I. 建… II. 潘… III. 故宫—古典园林—文物修整—英文
IV. K928.74 TU-87

中国版本图书馆CIP数据核字（2007）第179532号

责任编辑：章宏伟
设　　计：丘纬中／Semeiotics

建福宫花园重建记事
The Palace of Established Happiness:
Restoring a Garden in the Forbidden City

潘蔓著

紫禁城出版社出版发行
北京景山前街4号故宫博物院内
北京雅昌彩色印刷有限公司制版印刷

开本：889×1194　1/16　字数：66千　印张：14　图版：300幅
2008年3月第一版第一次印刷　印数 1—3000册
ISBN 978-7-80047-331-9

定价：380.00元